Vojtěch Novotný

Cur homo?
A history of the thesis
concerning man
as a replacement
for fallen angels

CHARLES UNIVERSITY IN PRAGUE
KAROLINUM PRESS 2014

Reviewed by: Prof. Dr. Achim Schütz (Pontificia Universitas Lateranensis, Vatican)
Prof. Dr. Fr. Emery de Gaál (University of St Mary of the Lake, Chicago)
Prof. Dr. Inos Biffi (Facoltà Teologica dell'Italia Settentrionale, Milano)

CATALOGUING-IN-PUBLICATION – NATIONAL LIBRARY
OF THE CZECH REPUBLIC

Novotný, Vojtěch
  Cur homo? A history of the thesis concerning man as a replacement
for fallen angels / Vojtěch Novotný ; [English translation by Pavlína
and Tim Morgan]. – 1st English ed. – Prague: Karolinum, 2014
Published by: Charles University in Prague
ISBN 978-80-246-2519-5

2-18 * 27-181.5 * 14:2 * 27-278 * 27 * 27-1 * 14:27
– human beings – Christian approach
– creation of man – Christian approach
– Biblical theology
– theological anthropology – 4th–13th centuries
– Christian theology – 4th–13th centuries
– Christian philosophy – 4th–13th centuries
– monographs

230 – Christian theology, Christian doctrinal theology [5]

ISBN 978-80-246-2519-5
e-ISBN 978-80-246-2586-9 (pdf)

To Tomáš Machula
In gratitude and friendship

Contents

Introduction

The following pages aim to fulfil a modest goal: to examine, outline, elucidate, and supplement the existing body of knowledge concerning a seemingly minor area of patristic and medieval theology, and that is the assertion that man was created as a replacement for fallen angels. Yves Congar has suggested, however, that the significance of this idea cannot be overstated.[1]

We are going to build upon the prompt provided by Marie-Dominique Chenu, who in 1953 drew attention to this all-but-forgotten controversy of the twelfth century.[2] Chenu noticed that the school of Laon, in the collection *Sententiae divinae paginate*, gave consideration to the assertion of St. Anselm of Canterbury – concerning a subject somewhat "outside his field" – in *Cur Deus homo* that God decided that the number of fallen angels would be replenished from human nature. Anselm also stated, however, that human nature was created for its own sake. They noticed this matter in Laon and made it a subject of much debate and disputation. In *De glorificatione Trinitatis,* Rupert of Deutz then linked the question to reflections upon God's mysterious intention

1   Yves CONGAR, L'Église chez S. Anselme, in *Spicilegium Beccense*, tome I, *Congrès international du IXe centenaire de l'arrivée d'Anselme au Bec*, Paris: J. Vrin, 1959, 372.

2   Marie-Dominique CHENU, Cur homo? Le sous-sol d'une controverse au XIIᵉ siècle, *Mélanges de sciences religieuses* 10 (1953), 197–204. Included in ID., *La théologie au douzième siècle*, Paris: J. Vrin, 1957, 52–61. Before Chenu, who should be credited with noting the importance of this problematic subject and incorporating it into the wider horizon of the "twelfth century Renaissance," the matter was noted only by scholars researching particular authors or texts in which it is alluded to. See, for example, Joseph Anton ENDRES, *Honorius Augustodunensis: Beitrag zur Geschichte des geistigen Lebens im 12. Jahrhundert*, Kempten-München: Verlag der Josef Kösel'schen Buchhandlung, 1906, 114–120; Ludwig OTT, *Untersuchungen zur theologischen Brief- literatur der Frühscholastik, unter besonderer Berücksichtigung des Viktorinerkreises*, Münster i. W.: Aschendorff, 1937, 456–484; Felix SCHEIDWEILER, Studien zum Anegenge, *Zeitschrift für deutsches Altertum und deutsche Literatur* 1/2 (1944), 33–35.

for creation, which looks forwards to the incarnation, and claimed that not only angels but everything – including angels – was created for man (that is, for the God-man). According to Chenu, the most notable contribution to this question and the controversy surrounding it was made by Honorius of Autun, to whose work he therefore paid a significant amount of attention. Chenu also pointed out that the whole theme was somehow backed up by the authority of St. Gregory, according to whom human beings will make up a tenth order in the heavenly kingdom, thus completing the existing nine angelic orders (*Homiliae in Evangelia* II,34).

Since that period, man as a "replacement creature" (*créature de remplacement*) has all but vanished as a subject of theological instruction, being referred to only occasionally and even then as something of a token. This was the case in Peter Lombard's *Summa sententiarum*, a work which nonetheless prompted a number of other authors, including Thomas Aquinas, to enter their opinion on the matter. But this was also a time of a new awareness of nature and of natures, including human nature, which appeared to be a synthesis of both a material and a spiritual entity (*mikrokosmos*) and so also the goal of the universe (*makrokosmos*). This is apparent not only in works from the school of Chartres but also in those of students of Gilbert de la Porrée, among whom featured Alain of Lille, whose view on our subject was not that man comes in order to replace fallen angels, but that through him all levels of creation should enter the heavenly Jerusalem and that matter itself should participate in the divine.

The whole discussion began at a time characterised by the awareness that man is, according to Louis Bouyer, a kind of *ange de remplacement*.[3] According to this *anthropologie angélique*, as Yves Congar put it, man is called, through resurrection, to become like the heavenly angels (Mark 12:25; Matt 22:30; Luke 20:36). This call is conditional upon his anticipating, here and now, the angels' way of life by serving God through unceasing praise, gazing upon God in contemplation, and becoming like him in his sanctity and in the purity of a virtuous life in which the spirit has supremacy over the body. And so, man – who inhabits *civitas terrenis* – and the angels – who inhabit *civitas caelestis* – will be, here and now and for all time, one together in *civitas Dei*. The "model" man in this respect is an ascetic sexually chaste monk, who already, here on the earth, leads *bios angelikos* and thus anticipates the goal towards which all predestined, redeemed people are headed.[4]

---

3   Louis BOUYER, *Le Sens de la vie monastique*, Paris: Les Éditions du Cerf, 2008, 56 (orig. 1950).
4   Yves-Marie-Joseph CONGAR, *Église et Cité de Dieu chez quelques auteurs cisterciens à l'époque des croisades en particulier dans le De Peregrinante civitate Dei d'Henri d'Albano,*

The discussion concerning whether man was created as a replacement for fallen angels or was willed as an "original" being thus touched upon a key understanding of the day concerning spirituality, social order, and the concept of man. Ultimately, the discussion resulted in a fundamental modification of that concept, positing man as an "original" being, that is, as a being created for its own sake, and for whom, furthermore, God created this world, a world which together with – and through – man is to proceed towards the heavenly Jerusalem.[5] If we put the question another way and ask whether man would have been created if the angels had not sinned, we enter the realm of another controversy, the origins of which can also be traced to the twelfth century, and that is whether the Son of God would have become incarnate if man had not sinned.[6] Thus, those who entered the debate began to see a connection between the purpose behind creation and the purpose behind the incarnation, something which clearly applies to Rupert of Deutz. Chenu rightly, therefore, by analogy to the christological question *cur Deus homo,* encapsulated our subject in the anthropological question *cur homo.*

This question brings us to the title of our paper, the aim of which, as we have said, is to examine, outline, elucidate, and supplement the claims by which Marie-Dominique Chenu re-introduced the question of man as a replacement angel, and which the research community, barring a small

---

in *Mélanges offerts à Étienne Gilson de l'Académie française,* Paris: Librairie philosophique J. Vrin, 1959, 177. See Robert BULTOT, *Christianisme et valeurs humaines: La doctrine du mépris du monde, en Occident, de S. Ambroise à Innocent III,* tome IV, *Le XI siècle,* vol. 1, *Pierre Damien,* Louvain-Paris: Éd. Nauwelaerts, 1963, 40: "'Angelic anthropology' – we do indeed have to use this contradictory expression – perceives man much less as a 'being-in-the-world' who is inseparably carnal and spiritual (a biblical concept) than as a spiritual and acosmic being (a concept borrowed from Hellenistic philosophy), the data from Genesis which prevent this metaphysical interpretation being either overlooked or interpreted in such a way as to empty them of their actual anthropological content." (Translated from the French.)

5   Marie-Dominique CHENU, *La théologie au douzième siècle,* 60: "Man is not a 'replacement creature,' but the demiurge of this world, which in revealing itself reveals man to himself. Consequently, the 'antique' reference to angelic life has lost its foundation and can no longer doctrinally define the monastic state; the comparison is no more than a matter of pious superiority, with neither bite nor structure, insufficient for sustaining such eschatological humanism." (Translated from the French.)

6   See J. M. BISSEN, La tradition sur la prédéstination absolue de Jésus-Christ du VIIe au XIVe siècles, *La France Franciscain* 22 (1939), 9–34; J. F. BONNEFOY, La question hypothétique: Utrum si Adam non peccasset... au XIIIe siècle, *Revista Española de Teología* 14 (1954), 327–368; Werner DETTLOFF, Die Geistigkeit des hl. Franziskus in der Christologie des Johannes Duns Scotus, *Wissenschaft und Weisheit* 22 (1959), 17–28; Daniel HORAN, How Original Was Scotus on the Incarnation? Reconsidering the History of the Absolute Predestination of Christ in Light of Robert Grosseteste, *The Heythrop Journal* 52 (2011), 374–391.

number of clarifications of an evidential or hypothetical nature, accepted without fundamental reservations. We will show that our subject was originally introduced by St. Augustine, then taken on by his scholarly successors and by St. Gregory the Great, whose authority added further to the authority of the bishop of Hippo. We will identify the typical contexts in which the subject was raised by the authors of the early Middle Ages, but will dwell for longer on the discussion that developed during the twelfth century, which represents the high point of the ideas under consideration here. We will show that St. Anselm, who quite intentionally used the notion that man was created as a replacement for fallen angels in his reflections upon the reasons for the incarnation, also suggested the idea that human nature was created *pro se ipsa*. We will further show that independently of Anselm, although in a not dissimilar way, the school of Laon arrived at this same conclusion and had a significant impact on the subsequent fate of the theme we are following. We will demonstrate that Rupert of Deutz elevated the subject to the christological level, but also that he did not, sadly, find any worthy successors, among whom cannot therefore be numbered, despite everything, Honorius of Autun. We will show that the idea that man was created for his own sake ultimately won through, although among authors of the monastic tradition the original claim remained intact. In conclusion, we will point briefly to the surprisingly contemporary relevance of these reflections, which comes to light through a discussion concerning the statement in the pastoral constitution of the Second Vatican Council, *Gaudium et spes* 24, according to which the Creator desires human being *propter seipsam*.

The paper presents the genesis of the notion of man as a replacement angel in four main stages, which are addressed in four corresponding chapters. The first of these chapters seeks out the idea's patristic roots. The second describes the journey through which the problem of the "replacement angel" passed during the early Middle Ages, thus arriving, as the third part will show, in the twelfth century, during which the subject became problematized. The fourth of these chapters shows how the subject begins to gradually fade away through the twelfth and thirteenth centuries in both monastic and scholastic theology. The conclusion will summarize the findings and shed light on the contemporary relevance of the question as to whether and in what sense man is willed by God for his own sake.

Since our work is mainly expository in nature, the research method adopted consists of the exposition, analysis, and comparison of texts presented mainly diachronically.[7] Where necessary, we study the sources that the various authors drew upon, and also the immediate context of the ideas; wider contextualization is, however, avoided. It should be pointed out that although what we are exploring was only a marginal subject in the reflections of the church fathers and the thinkers of the Middle Ages, these reflections are set out in the middle of the paper in order to acquaint ourselves with them more fully; the major and pivotal theological themes are to be found elsewhere.

We do not, however, wish only to multiply findings about the sources of the thesis concerning man as a replacement angel, and its variants, or about the numerous ways in which it has been criticized. What we are doing here is devoting ourselves to the history of theology, and being led first and foremost by theological interests. We want to show that what we gained from the journey taken by the ideas we are investigating was a clearer – and still highly relevant – awareness that man was created for his own sake, since God wills him as an original being and not merely as a puppet in some divine drama or as a function of another creature. By this, we are not of course saying that man is not here for God. Although this is true, however, in the very particular sense that this finality is interpersonal and defined by free and selfless love – love that is not merely functional. All of the affection of the Father since the beginning of time came to dwell in the incarnate Son, which is why man is made for Jesus Christ. He, however, out of filial love, turns this directing of human being towards himself to the Father. This process too is not to be merely functional. Man is here as the very goal of Christ's self-giving, and Christ is here as the One in whom man is to freely and selflessly recognise his Lord and brother, so that he can, together with him forever in the Holy Spirit, "praise the glory" of the heavenly Father (Eph 1:3–14).

Vojtěch Novotný, Prague, 31 August 2013

---

7   Our research made use of electronic resources, especially the *Patrologia Latina* database (Chadwycks-Healey), the *Library of Latin Texts, Series A* (Brepols), and *Digitale Monumenta Historiae Germanica* (Bayerische StaatsBibliothek – Deutsche Forschungsgemeinschaft). The research was based on a detailed study of these databases using typically occuring phrases. This was complemented by the reading of a number of other published texts. Patristic and medieval texts and texts from the Middle Ages published in databases or in printed form that did not yield relevant findings are not mentioned in the bibliography.

I. Origins: the church fathers

The idea that man was created as a replacement for fallen angels originated in the patristic period, and research has identified a number of
texts of St. Augustine (350–430) and St. Gregory the Great (c. 540–604)
in which these origins are believed to be located. We therefore need to
examine these sources and see how the theme was established by each
of these fathers. First, we will see how it was introduced by Augustine,
and explore any earlier sources on which he may have drawn; we will
then see how the subject was dealt with by others of the fathers, up to
and including St. Gregory the Great.

1. Sources

Chenu believed that we need to look for the patristic origins of the
medieval disputations in St. Gregory the Great, namely in *Homiliae in
evangelia* II,34.[1] This opinion has since been corrected, however, with
almost complete consensus. Although Gregory undoubtedly belonged
to those fathers whose thinking exerted significant influence upon early
medieval theology, our subject had already, before Gregory, been addressed by Augustine.[2]

---

1   Marie-Dominique CHENU, *La théologie au douzième siècle*, 57. Similarly, Mariano MAGRASSI,
     Teologia e storia nel pensiero di Ruperto di Deutz, Roma: Apud Pontificiam Universitatem Urbani-
     anam de Propaganda Fide, 1959, 258, and also Novella VARISCO, Dal Cur homo al Cur Deus
     homo: un percorso sulla via della consapevolezza, in Paul GILBERT – Helmut KOHLEN-
     BERGER – Elmar SALMANN (eds.). *Cur deus homo: Atti del Congresso anselmiano internazionale
     Roma, 21–23 maggio 1998*, Roma: Centro studi S. Anselmo, 1999, 562–563.
2   For example, in 1947, in the 17th note to his translation of Augustine's *Enchiridion,* Jean Rivière
     had already established the succession Augustine – Gregory – Anselm – Peter Lombard: see

Congar, therefore, offered an alternative list of the possible sources used by St. Anselm: Augustine's *Enchiridion* c.19, c.56, c.61, c.62; *De civitate Dei* 22,1; and *Sermones post Maurinos reperti* (= *Sermo* 229/H = *Sermo Guelferbytanus*); and Gregory's *Homiliae in evangelia* II,21,2; II,34,6–7.11.[3] Schmitt, in an edition of Anselm's *Cur Deus homo,* noted Augustine's *Enchiridion* c.29, c.61; and *De civitate Dei* 14,26; 22,1; and Gregory's *Homiliae in evangelia* II,21,2; II,34,11.[4] Following Schmitt, Roques mentioned Augustine's *Enchiridion* c.29; and Gregory's *Homiliae in evangelia* II,21,2.[5] Lohse and Schmidt, in their studies on St. Augustine, referred to *Enchiridion* c. 9,29; and *De civitate Dei* 22,1.[6] Lamirande cited Augustine's *Enchiridion* c.9,28; *De civitate Dei* 16,62; 20,14; 22,1; and *Sermo Guelferbytanus* 12,2.[7] Orazzo, who researched our subject in the work of St. Bernard, referred to Augustine's *Enchiridion* c.29, c.56, c.61; and *De civitate Dei* 22,1; and Gregory's *Homiliae in evangelia* II,21,2; II,24,11.[8] Marabelli, in an edition of one of Anselm's lectures recorded by a student of his, referred to Augustine's *Enchiridion* c.9,26; c.16,61; and *De civitate Dei* 14,26; 22,1–2; and Gregory's *Homiliae in evangelia* II,21,2; II,34,6.11.[9] Judic, in an edition of Gregory's homilies, mentioned Augustine's *Enchiridion* c.9,29.[10] Finally, Fiedrowicz, in an edition of *Homiliae in evangelia* II,21,2, referred to elsewhere in Gregory: *Moralia in Iob* 28,34; and *In librum primum Regum expositionum Libri VI* 1,44; 3,166; 4,26.[11]

[AUGUSTINUS], *Oeuvres de saint Augustin* 9, *Exposés généraux de la foi,* texte, traduction, et notes par Jean Rivière, Paris: Desclée de Brouwer, 1947, 351.

3   Yves CONGAR, *L'Église chez S. Anselme,* 373.

4   *S. Anselmi Cantuariensis archiepiscopi Opera omnia,* tomus II, ed. Franciscus S. Schmitt, Romae, 1940, 74–75, 81–82, 84.

5   ANSELME DE CANTORBERY, *Pourquoi Dieu s'est fait homme,* Paris: Cerf, 1963 (SC 91), 128.

6   Bernhard LOHSE, Zu Augustins Engellehre, *Zeitschrift für Kirchengeschichte* 70 (1959), 278–279, now also in ID., *Evangelium in der Geschichte: Studien zur Theologie der Kirchenväter und zu ihrer Rezeption in der Reformation,* Göttingen: Vandenhoeck & Ruprecht, 1998, 99–116; Martin A. SCHMIDT, Augustins "Bürgerschaft Gottes", *Theologische Zeitschrift* (Basel) 11 (1955), 45–67 (66–67: Anhang: Zur Lehre von der Wiederergänzung der Gottesbürgerschaft).

7   Émilien LAMIRANDE, *L'Église céleste selon saint Augustin,* Paris: Études Augustiniennes, 1963, 144–147.

8   Antonio ORAZZO, Il mistero della Sposa nei Sermones sul Cantico dei Cantici di san Bernardo, in Enrico CATTANEO – Antonio TERRACCIANO (eds.), *Credo Ecclesiam: Studi in onore di Antonio Barruffo S. I.,* Napoli: M. D'Auria Editore, 245.

9   *Anselmo d'Aosta nel ricordo dei discepoli: parabole, detti, miracoli,* eds. Inos Biffi – Aldo Granata – Costante Marabelli – Davide Riserbato, Milano: Jaca Book, 2008, 521–523; an Italian edition of *Memorials of St Anselm,* eds. R. W. Southern – F. S. Schmitt, Oxford: Oxford University Press, 1991.

10 GRÉGOIRE LE GRAND, *Homélies sur l'Évangile,* tome II, Paris: Cerf, 2008 (SC 522), 31.

11 GREGOR DER GROSSE, *Homiliae in evangelia* = *Evangelienhomilien,* Bd. 2, Freiburg im Breisgau: Herder, 1998 (FC 28/2), 378.

The research community therefore arrived fairly unanimously at an identification of the basic texts, although the lists were not always identical in scope. If we look beyond the obvious errors and the differences in the numbering in the various editions, it is clear that research has, to date, pointed to the following places: Augustine's *Enchiridion* 9,29; 15,56; 16,61; 16,62; *De civitate Dei* 14,26; 22,1; and *Sermo* 229/H,2 (*Sermo Guelferbytanus* 22,1 = *Sermones post Maurinos reperti*); and Gregory's *Homiliae in evangelia* II,21,2; II,34,6–7.11; and *In librum primum Regum expositionum Libri VI* 1,44; 3,166; 4,26.

These are therefore the texts that will form the basis of our investigation. With respect to Augustine's texts, we will largely confirm the conclusions of our predecessors, but will attempt to offer a more detailed explanation of the question we are addressing; we will regard *Enchiridion* 15,56 as irrelevant to our research. From Gregory, we will add one further text, *Moralia in Iob* 31,49, but we will challenge the inclusion of *Homiliae in evangelia* II,34, and will reject *In librum primum Regum expositionum Libri VI* as inauthentic. In addition, we will attempt to answer the question concerning the sources from which both fathers drew, and will show how Augustine's idea appeared in authors who predated Gregory, an area that is yet to be addressed in specialist literature.

2. Augustine of Hippo

Augustine's reflections on God's intentions for creation and on the fall of man and the angels – and the relationship between the two – developed over a number of years. The core idea that this study will be following appeared relatively late. Chronologically, the first text in which the bishop of Hippo introduced this idea was *Sermo* 229/H, delivered at Eastertide in 412. This was followed by book 14 of *De civitate Dei* between 418 and 420, and it was developed in more detail in *Enchiridion* between 421 and 423. The final text in which Augustine commented on the subject was book 22 of *De civitate Dei,* dated between 425 and 427. Subsequent writings make no further reference to the subject, so with respect to sources and chronology these appear to be the definitive references.

Augustine locates his statements on our subject in two specific contexts: in expositions on angelic and human begetting in the prelapsarian and postlapsarian states (*Sermo* 229/H,2; *De civitate Dei* 14,26; *Enchiridion* 9,29); and in expositions on resurrection and eternal life, or, more precisely, on the church after the final judgement and on the communion of men and angels (*Enchiridion* 16,61–62; *De civitate Dei* 22,1). The overall context of ideas that are implied is much broader, however, but before we proceed in this direction, we should add that from the list of sources identified in the research mentioned above we should rule out *Enchiridion* 15,56. Although this text speaks about one holy church consisting of the church on earth and the church of angels, it does not do so in the context we are exploring here, which constitutes a narrative we can describe in the following manner:

In his eternal plan, God decided, immutably, on the number of creatures that would dwell with him in eternal bliss in the heavenly church – a definitive number that would neither increase nor decrease. The logic and dynamics of the whole drama of history are written into and evolve from this framework. The final destiny of all rational creatures is determined by this decision of the Creator, who allotted their place for them and who also, in accordance with this plan, responds to the manner in which those beings used their freedom. *Numerus certus est, pertinens ad illam coelestem Ierusalem.* The Lord knows who are his (2 Tim 2:19): *ipsi ad numerum pertinent*; he also knows who are *super numerum*.[12]

First, God created a certain number of angels, and by a single act of their free will these beings attained a definitive state: some of them sinned, through their pride, and fell into eternal damnation; the others remained obediently with God in eternal bliss. The number of beings who dwelt in communion with God had now, therefore, been reduced, and as angels do not multiply by begetting, this number could not be replenished from among their own ranks. God therefore created man as a replacement for the fallen angels: *pro ipsis qui ceciderunt angelis homines illuc venturi sunt, et implebunt locum eorum qui ceciderunt.*[13]

More accurately, this is why God created man male and female, as from their union as many human beings are to be born as are required to complete the number of citizens in the heavenly city. Thus it was to have been in the prelapsarian state, and thus it will be in the postlapsarian

---

12 Augustine was speaking here about people, but doing so using the same logic he applied to angels. AUGUSTINUS, *Enarrationes in Psalmos* 39,10 (CCSL 38,433; PL 36,440). See ID., *De correptione et gratia* 12,39 (PL 44,940).

13 AUGUSTINUS, *Sermo* 229/H, 2 = *Sermo Guelferbytanus* 12,2, in *Sermones post Maurinos reperti*, ed. G. Morin, Romae: Typis polyglottis Vaticanis, 1930 (Miscellanea Agostiniana 1), 480: "Verumtamen hoc ipsum nasci et mori, non de universo mundo, sed de ista parte infima mundi; in caelis enim non est nasci et mori, ex quo ibi condita sunt omnia. Cadere inde potuit princeps quidam angelorum cum sociis suis; sed pro ipsis qui ceciderunt angelis homines illuc venturi sunt, et implebunt locum eorum qui ceciderunt. Quia ergo diabolus vidit hominem ascensurum unde ipse ceciderat, vidit, et invidit: cecidit, et deiecit."

state: the number of the elect required to build the city of God would have been the same without human sin as it is now, when out of God's grace it is being completed from among sinners born of the union of a man and a woman.[14]

So God was not in lack of a plan for completing the predetermined number of citizens of the heavenly city. He decided to call men, whose equality with angels lies in their also being *creatura rationalis*, into the place of the fallen angels. God decided to create man, even though he foreknew that man would sin. Through sin, original and personal, all men fell into damnation, and it would be only just if the Creator abandoned them forever, and if *totius humani generis massa damnata* served eternal punishment, just like the fallen angels. But God decided that it would be better for him to bring good out of evil than not to allow evil at all; this way he is able to demonstrate that he is not only just but also merciful, and precisely through this rescuing of the unworthy his selfless mercy would be expressed yet more clearly.

He reckoned on demonstrating, through them, exactly what their guilt deserves and what his grace bestows. Men, who will be lifted out from the community of those with whom they should share in a just punishment, will see that they have received the goodness they had no right to receive but which is nonetheless freely given. The wickedness of the guilty cannot pervert the order of things established by the Creator, as he, having out of his mercy rescued men from the great mass of the condemned, follows his original intentions for them: that through them he will complete the predestined number of citizens in his city (*consilium, quo certum numerum civium in sua sapientia praedestinatum etiam ex damnato genere humano suae civitatis impleret*).[15]

---

14 AUGUSTINUS, *De civitate Dei* 14,23 (CCSL 48,444–445; PL 41,430): "Quisquis autem dicit non fuisse coituros nec generaturos, nisi peccassent, quid dicit, nisi propter numerositatem sanctorum necessarium hominis fuisse peccatum? Si enim non peccando soli remanerent, quia, sicut putant, nisi peccassent, generare non possent: profecto ut non soli duo iusti homines possent esse, sed multi, necessarium peccatum fuit. Quod si credere absurdum est, illud potius est credendum, quod sanctorum numerus quantus complendae illi sufficit beatissimae civitati, tantus existeret, etsi nemo peccasset, quantus nunc per Dei gratiam de multitudine colligitur peccatorum, quo usque filii saeculi huius generant et generantur." See ID., *Retractationum libri duo* I,13,8 (CCSL 57,40; PL 32,605); ID., *De Genesi ad litteram libri duodecim* 9,7,12 (CSEL 28/1,275; PL 34,397).

15 AUGUSTINUS, *De civitate Dei* 14,26 (CCSL 48,450; PL 41,435): "Verumtamen omnipotenti Deo, summo ac summe bono creatori omnium naturarum, voluntatum autem bonarum adiutori et remuneratori, malarum autem relictori et damnatori, utrarumque ordinatori, non defuit utique consilium, quo certum numerum civium in sua sapientia praedestinatum etiam ex damnato genere humano suae civitatis impleret, non eos iam meritis, quando quidem universa

God thus foresaw the fall of men and of angels but allowed it as he knew the good he would bring out of evil. He decided to substitute fallen angels with sinful but redeemed men, who are, through Christ's sacrifice, gathered into the heavenly church. Together they will make one holy Catholic Church, the temple of the tri-personal God, and thus will be fulfilled God's eternal plan, according to which, through Christ's sacrifice, things in heaven and things on earth are to be reconciled and recapitulated (Col 1:19–20; Eph 1:10).

Although Christ died not for the angels but for the redemption of man, his death does also concern the angels, as by recalling man into grace he put an end to the enmity between sinful men and the holy angels, and by men's redemption the damage caused by the angels' fall is repaired (*ex ipsa hominum redemptione ruinae illius angelicae detrimenta reparantur*).[16] In heaven, this restoration takes place when that which fell in the angels is returned from among men (*id quod inde in angelis lapsum est ex hominibus redditur*). On earth, it takes place when men who were predestined to eternal life are rescued from their corruption[17] and gathered by God's grace into the earthly church, which God created so that through it he might supplement and restore the portion of angels that fell (*ut inde suppleat et instauret partem, quae lapsa est angelorum*).[18]

---

massa tamquam in vitiata radice damnata est, sed gratia discernens et liberatis non solum de ipsis, verum etiam de non liberatis, quid eis largiatur, ostendens. Non enim debita, sed gratuita bonitate tunc se quisque agnoscit erutum malis, cum ab eorum hominum consortio fit immunis, cum quibus illi iuste esset poena communis. Cur ergo non crearet Deus, quos peccaturos esse praescivit, quando quidem in eis et ex eis, et quid eorum culpa mereretur, et quid sua gratia donaretur, posset ostendere, nec sub illo creatore ac dispositore perversa inordinatio delinquentium rectum perverteret ordinem rerum?"

16 AUGUSTINUS, *Enchiridion de fide et spe et caritate* 16,61 (CCSL 46,82; PL 40,261): "Non enim pro angelis mortuus est Christus. Sed ideo etiam pro angelis fit quidquid hominum per eius mortem redimitur et liberatur a malo, quoniam cum eis quodammodo redit in gratiam post inimicitias quas inter homines et sanctos angelos peccata fecerunt, et ex ipsa hominum redemptione ruinae illius angelicae detrimenta reparantur."

17 AUGUSTINUS, *Enchiridion de fide et spe et caritate* 16,62 (CCSL 46, 82; PL 40,261): "Propter hoc ait apostolus instaurari omnia in Christo, quae in caelis sunt et quae in terris in ipso. Instaurantur quippe quae in caelis sunt, cum id quod inde in angelis lapsum est ex hominibus redditur; instaurantur autem quae in terris sunt, cum ipsi homines qui praedestinati sunt in aeternam vitam a corruptionis vetustate renovantur. Ac sic per illud singulare sacrificium in quo mediator est immolatus, quod unum multae in lege victimae figurabant, pacificantur caelestia cum terrestribus et terrestria cum caelestibus. Quoniam, sicut idem apostolus dicit: in ipso complacuit omnem plenitudinem inhabitare, et per eum reconciliari omnia in ipsum, pacificans per sanguinem crucis eius, sive quae in terris sunt sive quae in caelis."

18 AUGUSTINUS, *De civitate Dei* 22,1 (CCSL 48,807; PL 41,752): "... qui de mortali progenie merito iuste que damnata tantum populum gratia sua colligit, ut inde suppleat et instauret partem, quae lapsa est angelorum, ac sic illa dilecta et superna civitas non fraudetur suorum

The resurrected saints receive the promise that they will be like the angels (Luke 20:36). The heavenly Jerusalem will not therefore be deprived of its original number of citizens. This number may even see increase as it is not known precisely how many men will be admitted into the place of the unclean spirits. Augustine accepted that, hypothetically, the final number of heavenly beings is not necessarily identical to the original number. The number is, however, known by the Creator, who calls things that are not as though they were (Rom 4: 17), and orders all things by measure and number and weight (Wis 11:20);[19] the angels also know, from God, the number of men who are to complete the number of citizens of the heavenly city.[20]

In short, Augustine's thesis is set out from the perspective of the purpose that God the creator has for his creation, and by which he defines the predetermined number of creatures that are to share eternal bliss with him. Augustine's idea is, however, more soteriological in character. It describes the narrative concerning rational creatures – both angels and men – by referring to God's foreknowledge and predestination. The fact that one part of the angels departed in one stroke from the plan set out for them by the Creator does not invalidate this foreknowledge and predestination. Since the status of both good and fallen angels is unchangeable, they are not included in the transformation implied in the term "redemption." Even so, this act that God accomplished in Jesus Christ does in some way concern those angels who remained faithful to

numero civium, quin etiam fortassis et uberiore laetetur." See *De civitate Dei* 20,14 (CCSL 48,724; PL 41,680): "An tantus angelorum numerus aderit, quantus hominum erit, et vitam suam quisque ab angelo sibi adhibito audiet recitari?"

19 AUGUSTINUS, *Enchiridion de fide et spe et caritate* 9,29 (CCSL 46,65; PL 40,246): "Placuit itaque universitatis creatori atque moderatori Deo ut quoniam non tota multitudo angelorum Deum deserendo perierat, ea quae perierat in perpetua perditione remaneret; quae autem cum Deo illa deserente perstiterat de sua certissime cognita semper futura felicitate gauderet; alia vero creatura rationalis, quae in hominibus erat, quoniam peccatis atque suppliciis et originalibus et propriis tota perierat, ex eius parte reparata quod angelicae societati ruina illa diabolica minuerat suppleretur. Hoc enim promissum est resurgentibus sanctis, quod erunt aequales angelis Dei. Ita superna Hierusalem mater nostra, civitas Dei, nulla civium suorum numerositate fraudabitur, aut uberiore etiam copia fortasse regnabit. Neque enim numerum aut sanctorum hominum aut immundorum daemonum novimus in quorum locum succedentes filii sanctae matris, quae sterilis apparebat in terris, in ea pace de qua illi ceciderunt, sine ullo temporis termino permanebunt. Sed illorum civium numerus, sive qui est, sive qui futurus est, in contemplatione est eius artifici, qui vocat ea quae non sunt tamquam quae sint, atque in mensura et numero et pondere cuncta disponit."

20 AUGUSTINUS, *Enchiridion de fide et spe et caritate* 16,62 (CCSL 46,82; PL 40,261): "Et utique noverunt angeli sancti, docti de Deo cuius veritatis aeterna contemplatione beati sunt, quanti numeri supplementum de genere humano integritas illius civitatis exspectat."

God, as into that place in the heavenly city that was to have been occupied by the angels who fell, God's grace places a pre-ordained number
of men redeemed by Christ's blood; the place of one kind of rational
creature is to be taken by another *creatura rationalis*: man. His being chosen for eternal bliss, his creation, and his redemption are, in God's eternal
plan, causally related both to the good angels and to the fall of the evil
angels; and presumably, without this prefiguration of angels and devils,
this choice, creation, and redemption would not even have happened.
It occurs as a function of adding to the number of good angels, that is,
as a function of the completeness of the heavenly church; as a function
of God's plan *instaurari omnia in Christo, quae in caelis sunt, et quae in
terris* (Eph 1:10); principally, however, as a function of the immutability
of God's will for creation and the sovereignty of this will over the will
of the creatures. A secondary but not unimportant aspect of redemption
is that of the reconciliation between God's creatures – between angels
and men. With respect to the definitive numerical consititution of God's
heavenly city, Augustine leaves open the question as to whether the
initial number of angels, depleted by the angels' fall, will be completed
by the equivalent number of men, or whether, in fact, a greater number
of men will be admitted into heaven. One way or another, the number
of predestined citizens of the city of God will be fulfilled.[21] A further

---

21 See Émilien LAMIRANDE, *L'Église céleste selon saint Augustin*, 146–147: "How to judge this
contribution? With W. Kamlah we would describe it as a childish myth, or simply as lacking
any foundation. It cannot be denied, however, that the idea inserts itself entirely naturally into
the great Augustinian concept of the 'universal' church and brings a new element of cohesion
to its two parts. We do not believe, however, that we could consider it a main part of the larger
whole. B. Lohse goes too far when he sees in this theory the explanation of the fact that a
defined number of men are predestined for salvation. The doctrine of predestination pre-oc-
cupied St. Augustine very early on, perhaps from *De libero arbitrio*. We cannot see anywhere
that his idea, on this point, is dependent on his concept of the city of angels. It is rather the
opposite that seems likely. St. Augustine always strongly held to the existence of a determined
number of the predestined. It seemed to him that the replacement of demons by men brought
an explanation on the one hand of the saving will of God and on the other of the fixed state
of the number of the elect. Freed from his over-rigid forms, the theory does not lack greatness
and harmonizes itself without difficulty with the whole of revealed truth" (Translated from the
French); Bernhard LOHSE, Zu Augustins Engellehre, 291: „We are dealing here, in fact, fairly
thoroughly, with a new form of angelology in connection with soteriology and the doctrine
of *civitas*. At the same time, the doctrine of angels is of great significance for the doctrine of
redemption, for it is that which determines the belief that only a certain number of people
are predestined for salvation. Thus Augustine's doctrine of predestination and his angelology
belong closely together, intertwined, as the doctrine of *civitas* is connected in turn. Yes, his
angelology in fact constitutes the link between the doctrines of predestination and of *civitas*,
because it embodies the notion of *societas* on the one hand and the fixed number of inhabitants
of the heavenly city on the other." (Translated from the German.)

question introduced in this context concerning the nature of the heavenly hierarchy also remains undecided.

3. Before Augustine

In the context of these ideas, what Congar called *"un thème lancé par Augustin, appelé à une grande fortune"*[22] was therefore established. Our investigation will follow what next befalls this theme, but first we need to ask whether the thesis concerning man as a replacement angel might in fact rest on an earlier tradition.

Several hypotheses have been put forward in this respect. Dudden was of the opinion that "almost the same idea" as that held by Augustine was expressed by Ambrose in *Expositio evangelii secundum Lucam* 7,126.[23] Bareille pointed to Hilary of Poitiers's *Commentaria in Mattheum* 18,6; Lefevre was in accord with Bareille.[24] Lohse, who made a thorough investigation of Augustine's sources, ruled out Judaism, Neo-Platonism, and Manichaeism, as he did Hilary and Ambrose.[25] Magrassi and Lamirande pointed to Athanasius's *Vita Antonii* 22.[26] Gribomont and Marabelli suggested that the teaching in question ultimately had its roots in "Origenism," particularly perhaps in *Vita Antonii*.[27] Nardi looked for the foundations of Gregory's exegesis in Origen but did not refer to any work in particular, mentioning only a theory that the physical world was created as a punishment for the sins of the fallen spirits.[28] Pont pointed into the same direction, that is, to the idea that man was created because of the fall of evil angels, adding a reference to Origen's *De principiis* 1,5,5;

22 Yves CONGAR, *L'Église: De saint Augustin à l'époque moderne*, Paris: Les Éditions du Cerf, 1997, 18.
23 Frederick Homes DUDDEN, *The Life and Times of St. Ambrose*, vol. 2, Oxford: Clarendon Press, 1935, 589.
24 Georges BAREILLE, Ange II. Angélologie d'après les Péres, in *Dictionnaire de théologie catholique*, ed. A. Vacant, tome I, Paris: Letouzey et Ané, 1909, 1205; Yves LEFÈVRE, *L'Elucidarium et les Lucidaires: Contribution, par l'histoire d'un texte, à l'histoire des croyances religieuses en France au moyen âge*, Paris: E. de Boccard, 1954, 114.
25 Bernhard LOHSE, Zu Augustins Engellehre, 287–291.
26 Mariano MAGRASSI, *Teologia e storia nel pensiero di Ruperto di Deutz*, 258; Émilien LAMIRANDE, *L'Église céleste selon saint Augustin*, 146.
27 Jean GRIBOMONT, Introduction, in RUPERT DE DEUTZ, *Les oeuvres du Saint-Esprit*, tome I, Paris: Cerf, 1967 (SC 131), 40; *Anselmo d'Aosta nel ricordo dei discepoli*, eds. Inos Biffi – Aldo Granata – Costante Marabelli – Davide Riserbato, 521.
28 Bruno NARDI, *Dante e la cultura medievale*, Bari – Roma: Edizioni Laterza 1985, 251.

4,22 and *Homiliae super Numeri* 12,4.[29] Fiedrowicz held that Gregory's model was indeed Origen, but from *Homiliae in Ezekielem* 13,2.[30]
We now need to examine these claims, which we will do in reverse order, beginning with the most recent.

In *Collationes* 8,10, dated between 426 and 428, Augustine's contemporary, John Cassian (c. 360–435), stated that the devil deceived man as he did not wish man, created from the dust of the earth, to be called to the glory from which he, the devil, had fallen;[31] the envy that this calling aroused in the devil led him to attempt to deprive man of heavenly glory. Can we deduce from this that Cassian was a direct source for Augustine? Not at all. Although predestination, creation, and redemption are implied here, Cassian's statement does not, in itself, correspond to the way the subject was approached by the bishop of Hippo.

Augustine is very close to Ambrose (339–397), which at least allows for the possibility of his having drawn on him. There are indeed a number of similarities in their understanding of the heavenly Jerusalem and of the relationship between men and angels.[32] *Expositio evangelii secundum Lucam* 7,126 (from around 377 to 389; final redaction from 390) suggests that through resurrection men will become like the angels and will expand the number of heavenly beings,[33] but the idea of any kind of "replacement" of angels by men is conspicuously absent. We will find the specifics of Augustine's thesis neither here nor in Ambrose's exposition on the parables of the lost sheep and the lost drachma in *Expositio evangelii secundum Lucam* 7,207–212.[34]

29 Jeanne-Marie PONT, Homo angelorum decimus ordo, *Cahiers de civilisation médiévale* 31–121 (1988), 44.
30 GREGOR DER GROSSE, *Homiliae in evangelia* = *Evangelienhomilien*, Bd. 2, 378.
31 JOANNES CASSIANUS, *Collationes XXIII* 8,10 (CSEL 13,226; PL 49,737): "Denique livoris ac seductionis materia, qua ut hominem deciperet instigatus est. De anterioris ruinae extitit causa, quod scilicet de limo terrae nuperrime figuratum ad illam eum gloriam cernere evocandum, unde, cum esset unus de principibus, se meminerat corruisse."
32 See Émilien LAMIRANDE, Le thème de la Jérusalem céleste chez saint Ambroise, *Revue d'Études Augustiniennes* 3–4 (1983), 209–232.
33 AMBROSIUS MEDIOLANENSIS, *Expositio Evangelii secundum Lucam* 7,126 (CCSL 14,257; PL 15,1732): "Ergo quoniam per resurrectionem erunt homines sicut angeli in caelis, nos quoque exemplo angelorum gloriae caelestis augmentum Dominus, qui et illis eam tribuit, sperare praecepit, quoad absorbeatur hoc mortale a vita; oportet enim corruptibile hoc induere incorruptelam, et mortale hoc induere immortalitatem." ID., *De fide ad Gratianum Augustum* 5,6 (CSEL 78,244–245; PL 16,664); ID., *Expositio Psalmi CXVIII* 12,12 (CSEL 62,257; PL 15,1364).
34 It is a different matter with the text of a lenten sermon, attributed to Ambrose, in which there are clear echoes of St. Augustine. *Sermones S. Ambrosio hactenus ascripti: Sermo XXXI. De sancta Quadragesima* XV,3 (PL 17,668): "Adventus enim Domini, eiusque incarnatio non solum hominum salus fuit in terra, sed etiam angelorum in coelo; quia dum homines in terra salvantur,

In *Vita Antonii* 22 (written around 360, and known in the West from the translation by Evagrius of Antioch from 373), Athanasius (c. 298–373) presents the idea that after they fall from heaven to earth, demons do harm to Christians, out of envy, in order that Christians might not enter the place from which they, the demons, had fallen (*hina mé hothen exepeson autoi anelthómen hémeis*).[35] This idea is similar to Cassian's but is not identical to Augustine.

In his interpretation of the parable of the lost sheep, Hilary (c. 315–367) states, in *Commentaria in Mattheum* 18,6 (353–356), that the number of those included in heavenly glory is completed by men.[36] He did not, however, mention anything that would go beyond the traditional patristic principles behind the interpretation of this parable. In *Tractatus super Psalmos*, Ps 138:39, he suggests that the number of those whose names are written in the "book of life" is fixed and includes men as well as angels.[37] There is nothing here, however, that would stand out as an obvious source of Augustine's thesis.

---

angelorum numerus qui diabolo cadente, minoratus fuerat, integratur in coelo." This is, however, a text written in Italy in the ninth century. See *Clavis Patrum Latinorum*, ed. E. Dekkers, Turnhout: Brepols, 1995, 56, n. 180.

35 ATHANASE D'ALEXANDRIE, *Vie d'Antoine* 22 (SC 400,194.196) = EVAGRIUS, *Vita Antonii* 22 (PL 73,137 ed. B. Montfaucon): "Primum itaque hoc nosse debemus daemones appellari daemones, non quod tales fuerint conditi: nihil enim mali condidit Deus: sed boni etiam ipsi facti sunt; lapsi vero a coelesti sapientia, post in terra volutati, gentiles phantasiis deceperunt, invidiaque in nos Christianos ardentes, nihil non movent, ut coelorum nobis aditum intercludant, ne eo nos ascendamus unde lapsi illi sunt." See PG 26,876 ed. H. Rosweyde; Pascal Henricus Elisabeth BERTRAND, *Die Evagriusübersetzung der Vita Antonii: Rezeption-Überlieferung-Edition: Unter besonderer Berücksichtigung der Vitas Patrum-Tradition* (Proefschrift University of Utrecht), [S.l.]: [s.n.], 2006, 168 <http://igitur-archive.library.uu.nl/dissertations/2006-0221-200251>.

36 HILAIRE DE POITIERS, *Sur Matthieu* 18,6 (SC 258,80; PL 9,1020): "Atque ut ingentem esse in caelis laetitiam reditu humanae salutis ostenderet, comparationis posuit exemplum eius qui oves nonaginta et novem in montibus reliquisset et errantem unam requisisset; qua inventa plus gaudii sit quam habebatur in nonaginta novem conservatione laetitiae. Ovis una homo intelligendus est et sub homine uno universitas sentienda est. Sed in unius Adae errore omne hominum genus aberravit; ergo nonaginta novem non errantes multitudo angelorum caelestium opinanda est, quibus in caelo est laetitia et cura salutis humanae. Igitur et quaerens hominem Christus est et nonaginta novem relicti caelestis gloriae multitudo est, cui cum maximo gaudio errans homo in Domini corpore est relatus. [...] In uno enim Abraham omnes sumus et per nos qui unum omnes sumus caelestis ecclesiae numerus explendus est. Atque ideo et creatura omnis revelationem filiorum Dei exspectat et ideo congemiscit et dolet, ut numerus, qui per alfa Abrahae additus est et qui consummatus in Sarra est ad caelestem constitutionem incrementum credentium impleatur."

37 HILARIUS PICTAVIENSIS, *Tractatus super Psalmos*, Ps. 138,39 (CSEL 22,772; PL 9,830–831): "Et ut ad Ecclesiae populos referri istud necessarium intelligeretur, adiecit: dinumerabo eos, et super arenam multiplicabuntur. Numquid numerus eorum incertus est, qui in libro Dei

We are therefore left with Origen (184/185–253/254). Origen's influence is certainly possible, at least in principle, as it has been reliably shown that Augustine came to know a number of Origen's works shortly after his conversion and gradually became acquainted with others, whether from the Latin translations of Rufinus and Jerome or from other information that came to him by whatever route.[38] Researchers refer to a variety of texts. *De principiis* 1,5 mentions Satan, or Lucifer, falling from heaven (where he had enjoyed a place among the saints, with whom he shared in the light that angels and apostles take from the Lord) to this earthly world, of which he became the "ruler"; the same can be found in *De principiis* 4,22. The text *Homiliae super Numeri* 12,4 is not connected with our subject in any way. It talks about the devil's fall, out of pride, and about Christians' rejection of him through baptism and their attempt to pass through this world to the holy land promised only to the saints. Only *Homiliae in Ezekielem* 13,2, which Augustine certainly knew,[39] deserves closer attention. Here, Origen states that man is to ascend to the place of the angels who fell (*in locum angelorum qui ruerunt, tu adscensurus es*) and to be entrusted with a mystery that was once entrusted to those angels: he will also become the light of the world – a kind of Lucifer (*tu pro illo factus es Lucifer*).[40]

scribuntur? Ergo nulla est difficultas in numero, quorum veritas maneat in scripto. Sed aliqui quod dictum est: super harenam multiplicabuntur, non ad homines tantum referendum existimaverunt, quia Abrahae dictum esset: et erit semen tuum sicut harena maris, ut, quia Abrahae semen sicut harena maris est, ad id, quod super harenam multiplicantur, amicis dei multitudo angelicae numerositatis accedat. Non enim aliter sibi convenire sicut harena maris et super arenam maris putaverunt, nisi hominum multitudini connumeraretur copia angelorum."

38 Anne-Marie LA BONNARDIÈRE, Jérôme "informateur" d'Augustin au sujet d'Origène, *Revue des Études Augustiniennes* 20 (1974), 42–54; Berthold ALTANER, *Kleine patristische Schriften*, Berlin: Akademie-Verlag, 1967, 237–239 (chapter, Augustinus und Origenes: Eine quellenkritische Untersuchung); Roland J. TESKE, Origen and St. Augustine's First Commentaries on Genesis, in Robert J. DALY (ed.), *Origeniana quinta: historica, text and method, biblica, philosophica, theologica, Origenism and later developments*, Leuven: Peeters, 1992, 179–185; György HEIDL, Did the young Augustine read Origen's homily on Paradise? in Wolfgang BIENERT – Uwe KÜHNEWEG (eds.), *Origeniana septima*, Leuven: Peeters, 1999, 597–604; György HEIDL, *Origen's Influence on the Young Augustine: A Chapter of the History of Origenism*, Piscataway: Georgias Press, 2003.

39 Martine DULAEY, L'apprentissage de l'exégèse biblique par Augustin. Première partie: Dans les années 386–389, *Revue des Études Augustiniennes* 48 (2002), 289; György HEIDL, *Origen's Influence on the Young Augustine*, 77.

40 ORIGÈNE, *Homélies sur Ézéchiel* XIII,2 (SC 352,412–414): "Videbitis enim coelum apertum, et angelos Dei ascendentes et descendentes super filium hominis. Et tu exspecta ascensionem tuam. Tantum a ruina consurge, et audi: Exsurge, Hierusalem, a ruina tua, spera quia scis ascensurus in coelum [...] vocatus es enim in eam spem de qua ille cecidit. Peccato Istrahel salus gentibus subintravit. [...] Audebo aliquid sacratius dicere: in locum angelorum qui ruerunt, tu

The manner in which we are to understand this reference can be illuminated by *Homiliae super Leviticum* 9,11. Here, Origen offers an interpretation of Lev 16:17, which states that no one may be present in the tent of meeting when the high priest enters. Origen interprets this as meaning that whoever is able to follow Christ into heaven will no longer be a man but will be like God's angels (Matt 22:30); through the glory of resurrection he will cross over to the order of angels (*per resurrectionis gloriam in angelorum ordinem transeat*).[41] Origen does not mean by this, however, that man would cease to be himself, but that he will stop being a man in the sense this word carries as a consequence of sin. An alternative interpretation suggests that what must be abandoned is the state of mortality, the substance of which – turning away from the Life that is God himself – is apparent in the devil. In itself, the human soul is neither mortal nor immortal. If it cleaves to Life, it will be immortal and will participate in Life; if it turns from Life, it will be mortal and will participate in death. Although death will not, even then, affect its substance, it will nonetheless be in some way dead.[42]

This reference brings us closer to the context in which Origen's reflections on our subject take place. What is implied here is, especially,

---

adscensurus es, et mysterium quod illis aliquando creditum est, tibi credendum erit, de quo dicitur: Quomodo cecidit Lucifer, qui mane oriebatur? Tu vero lux factus es mundi, tu pro illo factus es Lucifer; unus de stellis erat Lucifer, qui de coelo ruit, et tu si tamen de semine es Abraham, inter stellas coeli computaberis."

41   See also ORIGENES, *Commentarius in Matthaeum* XVII,30 (PG 13,1569–1570): "...qui a mortuis resurgunt, angelis coeli similes fiunt, et ex hominibus in ordinem angelorum migrant (*hósper eisin hoi anistamenoi ek nekrón hós hoi angeloi en tó ouranó, kai tagmati angelón metaballontes*)."

42   ORIGÈNE, *Homélies sur le Lévitique* IX,11 (SC 287,122–124): "Addit post haec Scriptura: Et non erit inquit homo, cum ingredietur pontifex, intra velamen interius in tabernaculo testimonii. Quomodo non erit homo? Ego sic accipio quod, qui potuerit sequi Christum et penetrare cum eo interius tabernaculum et caelorum excelsa conscendere, iam non erit homo, sed secundum verbum ipsius erit tamquam angelus Dei. Aut forte etiam ille super eum sermo complebitur, quem ipse Dominus dixit: Ego dixi, dii estis et filii Excelsi omnes. Sive ergo spiritalis effectus unus cum Domino spiritus fiat, sive per resurrectionis gloriam in angelorum ordinem transeat, recte iam non erit homo; sed unusquisque ipse sibi hoc praestat, ut vel excedat hominis appellationem vel intra conditionem huius vocabuli censeatur. Si enim factus homo ab initio servasset illud, quod ad eum Scriptura dicit: Ecce, posui ante oculos tuos mortem et vitam, elige vitam, si hoc fecisset, numquam profecto humanum genus mortalis conditio tenuisset. Sed quoniam derelinquens vitam mortem secutus est, homo factus est; et non solum homo, sed et terra, propter quod et in terram redire dicitur. [...] Unde et arbitror quod ipsa per se anima humana neque mortalis neque immortalis dici potest. Sed si contigerit vitam, ex participio vitae erit immortalis (in vitam enim non incidit mors); si vero avertens se a vita participium traxerit mortis, ipsa se facit esse mortalem. Et ideo propheta dicit Anima quae peccat, ipsa morietur, quamvis mortem eius non ad interitum substantiae sentiamus, sed hoc ipsum, quod aliena et extorris sit a Deo, qui vera vita est, mors ei esse credenda est."

the teaching on the connection between the human soul and the body in its prelapsarian and postlapsarian states, on which Origen reflected in his commentary on Gen 1:26, 2:7, and 3:21, particularly the last of these verses, which talks about how, after the first sin, God clothed man in garments of animal skin. This leads to a reflection on the fact that as a consequence of sin, man became mortal and fragile. With this reflection come statements that are perceived, by some church fathers and current researchers alike, as pertaining to the pre-existence of the soul (before the body), and as concerning the soul's connection to the body as a consequence of sin. Much, however, suggests that what Origen meant was rather that the state of the human soul has an effect on the form of the human body, which through sin has become somehow more solid, more material, and darker, while through faith and purification it becomes (again) lighter, brighter, and more spiritual. Resurrection is a process by which the same human body that belonged to the soul on earth becomes definitively spiritual, ethereal, luminous. In this sense of the word it is similar to the angels, so man thus passes over, as it were, to the order of angels.[43]

Augustine knew of Origen's teaching about the garments of skin and it was this that inspired his commentary in *De Genesi contra Manicheos* 2,21,32 (388–389). Here, Augustine interpreted Gen 3:21 as the transformation of heavenly human bodies into earthly bodies; into the present mortal nature that is similar to animal mortality and in which lying hearts are hidden. This implies that heavenly dwelling and transformation into angelic form (*habitationem illam et commutationem in angelicam formam*) is earned by those who, even though they could be hiding lies under their garments of skin, love the truth.[44] It is clear that Augustine does not speak here about the connection of the soul to the body as a consequence of sin. He knew that Jerome had attributed this teaching to Origen; he was interested in it, but refuted it in his own writings.[45]

---

43 Manlio SIMONETTI, Alcune osservazioni sull'interpretazione origeniana di Genesi 2, 7 e 3, 21, *Aevum* 36 (1962), 370–381; Pier Franco BEATRICE, Le tuniche di pelle: Antiche letture di Gen 3, 21, in Ugo BIANCHI (ed.), *La tradizione dell'Enkrateia: motivazioni ontologiche e protologiche*, Roma: Edizioni dell'Ateneo, 1985, 433–482; Mario MARITANO, Argomenti "filosofici" di Origene contro la metemsomatosi, in Lorenzo PERRONE (ed.), *Origeniana octava: Origen and the Alexandrian Tradition*, Leuven: Peeters, 2002–2003, 497–529; ID., L'argomentazione scritturistica di Origene contro la metemsomatosi, in Gilles DORIVAL – Alain LE BOLLUEC (eds.), *Origeniana sexta: Origène et la Bible*, Leuven: Peeters, 1995, 251–276.

44 AUGUSTINUS, *De Genesi contra Manicheos* 2,21,32 (PL 34,212–213).

45 Anne-Marie LA BONNARDIÈRE, Jérôme "informateur" d'Augustin au sujet d'Origène, 44–46.

This said, can we assume that Augustine found the source of his thesis in Origen? It is certainly possible to see some kind of parallel between Augustine's *pro ipsis qui ceciderunt angelis homines illuc venturi sunt, et implebunt locum eorum qui ceciderunt* and Origens's *in locum angelorum qui ruerunt, tu adscensurus es,* which appears in a work the bishop of Hippo undoubtedly knew.[46] Although a certain degree of inspiration cannot therefore be ruled out, we should emphasise that the contexts in which these statements appear are not identical. In Augustine, the angels who fell could not be replaced from among their own ranks as they do not multiply by begetting, hence God created man as a replacement for the fallen angels. A variation on this idea, in Augustine's *Enchiridion* 9,29, relates to the resurrection and is taken from Mark 12:25, and here, the bishop of Hippo appears to agree with Origen. On closer inspection, however, their understandings of this dynamic are not in fact in accord.

In addition to the authors we have already been referred to by the hypothesis concerning the sources that inspired Augustine, we should mention one further work that offers a similar idea, and that is the apocryphal *Vita Adae et Evae*. The ideas contained within this work, which are clearly echoed in the texts from the church fathers, originate in a Jewish tradition that reflected on the animosity between man and the fallen angels, which arose because of the angels' envy at the privileged position in the created order that God awarded to man (see Ps 8:5–8). This tradition is attested to in the deuterocanonical book of Wisdom (2:23–24) and in some pseudepigraphical and rabbinic texts.[47]

Vita Adae et Evae was preserved in six languages (Greek, Latin, Slavonic, Armenian, Georgian, and a fragment in Coptic), all of which differ in content. The texts originated between the third and fifth centuries but their common source could be from as early as the first century. The author was probably Jewish, although some believe that the whole work

46 AUGUSTINUS, *Sermo* 229/H, 2 = *Sermo Guelferbytanus* 12,2; ORIGÈNE, *Homélies sur Ézéchiel* XIII,2.
47 Peter SCHAFER, *Rivalität zwischen Engeln und Menschen: Untersuchungen zur rabbinischen Engelvorstellung*, Berlin: De Gruyter, 1975; Mark Stephen KINZER, *"All Things under his Feet": Psalm 8 in the New Testament and in other Jewisch Literature of Late Antiquity* (PhD dissertation), Ann Arbor, MI: University of Michigan, 1995, 61–79; Georg GÄBEL, *Die Kulttheologie des Hebräerbriefes: eine exegetisch-religionsgeschichtliche Studie*, Tübingen: Mohr Siebeck, 2006, 137–141; Claudia LOSEKAM, *Die Sünde der Engel: die Engelfalltradition in frühjüdischen und gnostischen Texten*, Tübingen: Franck Verlag, 2010, 335–336; Samuel VOLLENWEIDER, Luzifer – Herrlichkeit und Sturz des Lichtengels: Eine Gegengeschichte zu Demut und Erhöhung von Jesus Christus, in Jörg FREY – Gabrielle OBERHÄNSLI-WIDMER (eds.), *Das Böse*, Neukirchen-Vluyn: Neukirchener Theologie, 2012, 203–226.

is of Christian origin.[48] The theme we are following appears only in the Latin version (chap. 12–17), and even then not in all of the preserved redactions. Here, the devil explains to Adam why he harbours hostility and envy towards him: when man was created, the angels had to bow to this image of God; he, however, refused to do so, on the grounds that man was a creature that was inferior to, and that appeared later than, him. God became angry with the devil and so deprived him and his angels of glory and evicted them to the earthly world. The devil then deceived Eve so that man would be deprived of his joy in the same way that he, the devil, was deprived of his glory. Adam then turned to God with the urgent request that he should distance him from this enemy of his who was seeking the destruction of his soul, and should give Adam the glory that the devil had lost *(da mihi gloriam eius, quam ipse perdidit)*.[49] What these words are expressing, therefore, is the idea that Adam should be admitted to the place of the fallen angels. It is, however, merely a suggestion, and appears without further elaboration or reflection.

Overall, it seems justifiable to conclude, with Bernhard Lohse, that although Augustine's idea had parallels in the earlier fathers, these were only ever expressed here and there, in hints, and never in a fully-formed concept that could have served him as a model.[50] The closest parallel appears to be Origen in *Homiliae in Ezekielem* 13,2, as noted by Fiedrowicz when researching possible sources for Gregory.[51] Essentially, however,

---

48 Johannes TROMP, *The Life of Adam and Eve in Greek: A Critical Edition*, Leiden-Boston: Brill, 2005; Marinus DE JONGE, *Pseudepigrapha of the Old Testament as Part of Christian Literature: The Case of the Testaments of the Twelve Patriarchs and the Greek Life of Adam and Eve*, Leiden: Brill, 2003, 181–201; J. P. PETTORELLI, La vie latine d'Adam et Eve, *Archivum Latinitatis Medii Aevi* 56 (1998), 18–67; Gary A. ANDERSON, The Exaltation of Adam and the Fall of Satan, in Gary A. ANDERSON – Michael E. STONE – Johannes TROMP, *Literature on Adam and Eve*, Leiden: Brill, 2000, 83–110.

49 Wilhelm MEYER, Vitae Adae et Evae, *Abhandlungen der königlich bayerischen Akademie der Wissenschaften, Philosophische-philologische Klasse* 14.3 (1878), 226: "17. Haec audiens Adam a diabolo exclamavit cum magno fletu et dixit: domine Deus meus, in manibus tuis est vita mea. Fac ut iste adversarius meus longe sit a me, qui quaerit animam meam perdere, et da mihi gloriam eius, quam ipse perdidit. Et statim non apparuit diabolus ei." Alternative redaction: J. H. MOZLEY, The Vita Adae, *Journal of Theological Studies* 30 (1928–1929), 133: "17. Hec audiens Adam exclamavit cum fletu magno et dixit, Domine Deus, vita mea in manibus tuis est; fac ut iste adversarius longe sit a me, qui querit animam meam perdere. Da mihi gloriam Domine de qua proiectus est. Et diabolus ab oculis eius evanuit."

50 Bernhard LOHSE, Zu Augustins Engellehre, 290.

51 GREGOR DER GROSSE, *Homiliae in evangelia = Evangelienhomilien*, Bd. 2, 378. Here (646) Fiedrowicz noted: „Although the traditional exegesis of parables was firmly moulded by Origen, and Gregory's proposition sounds like a distant echo of Origen's idea of the angelic pre-existence of early humanity, Gregory himself contemplates only the first humans' participation

Augustine's thesis does not derive from the texts of the earlier fathers, so we must assume that it is the fruit of his own reflections.

4. Between Augustine and Gregory

The first evidence of the tradition of Augustine's thesis was presented by Eucherius of Lyon (c. 380–449/450). In his *Instructiones* (428–434), he reflects on Eph 1:10 and points to the "assumptions of some," according to whom there is a remedying of the predicament that resulted from the angels' fall, *per augmentum societatemque sanctorum*.[52] This is a clear reference to *Enchiridion* 16,62.

There is also a clear echo of Augustine in the words of the North African bishop, St. Fulgentius of Ruspe (462/467–527/533), who in *Liber de Trinitate ad Felicem* (c. 508–515) speaks about the substitution of angels (*in hominis formatione et in angelorum similiter substitutione*)[53] and states explicitly that after the fall of the evil angels God created another rational creature, man, by whom the number of angels who fell from heaven is replenished (*per quam numerus ille angelorum de caelo labentium qui perierat suppleretur*).[54] This echoes *Enchiridion* 9,29.

---

in the life of the angels in the vision of God, not possession of their nature." (Translated from the German.)

52 EUCHERIUS LUGDUNENSIS, *Instructionum ad Salonium libri II* I,2 (CCSL 66,168; PL 50,806): "Quomodo intelligendum est hoc, quod apostolus scribit, quod proposuerit Dominus in dispensationem plenitudinis temporum, instaurare omnia in Christo, quae in caelis, et quae in terra sunt in ipsum? Vere mirum est quid nunc reparetur in caelo. Reparatur ergo secundum opinionem quorumdam illa quae cum principe suo cecidit angelorum portio per augmentum societatem que sanctorum de quibus scribitur: Sed sunt sicut angeli in coelo. Reparantur quoque omnia in terra, cum etiam in locum deficientium Iudaeorum admittuntur credentes ex gentibus. Et aliter: instaurantur quae sunt in terra, dum nos per mediatoris nostri sanguinem conciliationem que reparamur; reparantur caelestia, cum de salute nostra gaudium nascitur angelorum." See CASSIODORI DISCIPULUS, *Commentaria in epistulas sancti Pauli – Ad Ephesios* 1 (PL 68,609).

53 FULGENTIUS RUSPENSIS, *Liber de Trinitate ad Felicem* 6,3 (CCSL 91A,640): "Et cum in Genesi hominem Deus ad imaginem suam dicat esse formatum, et Iob sese a Sancto Spiritu narret esse plasmatum (spiritus, inquit, diuinus qui finxit me) liquide claret cooperatorem esse Patri ac Filio Spiritum Sanctum, et in hominis formatione et in angelorum similiter substitutione, secundum illud psalmographi: verbo domini caeli firmati sunt, et spiritu oris eius omnis virtus eorum."

54 FULGENTIUS RUSPENSIS, *Liber de Trinitate ad Felicem* 9,1 (CCSL 91A,642): "Ergo post lapsum malorum et stabilitatem bonorum, placuit omnipotenti Deo aliam condere creaturam rationalem, libero arbitrio exornatam, per quam numerus ille angelorum de caelo labentium qui perierat suppleretur."

A further resonance can be seen in the words of Boethius (c. 480–524), who in *De fide catholica,* probably from 512, states that when certain of the angels demanded more than their creator had assigned them they were cast out of their heavenly abode. Therefore, as the Creator did not wish the number of citizens in the heavenly city to be depleted, he made man (*et quoniam angelorum numerum, id est supernae illius civitatis cuius cives angeli sunt, imminutum noluit conditor permanere, formavit ex terra hominem*). Man was, however, through his wife, misled by the devil, who did not wish man to ascend to that place where he himself was not worthy of remaining.[55] Boethius's sources are not completely clear. Although it seems obvious to seek an origin in Augustine, his thesis is presented in a manner that does not entirely correspond with Augustine's texts, and is probably more closely connected to the tradition expressed in *Vita Adae et Evae* and in John Cassian.

We should also mention Martin of Braga (c. 510/515–579/580), who after a sojourn in Palestine became a monk, then a missionary in Galicia, and then archbishop of Braga. Around 573, he wrote a letter in which he suggested the manner in which the kerygma should be presented in rural areas, which were still largely pagan. He stated, in addition to much else, that after the fall of the angels, God created man and said to him, in paradise, that if he kept his commands he would remain immortal – in that heavenly place from which the angels had fallen. When the devil saw that man had been created to proceed in his stead into the kingdom of God from which he had fallen (*propterea factus fuerat homo, ut in loco illius unde ipse cecidit, in regno Dei succederet*), out of envy he misled man into breaking God's law.[56] Again, the link with Augustine is not totally con-

---

55 BOETHIUS, *De fide catholica,* in ID., *De consolatione philosophiae;* Opuscula theologica, ed. Claudio Moreschini, editio altera, Monachii et Lipsiae: In aedibus K. G. Saur, 2005, 197–198: "De caelestibus autem naturis, quae universaliter vocatur angelica, quamvis illic distinctis ordinibus pulchra sint omnia, pars tamen quaedam, plus appetens quam ei natura atque ipsius auctor naturae tribuerat, de caelesti sede proiecta est; et quoniam angelorum numerum, id est supernae illius civitatis cuius cives angeli sunt, imminutum noluit conditor permanere, formavit ex terra hominem atque spiritu vitae animavit, ratione composuit, arbitrii libertate decoravit eumque praefixa lege paradisi deliciis constituit, ut, si sine peccato manere vellet, tam ipsum quam eius progeniem angelicis coetibus sociaret, ut quia superior natura per superbiae malum ima petierat, inferior substantia per humilitatis bonum ad superna conscenderet. Sed ille auctor invidiae non ferens hominem illuc ascendere ubi ipse non meruit permanere, temptatione adhibita fecit etiam ipsum eius que comparem, quam de eius latere generandi causa formator produxerat, inoboedientiae suppliciis subiacere, ei quoque divinitatem adfuturum promittens, quam sibi dum arroganter usurpat elisus est."

56 MARTINUS BRACARENSIS, *De correctione rusticorum* 4, in Claude W. BARLOW, *Martini episcopi Bracarensis opera omnia,* New Haven, CT: Yale University Press, 1950, 185: "Post istam

vincing. Although the quoted text and its context were probably inspired by *De catechizandis rudibus* 18, the idea we are emphasising does not appear there.[57] Simonetti, who admits the difficulty in establishing Martin's sources, nonetheless believes the background to be *Enchiridion* and *De civitate Dei*. Although there is some similarity with Boethius, Simonetti adds that as Boethius's treatise had not by that time been widely disseminated, Martin could hardly have known it.[58] It should be stressed, however, that Martin's work is closer to Boethius than it is to Augustine.

5. Gregory the Great

A further, and for the later period decisive, echo of the theme we are investigating occurs in St. Gregory the Great.[59] The relevant texts have been pointed out most comprehensively by Michael Fiedrowicz,[60] and these are: *Moralia in Iob* 28,34 (we should also add 31,49); *Homiliae in evangelia* II,21,2; II,34,3ff; and *In librum primum Regum expositionum Libri VI* 1,44; 3,166; 4,26. The authorship of *In librum* is, however, uncertain. Adalbert de Vogüé, who initially agreed with the traditional attribution to Gregory, ultimately concluded that the author of this commentary was Peter, abbot of the Benedictine abbey at Cava de' Tirreni (12th century),

---

ruinam angelicam placuit Deo de limo terrae hominem plasmare, quem posuit in paradiso; et dixit ei ut, si praeceptum Domini servasset, in loco illo caelesti sine morte succederet, unde angeli illi refugae ceciderunt, si autem praeterisset Dei praeceptum, morte moreretur. Videns ergo diabolus quia propterea factus fuerat homo, ut in loco ipsius, unde ipse cecidit, in regno Dei succederet, invidia ductus suasit homini ut mandata Dei transcenderet." See PIRMINIUS, *Scarapsus de singulis libris canonicis* (PL 89,1031); Yitzhak HEN, Martin of Braga's De correctione rusticorum and its uses in frankish Gaul, in Esther COHEN – Mayke B. DE JONG (eds.), *Medieval Transformations: Texts, Power, and Gifts in Context*, Leiden-Boston-Köln: Brill, 2001, 35–49.

57 See AUGUSTINUS, *De catechizandis rudibus* 18 (CCSL 46,154–155; PL 40,332–333).

58 Manlio SIMONETTI, Longus per divinas scripturas ordo dirigitur: Variazioni altomedievali su un tema catechetico agostiniano, *Romanobarbarica: contributi allo studio dei rapporti culturali tra mondo latino e mondo barbarico* 6 (1981–1982), 315.

59 On the angelology of Gregory in general see Leopold KURZ, *Gregors des Großen Lehre von den Engeln*, Rottenburg: Bader'sche Verlagsbuchandlung, 1938; Claude CAROZZI, Hierarchie angelique et tripartition fonctionnelle chez Grégoire le Grand, in Claude CAROZZI – Huguette TAVIANI-CAROZZI (ed.), *Hiérarchies et services au Moyen-Age*, Aix-en-Provence: Publications de l'université de Provence, 2001, 31–51; Bruno JUDIC, Hiérarchie angélique et hiérarchie ecclésiale chez Grégoire le Grand, in François BOUGARD – Dominique IOGNA-PRAT – Régine LE JAN (eds.), *Hiérarchie et stratification sociale dans l'Occident médiéval (400–1100)*, Turnhout: Brepols, 2008, 39–54; Rade KISIC, *Patria Caelestis: Die eschatologische Dimension der Theologie Gregors des Grossen*, Tübingen: Mohr Siebeck, 2011, 240–242.

60 See GREGOR DER GROSSE, *Homiliae in evangelia*, Bd. 2, 378.

albeit strongly inspired by the works of St. Gregory.[61] Not everyone shares this opinion.[62] It is only the first two works, therefore, that represent reliable sources. They are chronologically close: although *Moralia in Iob* originated between 579 and 585, it was revised after 590, re-issued with an accompanying document from 595, and subjected to further alterations in 596;[63] both *Homiliae in evangelia* were delivered in 591.[64]

The first of Gregory's works in which the idea of man as a "replacement angel" appears is *Moralia in Iob*. First, he states that angels, together with men, praise God for the mystery of the incarnation and redemption as when they see how men are accepted by God, they rejoice that their number will be complete (*dum nos conspiciunt recipi, suum numerum gaudent repleri*).[65] Later, the same idea returns yet more clearly: because of the sin of certain of their number, the choir of angels was divided, and this predicament also affected those who remained faithful: they are "complete" (*integri*) in terms of the quality of their merits, but divided, or "broken off" (*praerupti*), with respect to quantity. And so the Mediator comes, who desires to repair this "breaking off" through the redeemed human race, and even perhaps to increase the measures of the heavenly country (*hanc praeruptionem restituere mediator venit ut redempto humano genere illa angelica damna sarciret, et mensuram coelestis patriae locupletius*

61 See Adalbert de VOGÜÉ, Introduction, in GRÉGOIRE LE GRAND, *Commentaire sur le Premier livre des Rois*, tome 1, Paris: Cerf, 1989 (SC 351), 18–125; ID., Avertissement, in GRÉGOIRE LE GRAND, *Commentaire sur le premier livre des Rois*, tome 3, Paris: Cerf, 1998 (SC 432), 9–10; ID., Introduction, in GRÉGOIRE LE GRAND, *Commentaire sur le premier livre des Rois*, tome 4, Paris: Cerf, 2000 (SC 449), 9–23.
62 See Lellia CRACCO RUGGINI – Giorgio CRACCO, Gregorio Magno e i "Libri dei Re", in Philip ROUSSEAU – Emmanuel PAPOUTSAKIS (eds.), *Transformations of Late Antiquity: Essays for Peter Brown*, Farnham, England; Burlington, VT: Ashgate Publishing Limited, 2009, 223–258.
63 On dating see Robert GILLET, Introduction, in GRÉGOIRE LE GRAND, *Morales sur Job*, tome I, Paris: Cerf, 1974 (SC 32 bis), 9–10.
64 On dating see Bruno JUDIC, Introduction, in GRÉGOIRE LE GRAND, *Homélies sur l'Évangile*, tome I, Paris: Cerf, 2005 (SC 485), 42–50; ID., Avant-propos au Livre II, in GRÉGOIRE LE GRAND, *Homélies sur l'Évangile*, tome II, Paris: Cerf, 2008 (SC 522), 7–17.
65 GREGORIUS MAGNUS, *Moralia in Iob* 28,34 (CCSL 143B,1421; PL 76,467–468): "Cum me laudarent simul astra matutina. Quia enim prima in tempore condita natura rationabilium spirituum creditur, non immerito matutina astra angeli vocantur. [...] Nec neglegenter audiendum est quod additur simul; quia nimirum astra matutina etiam cum vespertinis redemptoris potentiam laudant, dum electi angeli etiam cum redemptis in mundi fine hominibus largitatem gratiae supernae glorificant. Ipsi quippe ut nos ad laudem conditoris accenderent, hoc quod superius diximus, orta per carnem luce, clamaverunt: gloria in excelsis Deo et in terra pax hominibus bonae voluntatis. Simul ergo laudant, quia redemptioni nostrae voces suae exultationis accommodant. Simul laudant, quia dum nos conspiciunt recipi, suum numerum gaudent repleri."

fortasse cumularet), just as the words of the letter to the Ephesians (1:10) declare: in Christ everything on earth is restored when sinners are re-turned to righteousness, and everything in heaven is restored when humbled men return to the place from which the angels fell by their pride (*homines redeunt unde apostatae angeli superbiendo ceciderunt*).[66]

Homiliae in evangelia is a further work of Gregory's for which in-spiration came from Augustine's idea about man completing the number of angelic citizens of the heavenly Jerusalem. In the twenty-first homily (Eastertide 591), he presented a commentary on the pericope in Mark 16:1–7, and in it reflected upon the angel who was sitting in the empty tomb. The resurrection of the Redeemer is a cause for celebration for men and angels alike: for men because by it he leads them to immortality; and for angels because by calling men into the heavenly country, he com-pleted their number (*nos revocando ad coelestia eorum numerum implevit*) and repaired the damage done there (*dum nos per resurrectionem Domini-cam ad superna reducimur, coelestis patriae damna reparantur*).[67]

In November the same year, in his thirty-fourth homily, Gregory turned his attention to the pericope in Luke 15:1–10. In the first part, Jesus tells the story of the shepherd who left the ninety-nine sheep in or-der to look for the one that was lost. Gregory comments on this parable in the following terms: the one hundred sheep symbolize the "perfect" number of angels and men created by God (*quia enim centenarius perfectus est numerus, ipse centum oves habuit cum angelorum substantiam et hominum*

---

66 GREGORIUS MAGNUS, *Moralia in Iob* 31,49 (CCSL 143B,1618; PL 76,627–628): "Qui enim sunt alii praerupti silices, nisi illi fortissimi angelorum chori, qui quamvis non integri, sed tamen in proprio statu fixi, cadente cum suis angelis diabolo remanserunt? Praerupti enim sunt, quia pars eorum cecidit, pars remansit. Qui integri quidem stant per qualitatem meriti, sed per numeri quantitatem praerupti. Hanc praeruptionem restituere mediator venit ut re-dempto humano genere illa angelica damna sarciret, et mensuram coelestis patriae locupletius fortasse cumularet. Propter hanc praeruptionem de Patre dicitur: proposuit in eo, in dispen-satione plenitudinis temporum, instaurare omnia in Christo, quae in caelis, et quae in terra sunt in ipso. In ipso quippe restaurantur ea quae in terra sunt, dum peccatores ad iustitiam convertuntur. In ipso restaurantur ea quae in coelis sunt, dum illuc humiliati homines redeunt unde apostatae angeli superbiendo ceciderunt."
67 GREGORIUS MAGNUS, *Homiliae in evangelia* II,21,2 (CCSL 141,175; PL 76,1171): "Quia ergo Redemptor noster iam praesentis vitae corruptionem transierat, recte angelus qui nun-tiare perennem eius vitam venerat in dextera sedebat. Qui stola candida coopertus apparuit, quia festivitatis nostrae gaudia nuntiavit. Candor etenim vestis splendorem nostrae denuntiat sollemnitatis. Nostrae dicamus an suae? Sed ut fateamur verius, et suae dicamus et nostrae. Illa quippe Redemptoris nostri resurrectio et nostra festivitas fuit, quia nos ad immortalitatem reduxit; et angelorum festivitas exstitit, quia nos revocando ad caelestia eorum numerum implevit. In sua ergo ac nostra festivitate angelus albis vestibus apparuit, quia dum nos per resurrectionem Dominicam ad superna reducimur, caelestis patriae damna reparantur."

creavit); the ninety-nine sheep symbolize the angelic choirs that remained in heaven while the shepherd (that is, Jesus, the Good Shepherd of John 10) was searching on the earth for the single lost sheep, that is, man (or fallen human nature), who became lost when he sinned. He found the sheep and put it on his shoulders; he took on human nature and carried our sins. This interpretation is supplemented by a further explanation: through the lost sheep the number of beings – angels and men – who were created in order to see God was diminished, but with that sheep's return the perfect number of sheep in heaven is restored (*quia rationalis creaturae numerus, angelorum videlicet et hominum, quae ad videndum Deum condita fuerat, pereunte homine erat imminutus, et ut perfecta summa ovium integraretur in caelo, homo perditus quaerebatur in terra*).[68]

Gregory interpreted the parable of the woman looking for the single lost drachma from the ten she owned in a similar way. The woman represents God – God's wisdom. The nine coins she did not lose symbolize nine angelic choirs. In order that the number of the elect might be completed, man was created as a tenth (*ut compleretur electorum numerus, homo decimus est creatus*), whom the eternal Wisdom found – after man had through his own fault become lost – in the light of the earthen vessel, that is, in the body.[69]

---

68 GREGORIUS MAGNUS, *Homiliae in evangelia* II,34,3 (CCSL 141,301; PL 76,1247–1248): "Quia enim centenarius perfectus est numerus, ipse centum oves habuit cum angelorum substantiam et hominum creavit. Sed una ovis tunc periit quando peccando homo pascua vitae dereliquit. Dimisit autem nonaginta novem oves in deserto, quia illos summos angelorum choros reliquit in caelo. Cur autem caelum desertum vocatur, nisi quod desertum dicitur derelictum? Tunc autem caelum homo deseruit cum peccavit. In deserto autem nonaginta novem oves remanserant, quando in terra Dominus unam quaerebat, quia rationalis creaturae numerus, angelorum videlicet et hominum, quae ad videndum Deum condita fuerat, pereunte homine erat imminutus, et ut perfecta summa ovium integraretur in caelo, homo perditus quaerebatur in terra. Nam quod hic evangelista dicit in deserto, alius dicit in montibus, ut significet in excelsis, quia nimirum oves quae non perierant in sublimibus stabant. Et cum invenerit ovem, imponit in umeros suos gaudens. Ovem in umeris suis imposuit, quia humanam naturam suscipiens peccata nostra ipse portavit. Et veniens domum convocat amicos et vicinos dicens illis: Congratulamini mihi, quia inveni ovem meam quae perierat. Inventa ove ad domum redit, quia Pastor noster, reparato homine, ad regnum caeleste rediit. Ibi amicos et vicinos invenit, illos videlicet angelorum choros qui amici eius sunt, quia voluntatem eius continue in sua stabilitate custodiunt. Vicini quoque eius sunt, quia claritate visionis illius sua assiduitate perfruuntur. Et notandum quod non dicit: Congratulamini inventae ovi, sed mihi, quia videlicet eius gaudium est vita nostra, et cum nos ad caelum reducimur, sollemnitatem laetitiae illius implemus."

69 GREGORIUS MAGNUS, *Homiliae in evangelia* II,34,6 (CCSL 141,304; PL 76,1249): "Sed inter haec nequaquam relinquere negligenter debemus cur ista mulier, per quam Dei sapientia figuratur, decem drachmas habuisse perhibetur, ex quibus unam perdidit, quam cum quaereret invenit. Angelorum quippe et hominum naturam ad cognoscendum se Dominus condidit,

The bishop of Rome follows this with an exposition on the angelic hierarchy, concluding with a question as to why this matter is beneficial for man, which he answers as follows: the heavenly city consists of angels, and we believe that as many men will enter it as there are angels who remained there *(quia enim superna illa civitas ex angelis et hominibus constat, ad quam tantum credimus humanum genus ascendere, quantos illic contigit electos angelos remansisse)*. Gregory substantiated this claim by referring to Deut 32:8 (LXX): "He fixed boundaries of nations according to the number of divine sons."[70] But there is a parenthetical adjunct: it is necessary, however, for man to adopt the virtues of the particular angelic orders as only this will make him like them and join him to them.[71]

Gregory uses St. Augustine's idea in various contexts evoked for him by certain passages of Scripture. The theme appears in two variants. The first is a direct echo of Augustine and can be found in *Homiliae in evangelia* II,21,2 and, in particular, in *Moralia in Iob* 31,49. It has been shown quite clearly that when Gregory was writing this latter work he used Augustine, certainly *Enchiridion,*[72] with which the passage in question very obviously corresponds. From chapter 62, Gregory used the whole of the main idea, including the reference to Eph 1:10, and from chapter 29 he took the hypothesis that the final number of heavenly citizens

---

quam dum consistere ad aeternitatem voluit, eam procul dubio ad suam similitudinem creavit. Decem vero drachmas habuit mulier, quia novem sunt ordines angelorum. Sed ut compleretur electorum numerus, homo decimus est creatus, qui a conditore suo nec post culpam periit, quia hunc aeterna sapientia per carnem miraculis coruscans ex lumine testae reparavit."

70 Rupert of Deutz noted that Gregory did not quote from the Vulgate: RUPERTUS TUITIENSIS, *De glorificatione Trinitatis* III,20 (PL 169,71). This English translation of the LXX is from *A New English Translation of the Septuagint,* (c) 2007, by the International Organization for Septuagint and Cognate Studies, Inc., used by permission of Oxford University Press, all rights reserved.

71 GREGORIUS MAGNUS, *Homiliae in evangelia* II,34,11 (CCSL 141,309; PL 76,1252): "Sed quid prodest nos de angelicis spiritibus ista perstringere, si non studeamus haec etiam ad nostros profectus congrua consideratione derivare? Quia enim superna illa civitas ex angelis et hominibus constat, ad quam tantum credimus humanum genus ascendere, quantos illic contigit electos angelos remansisse, sicut scriptum est: Statuit terminos gentium secundum numerum angelorum Dei, debemus et nos aliquid ex illis distinctionibus supernorum civium ad usum nostrae conversationis trahere, nos que ipsos ad incrementa virtutum bonis studiis inflammare. Quia enim tanta illic ascensura creditur multitudo hominum, quanta multitudo remansit angelorum, superest ut ipsi quoque homines qui ad caelestem patriam redeunt ex eis agminibus aliquid illuc revertentes imitentur. Distincte namque conversationes hominum singulorum agminum ordinibus congruunt, et in eorum sortem per conversationis similitudinem deputantur."

72 See Robert GILLET, Introduction, 86–89. More generally on the influence of Augustine on Gregory see Carole STRAW, Gregory I, in Allan D. FITZGERALD (ed.), *Augustine through the Ages: An Encyclopedia*, Grand Rapids, MI: W. B. Eerdmans, 1999, 402–405.

might be higher than the initial number. Here, therefore, Gregory was not contributing anything new. It is worth noting, however, that he did not speak of men as having been created in order to replace the fallen angels, but of the Redeemer having come to man who had sinned in order to replenish from among the ranks of those who had been saved the number of angels that had fallen. The pope thus shifted Augustine's thesis from the context of creation to the context of redemption.

The second variant appears in *Homiliae in evangelia* II,34. Although the idea appears at first to be outlined in a similar way to Augustine – whose authority is more than likely in the background – it is nonetheless different. Gregory avoids the notion of man's having being created as a replacement for fallen angels, as well as the idea that man was redeemed in order to complete the number of heavenly citizens diminished by the angels' fall. Like Augustine, he saw the initial affinity of angels and men in their both being *creatura rationalis*, created in the eternal likeness of God. Gregory describes this original unity in the following terms: *angelorum substantiam et hominum creavit – rationalis creaturae numerus, angelorum videlicet et hominum, quae ad videndum Deum condita fuerat – angelorum quippe et hominum naturam ad cognoscendum se Dominus condidit, quam dum consistere ad aeternitatem voluit, eam procul dubio ad suam similitudinem creavit.*[73]

Augustine, however, assumed that God first created angels, and only subsequently, after their number had been diminished when some of them fell, did he additionally create man, from among whom the number of rational beings that are with God in the heavenly city was to be replenished. Gregory's starting point, however, in his interpretation of the parable of the lost sheep, is that the initial number of beings God created to behold his face consisted of both angels and men, which is symbolized by the flock of one hundred sheep gathered around the Shepherd. In his interpretation of the parable of the lost drachma, Gregory speaks of the creation of nine orders of angels to which, ultimately, man was added as the tenth in order to complete the perfect number of elect heavenly citizens. Here, therefore, the idea of man being created as a replacement for the fallen angels is clearly absent.

There is a further difference between the two fathers. According to Augustine, the original number of heavenly citizens was reduced

---

73 See GREGORIUS MAGNUS, *Expositio in Canticum canticorum* I,25 (CCSL 144,39; PL 79,488): "... in omni creatura duae creaturae rationales sunt conditae, humana et angelica. Cecidit angelus; persuasit homini. Mater enim omnis creaturae benignitas et potentia Dei. Nos ergo et angeli, ex eo quod rationales conditi sumus, quasi quamdam societatem fraternitatis habemus."

when the angels sinned. According to Gregory, however, this reduction happened when man sinned: *Tunc autem caelum homo deseruit cum peccavit [...] rationalis creaturae numerus [...] pereunte homine erat imminutus.* The original perfect number is completed at the moment the Shepherd takes on human nature and finds lost man: *ut perfecta summa ovium integraretur in caelo, homo perditus quaerebatur in terra.* The redemptive effect of the incarnation concerns people only, not angels. Neither does Gregory claim that redemption would bring the reconciliation of men and angels, although this idea was not foreign to him.[74] Finally, there is nothing in Gregory to suggest the possibility of there being a difference between the original number of citizens in the heavenly city and the final number. In the parable of the lost sheep the ratio of angels to man is 99:1; in the parable of the lost drachma it is 9:1; in Gregory's exposition of the angelic hierarchy it is 1:1. In the same homily, therefore, three different assertions can be heard. It is therefore clear that Gregory did not have any precise numbers in mind but rather allowed himself to be guided by what Scripture suggested to him,[75] or by the traditions he relied upon.[76]

---

74 See GREGORIUS MAGNUS, *Homiliae in evangelia* I,8,2 (CCSL 141,55; PL 76,1104): "Regem vero natum angelus nuntiat, eius que voci angelorum chori concinunt et congaudentes clamant: Gloria in excelsis Deo, et in terra pax hominibus bonae voluntatis. Prius quippe quam Redemptor noster per carnem nasceretur, discordiam cum angelis habuimus, a quorum claritate atque munditia per primae culpae meritum, per cotidiana delicta longe distabamus. Quia enim peccando extranei eramus a Deo, extraneos nos a suo consortio deputabant angeli cives Dei. Sed quia nos cognovimus regem nostrum, recognoverunt nos angeli cives suos. Quia enim caeli rex terram nostrae carnis assumpsit, infirmitatem nostram illa iam angelica celsitudo non despicit. Ad pacem nostram angeli redeunt, intentionem prioris discordiae postponunt, et quos infirmos prius abiectos que despexerant, iam socios venerantur."

75 Rade KISIC, *Patria Caelestis*, 242. These calculations, which appear in the exegesis of both Eastern and Western fathers, were also researched by PSEUDO-ATHANASIUS, *Quaestiones ad Antiochium ducem* VI (PG 28,602–603) – perhaps Anastasios of Sinai, active in Egypt and Syria c. 640–700: see Shaun O'SULLIVAN, Anti-Jewish Polemic and Early Islam, in David RICHARD (ed.), *The Bible in Arab Christianity*, Leiden: Koninklijke Brill NV, 2007, 49–50.

76 See Bruno JUDIC, Introduction, 26–30; ID., Hiérarchie angélique et hiérarchie ecclésiale chez Grégoire le Grand, 44–48; Joan M. PETERSEN, Greek influences upon Gregory the Great's exegesis of Luke 15:1-10 in *Homelia in evang.* II, 34, in Jacques FONTAINE (ed.), *Actes du colloque international CNRS Grégoire le Grand*, Paris: Éditions du CNRS, 1986, 521–529; ID., Homo omnino latinus? The Theological and Cultural Background of Pope Gregory the Great, in *Speculum* 62 (1987), 529–551; ID., Did Gregory the Great Know Greek? in *Studies in Church History* 13 (1976), 121–134; Ludwig EISENHOFER, Augustinus in den Evangelien-Homilien Gregors des Großen: Ein Beitrag zur Erforschung der literarischen Quellen Gregors des Großen, in Heinrich M. GIETL – Georg PFEILSCHIFTER (eds.), *Festgabe Alois Knöpfler zur Vollendung des 70. Lebensjahres gewidmet*, Freiburg im Breisgau: Herder, 1917, 56–66; Vincenzo RECCHIA, La memoria di Agostino nella esegesi biblica di Gregorio Magno, *Augustinianum* 25 (1985), 405–434.

Since Origen's time, the Greek fathers' interpretation of the pericope concerning the lost sheep had agreed that the ninety-nine sheep symbolize the good angels, and that the lost hundredth sheep symbolizes sinful man. The Good Shepherd's quest signifies the work of redemption: incarnation, suffering, and exaltation.[77] The Good Shepherd's return to the sheepfold with the lost sheep was understood as the completion of the original number of sheep. Origen (184/185–253/254) already understood it this way,[78] and it was Origen who spoke of the number "one hundred" denoting the perfection of rational beings (*totius rationalis creaturae continens sacramentum*).[79] The exegesis of Methodius of Olympus († 311/312) focused on Christ, who counts the blessed angels (*arithmón ta pléthé tón makarión angelón*) and completes the number of immortal living beings, divided according to their races and tribes, by adding man to their flock (*houtos gar isos kai teleios aritmos athanatón zóón kata gené kai fyla diérémenón,*

---

77 See the set of references to the Greek fathers in Bernhard LOHSE, Zu Augustins Engellehre, 287. For Augustine himself see AUGUSTINUS, *Enarrationes in Psalmos* 8,12 (CCSL 38,55; PL 36,114): "Sed unde probabimus oves posse accipi etiam sublimiter beatos, non homines, sed angelicae creaturae spiritus? An ex eo quod Dominus dicit reliquisse se nonaginta novem oves in montibus, id est in sublimioribus locis, et descendisse propter unam. Si enim unam ovem lapsam humanam animam accipiamus in Adam, quia etiam Eva de illius latere facta est, quorum omnium spiritualiter tractandorum et considerandorum nunc tempus non est, restat ut nonaginta novem relictae in montibus, non humani, sed angelici spiritus intelligantur." ID., *Collatio cum Maximino episcopo Arianorum* (PL 42,727): "Nam si angeli secundum naturae suae substantiam invisibiles habentur; quanto magis creator angelorum, qui tanta ac talia fecit, angelos, archangelos, sedes, dominationes, principatus, potestates, cherubim, seraphim? Ad quorum multitudinem, ut legimus in evangelio, omne genus humanum ad unam comparavit ovem, dicens: relictis nonaginta novem in montibus, venit quaerere unam errantem. Nam denique, sic erit gaudium, ait, in coelo super uno peccatore poenitentiam agente, quam in nonaginta novem iustis qui non indigent poenitentia. Nam qui non indigent poenitentia qui sunt, nisi utique illae coelestes virtutes, quibus nihil est cum humana natura commune? Consideranda est virtus unigeniti Dei, et in ipso admiranda est magnitudo omnipotentiae Dei Patris, qui tantum ac talem genuit Filium, tam potentem, tam sapientem, sic plenum, qui tantas ac tales coelestes virtutes fecit."

78 ORIGENES, *In Numeros homilia* 19,4 (PG 12,725): "Et quidem periit aliquando et una ovis ex centum ovibus: sed hanc ovem pastor bonus, relictis nonaginta novem in montibus, descendens ad vallem hanc nostram, vallem lacrymarum, et requirens invenit, atque impositam humeris suis reportavit, et illi numero qui in superioribus salvus manebat, adjunxit." ID., *In Genesim homilia* 13,2 (PG 12,231): "... et ovem quae erraverat, humeris suis reportet ad montes, et restituat ad alias nonaginta novem, quae non erraverunt."

79 ORIGENES, *In Genesim homilia* 2,5 (PG 12,171): "Centenarius autem numerus, plenus in omnibus et perfectus ostenditur, et totius rationalis creaturae continens sacramentum: sicut in Evangeliis legimus, ubi dicit quia habens quis centum oves, ex quibus cum perisset una, relictis nonaginta novem quae in montibus, descendit quaerere eam quae perierat, et posuit cum illis nonaginta novem quae non perierant. Hic ergo centenarius totius creaturae rationalis numerus..."

symparaléfthentos entautha té poimné kai tou anthrópou) when he creates and redeems him.[80] Cyril of Alexandria (375/80–444) interprets the "one hundred" sheep as a perfect number, and the mercy over the single sheep as the completion of this perfect number.[81] And so we could continue. It is clear that in their exegesis of our pericopes the fathers understood the creation and redemption of man in terms of the completion of the original number of rational creatures, angels and men, or as the completion of their final – perfect, ideal – number, without, however, implying Augustine's idea of man having been created as a replacement for the fallen angels. Gregory's interpretation, which culminates in the claims *ut perfecta summa ovium integraretur in caelo, homo perditus quaerebatur in terra*, and *ut compleretur electorum numerus, homo decimus est creates,* is in this respect traditional.

We must conclude, therefore, that *Homiliae in evangelia* II,34 does indeed differ from the bishop of Hippo's thesis, but that because of its apparent similarity it has often been closely linked with it, and this is how it has made its journey through history.

---

80   METHODIUS, *Convivium decem virginum* 3,6 (PG 18,68–69).

81   CYRILUS ALEXANDRINUS, *Commentarius in Lucam* 15,4 (PG 72,797–798): "Centum ait esse oves, ad plenum et perfectissimum cumulum referens rationalium sibi subjectorum numerum. Semper enim perfectus est centenarius numerus, ex decadibus decem conflatus. (*Hekaston men gar einai fesi ta probata, eis pléthyn anaferón tén artiós echousan kai teleiotatén, tón hypezeugmenón autó logikón ton arithmon· aei gar pós esti teleios ho hekaston arithmos, ek deka dekadón synkeimenos.*) [...] Miseri autem potius oportebat ejus quae perierat, ut nihil reliquae multitudini deesse videretur: nam hac una reducta, pulchre compleretur centenarius numerus (*prosepenénegmenou de tou henos, eché to idion kallos hé hekatontas*)."

II. Consolidation: the early middle ages

St. Gregory the Great represents the last in the line of Latin church fathers. Medieval theology only began creatively developing the argument concerning man as a "replacement angel" from the end of the eleventh century (with the exception of Eriugena, who will be discussed later). Until then it was passed down in a number of more or less settled forms that combined the ideas and expressions of Augustine and Gregory. The various *loci communes* that follow have been reliably identified and substantiated as far as possible, but without claiming to represent an exhaustive list. The relevant time span runs from the seventh century up to the middle of the eleventh, in other words up to St. Anselm of Canterbury, with whom a new chapter in the life of our question will begin. A small number of later works are also referenced.

1. Eph 1:10

Augustine's interpretation of Eph 1:10 in *Enchiridion* 16,62 was followed by numerous authors, either in direct quotation or by close paraphrasing. It has already been mentioned that the earliest evidence of the tradition of this interpretation was offered by Eucherius of Lyon in *Instructiones* (428–434). Further evidence of the tradition appears in the sixth century in Gregory's *Moralia in Iob* 31,49.[1]

---

1   This brief summary is expanded in René WASSELYNCK, La part des "Moralia in Job" de S. Grégoire-le-Grand dans les "Miscellanea" victorins, *Mélanges de science religieuse* 10 (1953), 287–294; ID., Les compilations des "Moralia in Job" du VIIe au XIIe siècle, *Recherches de théologie ancienne et médiévale* 29 (1962), 5–32; ID., Les "Moralia in Iob" dans les ouvrages de morale du haut moyen âge latin, *Recherches de théologie ancienne et médiévale* 31 (1964), 5–31; ID., L'influence de l'exégèse de S. Grégoire le Grand sur les commentaires bibliques médiévaux

A greater response to the idea can be traced among the writers of the Carolingian Renaissance of the eighth and ninth centuries, who more or less all quote directly from Augustine.[2] Only a solitary piece of evidence has been found from the tenth century.[3] For the eleventh and twelfth centuries we need to locate the exegetic topos in the circle of people known to Anselm of Canterbury, namely Lanfranc of Canterbury (c. 1005–1089),[4] Bruno of Cologne [?] (c. 1030–1101),[5] and Hervaeus of Bourg-Dieu (c. 1075–1149/1150).[6]

2. Luke 15:8-10

Numerous authors followed Gregory's interpretation of the parable of the woman searching for the lost drachma (Luke 15:8-10) in *Homiliae in evangelia* II,34, in which he writes *ut compleretur electorum numerus, homo decimus est creates;* most of them quoted it directly.[7] Often, however, it was combined with Augustine's thesis of man as a "replacement angel."

Gregory gained an almost immediate response from Isidore of Seville (560/570–636),[8] and slightly later from Taio of Zaragoza (c. 600–c. 683),[9] who belongs to the same circle. From the beginning of the eighth century

(VIIe-XIIe s.), *Recherches de théologie ancienne et médiévale* 32 (1965), 157–204; ID., La présence des "Moralia" de S. Grégoire le Grand dans les ouvrages de morale du XIIe siècle, *Recherches de théologie ancienne et médiévale* 35 (1968), 197–240; 36 (1969), 31–45.

2 RABANUS MAURUS, *Enarrationes in epistolas B. Pauli* XVII – *Expositio in Epistolam ad Ephsesios* 1 (PL 112,390); HAYMO HALBERSTATENSIS, *De varietate librorum* 7 (PL 118,882); ID., *Expositio in D. Pauli epistolas – In epistolam ad Ephesios* 1 (PL 117,704); FLORUS LUGDUNENSIS, *De expositione missae* 25 (PL 119,35); SEDULIUS SCOTUS, *Collectanea in omnes B. Pauli epistolas – In epistolam ad Ephesios* 1 (PL 103,196).

3 ATTO VERCELLENSIS, *Expositio epistolarum S. Pauli – ad Colossenses* 1 (PL 134,616).

4 LANFRANCUS CANTUARIENSIS, *Commentarius in omnes epistolas Pauli – Epistola B. Pauli apostoli ad Ephesios* 1 (PL 150,288–289).

5 [BRUNO CARTHUSIANORUM?], *Expositio in epistolas Pauli – Epistola ad Ephesios* 1 (PL 153,321). On the question of doubts concerning authenticity see Artur Michael LANDGRAF, *Introduction à l'histoire de la littérature théologique de la scolastique naissante*, Paris: Librairie philosophique J. Vrin, 1973, 66.

6 HERVAEUS BURGIDOLENSIS, *Commentaria in epistolas Pauli – In epistolam ad Ephesios* 1 (PL 181,1212–1213).

7 The influence of Gregory's *Homiliae in evangelia* was outlined in Bruno JUDIC, Introduction, 50–88. Our method is complementary – it follows a single theme.

8 ISIDORUS HISPALENSIS, *Allegoriae sacrae Scripturae* 174 (PL 83,121).

9 TAIO CAESARAUGUSTANUS, *Sententiae* 13 (PL 80, 744).

we have Bede the Venerable (672/674–735),[10] and from the eighth and ninth centuries the writers of the Carolingian Renaissance.[11] The life and work of the Anglo-Saxon monk Ælfric (c. 955–c. 1025) spans the tenth and eleventh centuries.[12] Also in the eleventh century we find a text in which Gregory's exegesis of Luke 15:8–10 is referred to in an exposition on a different passage of Scripture.[13] Further references can also be found from the eleventh and twelfth centuries.[14] Bruno of Cologne [?][15] made a comparison of the two church fathers in the eleventh century. As we will see, Gregory's thesis also appears in other contexts.

3. Luke 2:14

Gregory quoted the angels' hymn of praise at the birth of the Saviour (Luke 2:14) in *Moralia in Iob* 28,34, adding a commentary that was quoted by several authors from the eighth to the tenth centuries.[16] The commentary was also used by Hildebert of Lavardin (c. 1056–1133).[17]

---

10 BEDA VENERABILIS, *In Lucae evangelium expositio* IV,15 (CCSL 120,287; PL 92,521).

11 SMARAGDUS S. MICHAELIS, *Collectiones in epistolas et evangelia* 15 (PL 102,362); RABANUS MAURUS, *Homiliae* 95 (PL 110,327); HAYMO HALBERSTATENSIS, *Homiliae* 114 (PL 118,613).

12 ÆLFRIC, *The Sermones Catholici, or Homilies of Ælfric: In the original Anglo-Saxon, with an English version*, ed. Benjamin Thorpe, vol. 1, London: Richard and John E. Taylor, 1844, 343.

13 GUIBERTUS S. MARIAE DE NOVIGENTO, *Tropologiae in prophetas Osee et Amos ac Lamentationes Jeremiae* 4 (PL 156,431): "...homo decimus in rationali creatura."

14 WERNERUS S. BLASII, *Libri deflorationum* II (PL 157,1031); ZACHARIAS CHRYSOPOLI-TANUS, *De concordia evangelistarum* 46 (PL 186,304).

15 [BRUNO CARTHUSIANORUM?], *Expositio in Psalmos* LXXXVIII (PL 152,1118). Landgraf assumes the work authentic; Morard does not; Mews does: see Artur Michael LANDGRAF, *Introduction à l'histoire de la littérature théologique de la scolastique naissante*, 67; Martin MORARD, Le Commentaire des Psaumes et les écrits attribués à saint Bruno le Chartreux: codicologie et problèmes d'authenticité, in Alain GIRARD – Daniel LE BLÉVEC – Nathalie NABERT (eds.), *Bruno et sa postérité spirituelle: Actes du colloque international des 8 et 9 octobre 2001 à l'Institut catholique de Paris*, Salzburg: Insitut für Anglistik und Amerikanistik, 2003, 21–39; Constant J. MEWS, Bruno of Rheims and Roscelin of Compiègne on the Psalms, in M. W. HERREN – C. J. MCDONOUGH – R. G. ARTHUR (eds.), *Publications of The Journal of Medieval Latin*, t. II: *Latin Culture in the Eleventh Century*, Turnhout: Brepols, 2002, 129–152.

16 BEDA VENERABILIS, *In Evangelium S. Lucae* 2 (PL 92,333); SMARAGDUS S. MICHAELIS, *Collectiones in epistolas et evangelia – Evangelium Lucae* 2 (PL 102,26); ODO CLUNIACENSIS, *Moralia in Iob* 28,38 (PL 133,432). See WERNERUS S. BLASII, *Libri deflorationum* (PL 157,972): "Gloria erat apud angelos in excelsis: De restauratione diminuti ordinis. Laudant Deum de reparatione hominum ad restaurationem angelorum."

17 HILDEBERTUS CENOMANENSIS, *Sermones* 9 (PL 171,382), *Sermones* 11 (PL 171,392).

4. Mark 16:1-7

In *Homiliae in evangelia* II,21, Gregory presented a commentary on the pericope from Mark 16:1–7, in which the women meet an angel in Jesus' empty tomb. The commentary was quoted by authors from the eighth to the tenth centuries.[18]

5. Rev 11:13

Gregory's words concerning *homo decimus*, in relation to Augustine's thesis, found their echo in interpretations of Rev 11:13, which speaks of the great earthquake that led to the collapse of a tenth (*decima pars*) of the city that is "allegorically called Sodom and Egypt, where their Lord was crucified," (11:8) and those who survived gave glory to God in the heavens. Here, Carolingian writers found occasion to speak of the fall of the tenth order of angels and of its replacement by a tenth order of men.[19] As we will discover, some later authors proceeded in a similar vein.[20]

6. The Missal

From the beginning of the ninth century, commentaries on the holy mass developed in the context of the Carolingian Renaissance. The words from the preface, *Per quem maiestatem tuam laudant angeli*, recall the Augustinian-Gregorian tradition. The question of the exact filiation is not significant. What is certain is that at the heart of this tradition stands Gregory's *Homiliae in evangelia* II,34, which mentions nine angelic orders and adds that *ut compleretur electorum numerus, homo decimus est creatus.* In the Middle Ages, Isidore of Seville presented this quantification of

---

18   BEDA VENERABILIS, *In Marci evangelium expositio* IV,16 (CCSL 120,640–641; PL 92,296); ID., *Homiliae subditae* 61 (PL 94,426); SMARAGDUS S. MICHAELIS, *Collectiones in epistolas et evangelia – Evangelium Marci* cap. ultimo (PL 102,226); RABANUS MAURUS, *Homiliae* 4 (PL 110,141); RATHERIUS VERONENSIS (Leodiensis sive Lobiensis), *Sermones Monacenses* 1, in *Thesaurus Ratherii Veronensis necnon Leodiensis*, ed. F. Dolbeau, Turnhout: Brepols, 2005, XXXII (CC-LLS, Series A-B, Formae et lemmata).

19   AMBROSIUS AUTPERTUS, *Expositio in Apocalypsin* 5,11,13 (CCCM 27,433); ALCUINUS, *Commentaria in Apocalypsin* 11 (PL 100,1150); HAYMO HALBERSTATENSIS, *Expositio in Aposalypsin* 11 (PL 117,1077).

20   For example BRUNO ASTENSIS, *Expositio in Apocalypsim* 11 (PL 165,665).

angelic orders in his *Etymologiae*.[21] Such interpretations of the above words from the preface are derived indirectly from Isidore, where we are reminded that there were ten angelic orders in total, but that after the tenth order had fallen (*decimus ordo cecidit et versus est per superbiam in diabolum*), only nine remained.[22] Some of these commentaries in both the Carolingian and Ottonian contexts also carry an echo of Augustine's thesis.[23]

Bede the Venerable used our thesis in a Palm Sunday homily in which he commented on the words with which the crowds welcomed Jesus into Jerusalem: "Hosanna to the Son of David!" (Matt 21:9) From here, his words were transmitted into commentaries on the Missal hymn, "Hosanna."[24]

A further reference to Augustine's teaching appears in the eleventh century in Humbert of Silva Candida's (c. 1000–1061) exposition on why the "Alleluia" is left out of the liturgy for the nine weeks leading up to Easter. The number of weeks signifies the nine angelic orders, whose perfect joy was diminished by the fall of the tenth order. God therefore created the tenth order from among men as a replacement. The angels' joy at the completion of their ranks was disturbed once again, however, by the fall of man, and their praise of the Creator will not be perfected until the moment when, in the resurrected Christ, the first fallen man also rises. At that time the angelic choirs, full of joy at the expansion of their community and full of the hope that surpasses all expectations, will resound anew with *alleluia*. The church, which on the day of resurrection will devote itself, together with the angels, to the joyous *alleluia*, joins the silence of the angels during the preparations for Easter.[25]

21 ISIDORUS HISPANENSIS, *Etymologiae* 7,5,4 (PL 82,271).
22 ISIDORUS HISPANENSIS (incertus), *Expositio in missa* 9 (PL 83,1146). See Robert E. McNALLY, Isidoriana, *Theological Studies* 3 (1959), 439–440.
23 RABANUS MAURUS, *Liber de sacris ordinibus* 19 (PL 112,1181); FLORUS LUGDUNENSIS, *De expositione missae* 25 (PL 119,35); AUCTOR INCERTUS, *Expositio super missam* (PL 138,1165); REMIGIUS ALTISSIODORENSIS, *Expositio missae* 9, in Jean-Paul BOUHOT, Les sources de l'*Expositio missae* de Rémi d'Auxerre, *Révue des études augustiniennes* 1 (1980), 147.
24 BEDA VENERABILIS, *Homeliarum evangelii libri II* 2,3 (CCSL 122,197; PL 94,124); SEDULIUS SCOTUS, *In evangelium Matthaei* 2,3,21,9 (Vetus Latina 14,476); FLORUS LUGDUNENSIS, *De expositione missae* 42 (PL 119,42); HILDEBERTUS CENOMANENSIS, *Sermones* XXXII (PL 171,501). See Jean-Paul BOUHOT, Fragments attribués à Vigile de Thapse dans l'Expositio missae de Florus de Lyon, *Révue des études augustiniennes* 3–4 (1975), 313.
25 HUMBERTUS SILVAE CANDIDAE, *Adversus Graecas calumnias* 58 (PL 143,969).

7. Canon law

It was impossible for interpretations relating to liturgy not to enter canon law, especially when backed by the authority of Isidore of Seville, the leading mediator of the patristic heritage concerning liturgical and canonical order in the West. His treatment of Augustine's thesis in the work *Sententiae*[26] entered into the decretals.[27] Likewise, in the twelfth century, the commentary compiled by Humbert of Silva Candida was integrated into *Decretum Gratiani*.[28]

8. The tithe

Our thesis also provided inspiration for spiritual interpretation regarding the obligation of the tithe, that is, the payment of the church tax, amounting to around a tenth of a person's income. This, however, appears relatively late, probably not until the twelfth century.[29]

9. The number of the saved

Augustine's starting point was God's preordaining of the number of citizens in the heavenly Jerusalem – a number that was neither to decrease nor increase. The fall of some of the angels corrupted this number and man was created and redeemed so that this shortfall could be rectified. Initially, the idea is presented that the number of fallen angels is identical

---

26 ISIDORUS HISPALENSIS, *Sententiae* 1,10,13 (CCSL 111,33; PL 83,555–556): "Bonorum angelorum numerus, qui post ruinam angelorum malorum est diminutus, ex numero electorum hominum supplebitur. Qui numerus soli Deo est cognitus."

27 BURCHARDUS WORMACIENSIS, *Libri decretorum* 20,54 (PL 140,1034); IVO CARNOTENSIS, *Decretum* 65 (PL 161,990).

28 *Decretum Gratiani* 3,1,55 (*Corpus iuris canonici* 1, Graz: Akademische Druck- u. Verlagsanstalt, 1959, 1309).

29 BRUNO ASTENSIS, *Expositio in Pentateuchum* 18 (PL 164,487–488): "Decimas autem ideo damus, quoniam ipsi decimae sumus: nos enim sumus drachma decima, nos sumus et ovis centesima; quod enim centesimum est, decimum est: nos sumus et decimus ordo, quoniam novem sunt ordines angelorum. Quoniam igitur decimas damus, nosmetipsos quasi decimas in decimis Domini commendamus." ROBERTUS PULLUS, *Sententiae* 6 (PL 186,918): "Decimam offerimus ut simul cum novem ordinibus, quasi decimus ordo, loco corruentium computemur." *Emonis Chronicon* 1204–1234 (MGH SS 23,492). "Item decimam damus et novem retinemus, quia omnis imperfectio a nobs est, ut ostendamus nos ex illis esse, ex quibus decimus ordo angelorum replendus est."

to the number of people saved, and this is Augustine's usual assumption. Equivalence is not, however, the only solution he allows. God could have included – in the final number of creatures that will be, according to his plan, always with him – the number the fallen angels replaced by men, but increased it still further with additional people. Therefore, in *Enchiridion* 9,29 and *De civitate Dei* 22, Augustine leaves open the question as to whether the original number of heavenly citizens would be merely restored or actually exceeded.

In the ninth century, Johannes Scotus Eriugena (c. 810–c. 877) addressed the same issue in *Periphyseon* (*De divisione naturae*) 5,38, in which he focused on the infallible and universal efficacy of God's saving will and drew on an interpretation of the three parables from Luke 15: the parables of the prodigal son, the lost sheep, and the lost drachma. In each of these he saw the whole human race, whose salvation God realized in Christ. In his interpretation of the parable of the prodigal son, Eriugena followed Ambrose; in interpreting the other two parables, Dionysius the Areopagite is explicitly in the background, and Gregory and Augustine implicitly. What is worth noting is that Eriugena shifted Gregory's idea onto the christological level: the perfect number in the heavenly Jerusalem, reduced by the fall of human nature, is restored when humankind returns to the city in its Head, which is Christ (*cuius numerositas, veluti centenarii numeri latitudo, ad integrum implebitur, dum humanum genus in capite suo (quod est Christus) in eam revertetur*).[30]

This argument also implies Eriugena's idea that human nature was created with the same dignity as angelic nature but was later, as a consequence of sin, debased. In Christ, however, human nature was admitted into God and thus exalted above every creature, including the angels,

---

30 IOHANNES SCOTUS ERIUGENA, *Periphyseon (De divisione naturae)* 5,38 (CCCM 165,204; PL 122,1005–1006): "Eadem interpretatio est de dragma perdita et, post eversionem huius mundi veluti cuiusdam domus, inventa a muliere, Dei videlicet sapientia, quae eam fecit et possedit. Decima etiam ideo computatur, quoniam humana natura non solum novem ordinibus angelorum aequalis facta est, verum etiam nullus angelicus ordo est, cui humana natura post restaurationem suam iuxta intelligibiles gradus non interseratur, donec perfectum denarium caelestis compleat civitatis, teste Dionysio Ariopagita in libro De caelesti ierarchia. Quod etiam ei futurum erat, si non peccaret. Simili modo de ove centesima intellige, quae erraverat caelestem gregem deserens, quam bonus pastor (qui est Christus) quaesivit et repperit, repertam que in que humeros suos acceptam ad gregem quem errando deseruerat reportat. Quae propterea centesima connumeratur, quoniam post lapsum humanae naturae perfectio (quae per centenarium numerum innuitur) caelestis Hierusalem, quae est mater nostra, diminuta est. Cuius numerositas, veluti centenarii numeri latitudo, ad integrum implebitur, dum humanum genus in capite suo (quod est Christus) in eam revertetur."

and that which happened in the Head is to happen at the end of the ages, at the resurrection, also in the members.[31]

First and foremost, however, Eriugena was interested in Augustine's question as to whether the number of men who return to the heavenly city will be identical to the number of angels who fell from it.[32] He introduced a dilemma: either the number of people born in the period between the beginning and the end of the ages is identical to the number of fallen angels, in which case it can be assumed that all men will come to salvation; or there will be more people born than there were angels who fell, which implies that some people represent a superfluity and will not therefore come to salvation as they will not "fit" into heaven.[33]

Most Eastern and Western authors resolve this dilemma by leaning towards an equivalent number of fallen angels and redeemed people, and this therefore offers itself as an authoritative solution. But the other possibility, of there being more people born in the world than there were angels who fell, is the direction in which Eriugena leaned.[34] What he especially attempted to demonstrate, however, was that whichever possibility is true, nothing can prevent the belief that in Christ all humankind will be redeemed and returned to Jerusalem saved from the power of the devil, who had gained certain rights over man (the so called *ius diaboli*), but lost them with the unjust killing of the man Jesus Christ.[35]

---

31 IOHANNES SCOTUS ERIUGENA, *Periphyseon (De divisione naturae)* 2,23 (CCCM 165,66–68; PL 122,574–575): "... divina eloquia hominem ad imaginem Dei factum perhibeant. Quod de angelis dixisse aperte non reperitur. Astantes etiam et ministrantes Deo caelestes virtutes legimus, humanam vero naturam in Verbo Dei Deum factam et sedere ad dexteram Dei et regnare fides testatur catholica. [...] Vides ne quantum humana natura in primo homine post peccatum humiliata est, et quantum in secundo homine, in Christo dico, per gratiam exaltata est? Siquidem non solum ad pristinum naturae suae statum de quo cecidit homo restitutus est, verum etiam super omnes caelestes virtutes exaltatus est. Ubi enim abundavit peccatum, superabundavit gratia. Si igitur humana natura non solum ad dignitatem angelicam in Christo renovata pervenit verum etiam ultra omnem creaturam in Deum assumpta est, et quod factum est in capite in membris futurum esse impium est negare, quid mirum si humani intellectus nil aliud sint nisi ineffabiles incessabiles que motus – in his dico qui digni sunt – circa Deum, in quo viuunt et moventur et sunt?"

32 IOHANNES SCOTUS ERIUGENA, *Periphyseon (De divisione naturae)* 5,38 (CCCM 165,205; PL 122,1005–1006): "Quo in loco illa non parva quaestio oritur, iam divulgata sed non iam, ut arbitror, soluta; et si soluta, nondum in nostras manus venisse fatemur. Quaeritur enim: Si tantus numerus hominum in consortium caelestis civitatis (hoc est societatis beatae multitudinis sub uno Deo degentis) reversurus est, quantus praevaricantium angelorum inde lapsus..."

33 IOHANNES SCOTUS ERIUGENA, *Periphyseon (De divisione naturae)* 5,38 (CCCM 165,205; PL 122,1005-1006).

34 IOHANNES SCOTUS ERIUGENA, *Periphyseon (De divisione naturae)* 5,38 (CCCM 165,205–206; PL 122,1005–1006).

35 IOHANNES SCOTUS ERIUGENA, *Periphyseon (De divisione naturae)* 5,38 (CCCM 165,207;

Let us add that a little later Eriugena inserted into his treatise a reflection that is not explicitly inspired by our theme but which nonetheless clearly relates to it. In his exposition of the command, "Go into all the world and preach the gospel to all creation" (Mark 16:15; NASB), he embraced an interpretation foreshadowed by St. Gregory: by "all creation" is meant man, who has something in common with all creatures – from stones all the way up to angels – and is therefore, in a certain sense, "all creation."[36] After this assertion there follows a further reflection, according to which if man is "all creation," and the Word of God became a man, then salvation reached the entirety of the world: the one who is in his deity the cause of everything, descended in his humanity into the effects he had caused and so returned everything to its true causes, as that which happened in this way in the incarnate Word of God is to happen at the end of the ages with the whole world and with every creature.[37]

Therefore, when the Word accepted human nature it accepted every creature, and when it saved and restored (*salvavit et restauravit*) human nature, it restored all creatures, visible and invisible (*omnem profecto*

PL 122,1005–1006): "Sive itaque aequalis sit numerus praevaricantium hominum et angelorum, sive uberior et multiplicior, nil obstat credere totum genus humanum et in Christo redemptum et in caelestem Hierusalem reversurum. Si enim aequalis, ut multis qui de talibus tractant videtur, ad laudem redemptoris nostri suffecerit, cuius providentia tantum humanae numerositatis praeordinavit, quantum posset mundi huius principi insultare. A quo non solum totum regnum nostrae naturae abstulit, verum etiam eius haereditatem, ex qua inflatus superbia deiectus est, nobis in aeternam possessionem distribuit, ut duplicis tristitiae poena torqueretur, una quidem qua regni sui quod primum hominem seducendo adeptus est iuste amissione secundum hominem occidendo iniuste, altera qua inimicis suis caelestem suam haereditatem (quam deseruerat) possidentibus invidendo cruciatur. Sin vero uberior, uberiorem profecto laudem gratiae ipsius debemus solvere, qui non solum possessiones antiqui nostri hostis nobis in caelo divisit, verum etiam numerosiores nos ad habitationem caelestis patriae praeparavit his, qui ea lapsi sunt. De generali reditu in paradisum praefata sufficiunt paradigmata, ut opinor."

36 IOHANNES SCOTUS ERIUGENA, *Periphyseon (De divisione naturae)* 5,25 (CCCM 165,73; PL 122,912); GREGORIUS MAGNUS, *Homiliae in evangelia* II,29,2 (CCSL 141,245–246; PL 76,1214). See Richard C. DALES, A Medieval View of Human Dignity, *Journal of the History of Ideas* 4 (1977), 557–572; Marie-Dominique CHENU, *La théologie au douzième siècle*, 33–43.

37 IOHANNES SCOTUS ERIUGENA, *Periphyseon (De divisione naturae)* 5,25 (CCCM 165,74; PL 122,912): "N(UTRITOR): Fateris ergo Verbum Dei, in quo et per quod et ad quod facta sunt omnia secundum suam divinitatem, in effectus causarum descendisse secundum suam humanitatem. [...] Non aliam ob causam, ut opinor, nisi ut causarum, quas secundum suam divinitatem aeternaliter et incommutabiliter habet, secundum suam humanitatem effectus salvaret in que suas causas revocaret, ut in ipsis ineffabili quadam adunatione, sicuti et ipsae causae, salvarentur. A(LUMNVS): Totus itaque mundus in Verbo Dei unigenito, incarnato, inhumanato adhuc specialiter restitutus est, in fine vero mundi generaliter et universaliter in eodem restaurabitur. Quod enim specialiter in se ipso perfecit, generaliter in omnibus perficiet, non dico in omnibus hominibus solummodo, sed in omni sensibili creatura."

creaturam visibilem et invisibilem restauravit).[38] Thus, the incarnation of the Word of God benefitted both angels and men: angels by bringing them knowledge; men by bringing them salvation. The Word of God was incomprehensible to angels and men before the incarnation, but through it the abundant light of knowledge came to them, which is why angels and men, united in the incarnate Word into one universal church, sing together their song of praise to God.[39] In the incarnate Word, the visible and invisible creatures were called back to the ineffable unity which in him is already a reality, and in creatures is yet to be realised: *per inhumanationem Filii Dei omnis creatura in caelo et in terra salva facta est.*[40]

Eriugena's argument fits in perfectly with the theme of our study. It shows that he was particularly concerned with the universal nature of Christ's saving work and was seeking reasons for supporting the salvation of all people, all angels, and even all creatures. In this respect the thesis of man as a replacement angel was for Eriugena merely supportive – even deficient. He was not so much concerned with whether a certain number of people will take the place of the fallen angels, but whether all men and all angels will be saved when the Word of God becomes man, that is, the one who is in a certain sense all creatures, as he has something in common with all creatures, therefore also with angels.

It is in Eurigena that we encounter the first truly creative theological approach to Augustine and Gregory's theme. In the eleventh century, St. Anselm will take up precisely this question upon which Scotus Eriugena was reflecting.

---

38 IOHANNES SCOTUS ERIUGENA, *Periphyseon (De divisione naturae)* 5,25 (CCCM 165,74; PL 122,912): "Ipsum siquidem Dei Verbum, quando accepit humanam naturam, nullam creatam substantiam praetermisit, quam in ea non acceperit. Accipiens igitur humanam naturam, omnem creaturam accepit. Ac per hoc si humanam naturam, quam accepit, salvavit et restauravit, omnem profecto creaturam visibilem et invisibilem restauravit."
39 IOHANNES SCOTUS ERIUGENA, *Periphyseon (De divisione naturae)* 5,25 (CCCM 165,75; PL 122,912–913).
40 IOHANNES SCOTUS ERIUGENA, *Periphyseon (De divisione naturae)* 5,25 (CCCM 165,75; PL 122,913): "Ac per hoc breviter concludendum. In ipso omnia visibilia et invisibilia (hoc est sensibilis et intelligibilis mundus) restaurata in que unitatem ineffabilem revocata sunt, adhuc in spe, in futuro vero in re, adhuc in fide, in futuro in specie, adhuc in argumento, in futuro in experimento, iam in ipso homine quem specialiter accepit factum, in futuro in omnibus generaliter perficiendum. Non itaque quis parvi pendat quod Dei Verbum inhumanatum sit ac veluti humanam naturam solummodo salvarit, sed firmissime credat et purissime intelligat quod per inhumanationem Filii Dei omnis creatura in caelo et in terra salva facta est."

10. Other references

Our account of the means by which Augustine and Gregory's concept of man as a "replacement angel" spread in the early Middle Ages is not, of course, exhaustive. Direct reading of the works of both fathers also inspired authors entirely individually, unexpectedly, for example the reflections on our theme in Irish and Anglo-Saxon contexts.[41] Here and elsewhere it also found artistic expression,[42] as with the Carolingian poet Audradus Modicus of Sens († c. 853).[43] Later, Peter, the twelfth-century abbot of the Benedictine abbey at Cava de' Tirreni, returned to our subject repeatedly in his commentary on 1 Kings (which was, as mentioned above, ascribed to St. Gregory),[44] and a combination of the thoughts of St. Gregory and St. Anselm of Canterbury was presented to his monastic brothers by Hermann of Tournai.[45]

---

41   David F. JOHNSON, The Fall of Lucifer in Genesis A and two Anglo-Latin Royal Charters, *Journal of English and Germanic Philology* 4 (1998), 511.515; Damian BRACKEN, The Fall and the Law in Early Ireland, in Próinséas NÍ CHATHÁIN – Michael RICHTER (eds.), *Ireland and Europe in the Early Middle Ages: Texts and Transmissions*, Dublin: Four Courts Press, 2002, 166.

42   Jeanne-Marie PONT, Homo angelorum decimus ordo; Y. CHRISTE – R. BONVIN, Les neufs choeurs angéliques; une création tardive de l'iconographie chrétienne, *Les Cahiers de Saint-Michel de Cuxa* 15 (1984), 67–99; Alessandro ROVETTA – Serena COLOMBO, Analisi iconografica del ciclo antelamico, in Giorgio SCHIANCHI (ed.), *Il battistero di Parma: iconografia, iconologia, fonti letterarie*, Milano: Vita e Pensiero, 1999, 163; Giorgio SCHIANCHI, Iconologia del programma iconografico del cantiere antelamico, ibid., 226ff.

43   AUDRADUS MODICUS, *Carminum in honore Ecclesiae* VI (MGH Poetae 3,84): "Denique de superis decimus quia corruit ordo, / Dum nollet laudare Deum, locus ipse polorum / Auxiliante Deo Petro piscante repletur." ID., *Carminum de sancta Trinitate* (MGH Poetae 3,743): "Angelicosque choros fecit laudemque paravit / Ac sibi cum genito iussit cantare decorem. / Hisque novem laeti gaudent se subdere iussis / Factorique suo laudes sine fine referre; / Sed decimus cecidit nolens laudare tonantem, / Seque creatori similiam quia dixit, in imis / Damnatus miseram servat sine luce gehennam. / Denique cum genitor per natum conderet orbem, Post propriis hominem manibus plasmavit, ut illi / Deliciis utens paradisi pangeret odas..."

44   GRÉGOIRE LE GRAND, *Commentaire sur le premier livre des Rois* I,44,2 (SC 351,250): "Tunc immolavit sollemnem hostiam, cum se aeterno Patri per glorificatae carnis materiam in caelo exhibuit et angelorum naturam, sicut de redemptione nostra, ita etiam de eorum reparatione laetificavit." See GRÉGOIRE LE GRAND, *Commentaire sur le premier livre des Rois* III,166,1; IV,26,2 (SC 432,278. 346–348).

45   HERMANNUS TORNACENSIS, *De incarnatione Christi* 2–5 (PL 180,14–19).

III. Crisis: the eleventh and twelfth centuries

In the preceding chapters we have shown how the subject of man as a "replacement angel" originated among the church fathers, namely Augustine and Gregory, and how it then continued its journey through the early Middle Ages. From the ninth century, we were particularly interested in Johannes Scotus Eriugena, who developed the subject christologically, paying particular attention to the question as to whether the number of men who will return to the heavenly city is equal to the number of angels who fell from it. At the dawn of the eleventh and twelfth centuries, we noted our theme among the circle of contemporaries of St. Anselm, archbishop of Canterbury, and our attention now turns in that direction. We will notice, subsequently, how the question as to whether man was not perhaps created for his own sake – which Anselm introduced in passing, as it were, and to which he gave but a hesitant answer – appeared in the context of other theological enquiries in the school of Laon, which arrived at the opinion that both men and angels were created for their own sake in order that *laus perfecta* may be offered to God. We will also see how Rupert of Deutz connected the question of the goal of the creation of man (*cur homo*) with the question of the primary goal of the incarnation of the Word (*cur Deus homo*) and came to the conclusion that both men and angels were "original" creatures, made for the man Jesus Christ, the incarnate Son of God. Rupert inspired Honorius of Autun, a determined advocate of the idea that man was created for his own sake and will be admitted as such into the heavens: God has, since time immemorial, wished for man's deification and this is why, not only because of sin, the Son of God became incarnate. We are now at the very heart of our problematics.

1. Anselm of Canterbury

In the previous chapter we saw how our theme arrived in the milieu of St. Anselm of Canterbury (1033–1109). In the context of the exegesis of Eph 1:10 and Luke 2:14 we mentioned Lanfranc of Canterbury (c. 1005–1089), Bruno of Cologne (c. 1030–1101), Hervaeus of Bourg-Dieu (c. 1075–1149/1150) and Hildebert of Lavardin (c. 1056–1133). We can also add Osbern of Canterbury († c. 1090).[1]

Our theme appears repeatedly in Anselm's own work.[2] There is one brief mention in the context of Mary in *Oratio* 7, which is yet to be definitively dated.[3] More extensive references can be found in *De casu diaboli* from 1085/1090. In chapter 5, the author asks himself whether the good angels were capable of sin before the fall of the evil angels. He answers in the affirmative, arguing that if the good angels were not capable of sin, they would have remained just by default and would not therefore have deserved God's grace for what amounted to nothing more than preserving the reason they were unable to lose; for this they could not rightly be called just. If, however, the angels who fell had not sinned, despite being capable of doing so, they would have been better than those whose justness pertained to them simply because they were not capable of sin. From this it would follow either that elect men would be better than the good angels, or that the replacement of the reprobate angels would be imperfect since the men who would assume their places would not be the same as they, the reprobate angels, were to have become.[4]

1   OSBERNUS CANTUARIENSIS, *Vita S. Dunstani* 40 (PL 137,449): "O Rex Dominator gentium, salva genus Christianorum in terra adhuc perigrinantium, ut et ipsi post inimicitias ad gratiam revertantur, et angelicae ruinae per illos damna reparentur."

2   The relevant texts have been identified by Yves CONGAR, L'Église chez S. Anselme, 373. Of these we can omit ANSELMUS CANTUARIENSIS, *Oratio* 2 (S. Anselmi Cantuariensis Opera omnia III,7), where it appears in an inconclusive sentence: "Heu mihi, qui videre non potui dominum angelorum humiliatum ad conversationem hominum, ut homines exaltaret ad conversationem angelorum." Also on our motif in Anselm see Markus ENDERS, "Nichts liebt Gott mehr in dieser Welt als die Freiheit seiner Kirche": Anselm von Canterburys Verständnis der Kirche, kirchlicher Lebensformen und des Verhältnisses der kirchlichen zur weltlichen Gewalt, in Christoph STUMPF – Holger ZABOROWSKI (eds.), *Church as Politeia: The Political Self-Understanding of Christianity*, Berlin-New York: Walter de Gruyter, 2004, 29–46.

3   ANSELMUS CANTUARIENSIS, *Oratio* 7 (S. Anselmi Cantuariensis Opera omnia III,21): "Sed cur solum loquor, domina, beneficiis tuis plenum esse mundum? Inferna penetrant, caelos superant. Per plenitudinem enim gratiae tuae et quae in inferno erant se laetantur liberata, et quae supra mundum sunt se gaudent restaurata. Per eundem quippe gloriosum filium gloriosae virginitatis tuae, omnes iusti qui obierunt ante vitalem eius mortem exultant diruptione captivitatis suae, et angeli gratulantur restitutione semirutae civitatis suae."

4   ANSELMUS CANTUARIENSIS, *De casu diaboli* 5 (S. Anselmi Cantuariensis Opera omnia

In chapter 23, Anselm claims that just as it is certain that the evil angel could not have not known he *ought* to be punished if he sinned, it is also true that he did not necessarily know that he actually *would* be punished if he sinned. This is because the devil could not, in all his rationality, have known whether the mysterious God would actually do what he could with complete justice do, especially as up to that point no example had yet been given of justice punishing injustice. The unchangeable (*certus*) number of those created to enjoy God was fixed in advance by such wisdom that there is nothing superfluous in it, since if the number had been diminished it would have become imperfect, but God's work could not be imperfect in any respect. It does not follow from this, however, that the devil could have known that if he himself fell, God would replace angelic nature with human nature, or would restore each of them individually to that end for which each had been created in itself and not in regard to anything else. This would have been the case if man had already been created; and if he had not yet been created the devil would have been even less able to suppose that if he himself sinned, man would be created to substitute for the nature of another being.[5]

It appears that Anselm takes Augustine's thesis as fact and integrates it as such into his reflections, and at the same time returns to the perspective of God's eternal plan. He utilizes it, however, in a different way, and that is in order to better understand the fall of the evil angels. In this context, doubts gradually begin to appear concerning whether man was indeed created as a replacement for another nature, or rather whether each nature was created in some way for itself and was precisely in this manner to participate in the work of redemption. As will become clear, this hesitant idea (which betrays a certain preference of the author) is crucial.

1,243): "Unde sequitur quia aut electi homines meliores et maiores erunt angelis bonis, aut reprobi angeli perfecte non restaurabuntur, quoniam non tales erunt homines qui pro illis assumentur, quales illi futuri erant."

5   ANSELMUS CANTUARIENSIS, *De casu diaboli* 23 (S. Anselmi Cantuariensis Opera omnia 1,270): "... sed et si quis dicat quia nullatenus credere potuit Deum creaturam suam propter eius culpam damnaturum, quam tanta sua bonitate fecerat – praesertim cum nullum exemplum iustitiae ulciscentis iniustitiam praecessisset, et certus esset numerum in quo illi facti erant qui Deo frui deberent tanta sapientia esse praestitutum, ut sicut nihil habebat superfluum ita si minueretur imperfectus esset, nec tam praeclarum opus Dei ex aliqua parte permansurum imperfectum, nec ulla ratione scire posset si homo iam factus erat, Deum humanam naturam pro angelica aut angelicam pro humana si caderet substituturum, sed potius unamquamque in id ad quod facta erat pro se non pro alia restituturum, aut si factus nondum erat homo, multo minus putare posset ad substitutionem alterius naturae illum esse faciendum..."

Anselm returns once more to our theme in *Cur Deus homo* (1094–1098). The three chapters he devotes to it (I,16–18) represent about one seventh of the text; the theme also returns in subsequent chapters (I,19.23; II,6.15.16).[6] It is clear, therefore, that the subject matter is important to Anselm and not simply *"la digression imposée hors son sujet."*[7] *Cur Deus homo* starts with the question as to why, and out of what necessity, God became man and, through his death, returned life to the world, despite his being capable of achieving the same result by a different person (angelic or human) or by a simple act of his will.[8] The answer was to rest on *rationes necessariae,* the concatenation of which was to cover the whole of Christian faith.

The history of salvation therefore put Anselm in the position of needing to explain why God's honour, defamed by the fall of the angels, is to be restored by the Son of God becoming man. It was therefore necessary to move from the angels' sin to man's redemption, and here Anselm found to hand Augustine's thesis, which he understood as a kind of axiom: *Deum constat proposuisse ut de humana natura quam fecit sine peccato numerum angelorum qui ceciderant restitueret.* Even so, he attempted to support this assertion by using a form of argument: part of the universal order that God established (*dispositio, universitatis ordo*) is the number of citizens, that is, beings of a rational nature, in the heavenly city. It is impossible, after all, to suppose that God could not have known what number would be best, and because he knew it, it is also clear that he created that precise quantity. It is *numerus praescitus, praedestinatus, perfectus, integer;* it can be neither increased nor diminished. The fallen angels were created as part of this number, since if the opposite had been the case, they would have been created beyond its scope, in excess, and therefore necessarily destined to sin, which is nonsensical.[9] From this it

6   René ROQUES, Introduction, in ANSELME DE CANTORBERY, *Pourquoi Dieu s'est fait homme* (SC 91,126–130). See also, Attilio CARPIN, *La redenzione in Origene, s. Anselmo e s. Tommaso,* Bologna: Edizioni Studio Domenicano, 2000, 85–90.

7   Marie-Dominique CHENU, *La théologie au douzième siècle,* 53.

8   ANSELMUS CANTUARIENSIS, *Cur Deus homo* I,1; II,18 (S. Anselmi Cantuariensis Opera omnia II,126).

9   ANSELMUS CANTUARIENSIS, *Cur Deus homo* I,16 (S. Anselmi Cantuariensis Opera omnia II,74–75): "Rationalem naturam quae Dei contemplatione beata vel est vel futura est, in quodam rationabili et perfecto numero praescitam esse a Deo, ita ut nec maiorem nec minorem illum esse deceat, non est dubitandum. Aut enim nescit Deus in quo numero melius eam deceat constitui, quod falsum est; aut si scit, in eo illam constituet, quam ad hoc decentiorem intelliget. Quapropter aut angeli illi qui ceciderunt, facti erant ad hoc ut essent intra illum numerum; aut quia extra illum permanere non potuerunt, ex necessitate ceciderunt, quod absurdum est opinari."

follows that if they had fallen from this predetermined number by their own fault, then their number had somehow to be restored (*restaurandus*), otherwise the number of rational beings that had been foreknown as perfect would remain imperfect, which is not possible.[10]

The question is from whom the number was to be made up. It could not be from either the fallen angels or the good angels: Anselm had already proved this in *De casu diaboli* and returned to it briefly in *Cur Deus homo*.[11] Crucial for Anselm was the conclusion that rational nature could be made up only from human nature.[12] For the purposes of his investigation this was a decisive moment as it would help to explain why God became a man.

In order to restore his honour – honour that will brook no deviation from its original intentions – God set his work back on its original course by accepting men into the heavenly city in place of the fallen angels. These ought to have been the same as the good angels but because of their sin they were not, and they therefore needed to attain justification.[13] But man, permeated by sin, was not capable of this: he could not justify himself and thereby make up the number of heavenly beings even though he was made expressly for this purpose (*ad quem complendum factus est homo*).[14] It therefore holds that although it is man through whom the

---

10 ANSELMUS CANTUARIENSIS, *Cur Deus homo* I,16 (S. Anselmi Cantuariensis Opera omnia II,75): "Quoniam ergo de illo numero esse debuerunt: aut restaurandus est ex necessitate numerus eorum, aut in imperfecto remanebit numero rationalis natura, quae in numero perfecto praescita est; quod esse non potest."

11 ANSELMUS CANTUARIENSIS, *Cur Deus homo* I,17; II,21 (S. Anselmi Cantuariensis Opera omnia II,75–76; 132).

12 ANSELMUS CANTUARIENSIS, *Cur Deus homo* I,16 (S. Anselmi Cantuariensis Opera omnia II,75): "Necesse est ergo eos de humana, quoniam non est alia de qua possint, natura restaurari."

13 ANSELMUS CANTUARIENSIS, *Cur Deus homo* I,19 (S. Anselmi Cantuariensis Opera omnia II,84): "Tales ergo oportet esse homines in illa civitate superna qui pro angelis in illam assumentur, quales ibi futuri erant illi pro quibus ibidem erunt, id est quales nunc sunt boni angeli. Alioquin non erunt restaurati qui ceciderunt, et sequetur quia Deus aut non poterit perficere bonum quod incepit, aut paenitebit eum tantum bonum incepisse; quae duo absurda sunt. [...] Potesne cogitare quod homo, qui aliquando peccavit nec umquam Deo pro peccato satisfecit, sed tantum impunitus dimittitur, aequalis sit angelo qui numquam peccavit? [...] Non ergo decet Deum hominem peccantem sine satisfactione ad restaurationem angelorum assumere perditorum, quoniam veritas non patitur eum levari ad aequalitatem beatorum."

14 ANSELMUS CANTUARIENSIS, *Cur Deus homo* I,23 (S. Anselmi Cantuariensis Opera omnia II,91): "Nullatenus ergo debet aut potest accipere homo a Deo quod Deus illi dare proposuit, si non reddit Deo totum quod illi abstulit; ut sicut per illum Deus perdidit, ita per illum recuperet. Quod non aliter fieri valet nisi ut, quemadmodum per victum tota humana natura corrupta et quasi fermentata est peccato, cum quo nullum Deus assumit ad perficiendam illam civitatem caelestem, ita per vincentem iustificentur a peccato tot homines quot illum numerum

heavenly city is to be perfected, this is not possible without man offering to God perfect satisfaction, which he is obliged to do; but of this man is not capable, only God. It therefore follows that God's intentions cannot be fulfilled without the Son becoming incarnate and justifying men through his death on the cross.[15]

In chapter 18, Anselm inserts into his argument a lengthy aside in which he asks whether more men will be justified and admitted into heaven than there were angels who fell. Thus he returned to the idea introduced by Augustine and Gregory and developed by Eriugena, who attempted to think things through in such a way as to support his belief in the final salvation of all people. But Anselm used the idea in a different way: for him it became a means for reflecting upon whether there is any truth in the idea that man was created merely to replace the lost angels. We are therefore now at the very core of the thesis about man as a "replacement angel." It was a question that occupied Chenu, who within Anslem's problematic *cur Deus homo* recognized the question *cur homo*.

Anselm contended that if the foreknown number of rational beings that are to dwell in blissful contemplation of God corresponded exactly to the number of angels from among which those who fell are to be replenished by men, then man was created only as a replacement for those fallen angels (*non sunt homines facti nisi pro restauratione angelorum perditorum*). If, however, the intention was to create fewer angels than the foreknown total number of beings, and men were included in greater numbers than was necessary for the simple replenishing of the reprobate angels, then man was made not only for replenishing the depleted number but also in order to perfect an as yet imperfect number (*et sic dicemus quia non fuerunt homines facti tantum ad restaurandum numerum imminutum sed etiam ad perficiendum nondum perfectum*).[16]

---

completuri erant, ad quem complendum factus est homo. Sed hoc facere nullatenus potest peccator homo, quia peccator peccatorem iustificare nequit."

15 ANSELMUS CANTUARIENSIS, *Cur Deus homo* II,6.15 (S. Anselmi Cantuariensis Opera omnia II,101.116): "Si ergo, sicut constat, necesse est ut de hominibus perficiatur illa superna civitas, nec hoc esse valet, nisi fiat praedicta satisfactio, quam nec potest facere nisi Deus nec debet nisi homo: necesse est ut eam faciat Deus-homo. [...] Ecce vides quomodo rationabilis necessitas ostendat ex hominibus perficiendam esse supernam civitatem, nec hoc posse fieri nisi per remissionem peccatorum, quam homo nullus habere potest nisi per hominem, qui idem ipse sit Deus atque morte sua homines peccatores Deo reconciliet. Aperte igitur invenimus Christum, quem Deum et hominem confitemur et mortuum propter nos."

16 ANSELMUS CANTUARIENSIS, *Cur Deus homo* I,18 (S. Anselmi Cantuariensis Opera omnia II,76): "Si angeli, antequam quidam illorum caderent, erant in illo perfecto de quo diximus numero, non sunt homines facti nisi pro restauratione angelorum perditorum, et palam est quia non erunt plures illis. Si autem ille numerus non erat in illis omnibus angelis, complendum

It was this second possibility to which Anselm leaned in an argument that was further complicated by the question as to whether everything was created simultaneously (Sir 18:1) or gradually (Gen 1). We will not present here the way in which Anselm progressed his argument, which contains echoes of Augustine and Gregory's theses, but only the conclusion to which he returned over and over again: that there were more men created for eternal bliss than there were angels who fell. Within this complex argument we can detect the assertion that the perfection of creation (*perfectio mundanae creaturae*) lies not so much in the number of individuals but rather in the number of natures. It is therefore clear that man was created more in order to complete this aspect of the perfection of creation, which is why we must then assume that human nature was created for its own sake and not only in order to replace individuals of another, angelic nature (*quare pro se ipsa ibi facta est, et non solum pro restaurandis individuis alterius naturae*): man would have had his place in the heavenly city even if the angels had not fallen.[17]

That said, in chapter 19 Anselm returns to his previous interrupted exposition, following it up with his original starting point: *Constat Deum proposuisse, ut de hominibus angelos qui ceciderant restauraret. – Certum est.*[18] Later, he even added that the very reason man was created was to complete the number of the citizens of heaven.[19]

Chronologically, the final reference to our subject appears from a conference Anselm held in Cluny in 1100. Here he suggested that he who aspires to a virtuous life can be of benefit to the angels by completing, from among good people, the depleted number.[20]

---

est de hominibus et quod periit et quod prius deerat, et erunt electi homines plures reprobis angelis; et sic dicemus quia non fuerunt homines facti tantum ad restaurandum numerum imminutum, sed etiam ad perficiendum nondum perfectum."

17 ANSELMUS CANTUARIENSIS, *Cur Deus homo* I,18 (S. Anselmi Cantuariensis Opera omnia II,77–78): "Sed et si perfectio mundanae creaturae non tantum est intelligenda in numero individuorum quantum in numero naturarum, necesse est humanam naturam aut ad complementum eiusdem perfectionis esse factam, aut illi superabundare, quod de minimi vermiculi natura dicere non audemus. Quare pro se ipsa ibi facta est, et non solum pro restaurandis individuis alterius naturae. Unde palam est quia, etiam si angelus nullus perisset, homines tamen in caelesti civitate suum locum habuissent. Sequitur itaque quia in angelis, antequam quidam illorum caderent, non erat ille perfectus numerus. Alioquin necesse erat, ut aut homines aut angeli aliqui caderent, quoniam extra numerum perfectum ibi nullus manere poterat."

18 ANSELMUS CANTUARIENSIS, *Cur Deus homo* I,19 (S. Anselmi Cantuariensis Opera omnia II,84).

19 ANSELMUS CANTUARIENSIS, *Cur Deus homo* I,23 (S. Anselmi Cantuariensis Opera omnia II,91): "... ita per vincentem iustificentur a peccato tot homines quot illum numerum completuri erant, ad quem complendum factus est homo."

20 *Eadmeri Cantuariensis monachi Scriptum de beatitudine perennis vitae sumptum de verbis beati An-*

It is clear that Anselm worked with the Augustinian thesis repeatedly, diversely, and over a long period. In *Cur Deus homo* he considers as pivotal the idea that if God's honour was first defamed by the sin of the angels, which causally and perhaps chronologically predates the fall of man, this begs the question as to how God's Son by becoming man can be the very thing that restores this honour. Augustine's proposition – that God's original creative intention is achieved by creating man to replace the fallen angels – is used here as a kind of bridge to reflecting upon the redemption of sinful men through the incarnate Word. In *De casu diaboli* 23 and *Cur Deus homo* I,18, doubts are carefully introduced as to whether human nature was truly created as a replacement for angelic nature, or whether, rather, it was created for its own sake. Although Anselm leans in this latter direction, ultimately he returns to the traditional position of Augustine.

2. The school of Laon

Chenu noted that while Anselm of Canterbury was developing his theories, the school of Laon was also occupying itself with the question as to whether man was created as a replacement for the fallen angels.[21] The school's most renowned representative was Anselm of Laon (c. 1050–1117), erroneously considered to be a student of the archbishop of Canterbury while he was living at Le Bec Abbey, and perhaps correctly assumed to be a student of Bruno of Cologne. From about 1080 he became head of the cathedral school at Laon, which gained great renown during the time of his incumbency alongside his brother Ralph (c. 1060–c. 1133), partly because of its association with William of Champeaux (c. 1070–1121) and a number of other leading personalities of the time.

In works that have been connected with his name, our theme appears particularly in *Glossa ordinaria,* an interlinear gloss on Scripture

selmi 15, in *Anselmo d'Aosta nel ricordo dei discepoli*, eds. Inos Biffi – Aldo Granata – Costante Marabelli – Davide Riserbato, 520: "Qualiter autem bonus homo sit etiam angelis utilis, inde cognoscitur, quod ex societate bonorum hominum numerus illorum qui diminuitus erat redintegratur. Cum igitur aliquis per vitam bonam in societatem illorum currit, magnum quid ipsis praestat, quia quantum in ipso est, numerum eorum supplet et perficit. Omni quoque iusto homini, necnon omni creaturae iustum hominem utilem dimus."

21 Marie-Dominique CHENU, *La théologie au douzième siècle*, 53–54. Chenu, however, knew only *Sententie divine pagine* and *Sententiae Anselmi*, with which he worked in a different way to that descibed here. As far as we can see, no other researcher has noted anything of significance concerning the presence of our theme in works from the school of Laon.

penned by Anselm and some of his students.[22] Occasions for recalling the
ideas of St. Augustine and St. Gregory were the topoi of Luke 15:3–10
(Anselm of Laon or Ralph of Laon),[23] Eph 1:10 (Anselm of Laon [?]),[24]
and Rev 11:13 (Anselm of Laon or Gilbert de la Porrée [?]),[25] which was
commented on repeatedly.[26] There is no need to lay any great stress on
the influence this codification of the patristic thesis in *glossa ordinaria*
had on future exegesis as all of the places noted represent simple echoes
of Augustine and Gregory; they bring nothing original, and simply bear

22 Determining the genuiune authorship of individual glosses and biblical commentaries attributed to Anselm is still problematic. See Cédric GIRAUD, *Per verba magistri: Anselme de Laon et
son école au XIIe siècle*, Turnhout: Brepols, 2010, 84–101; Alexander ANDRÉE, *Gilbertus Universalis: Glossa ordinaria in Lamentationes Ieremie Prophete: Prothemata et Liber I: A Critical Edition with
an Introduction and a Translation*, Stockholm: Almqvist & Wiksell International, 2005, 20–24;
Lesley SMITH, *Glossa Ordinaria: The Making of a Medieval Bible Commentary*, Boston (MA): Brill
Academic Publishers, 2009, 17–38; Alexander ANDRÉE, Anselm of Laon unveiled: The Glossae Super Iohannem and the Origins of the Glossa Ordinaria on the Bible, *Mediaeval Studies*
73 (2011), 217–260; Atria A. LARSON, The Influence of the School of Laon on Gratian: The
Usage of the Glossa Ordinaria and Anselmian Sententiae in de Penitentia (Decretum C. 33
q. 3), *Mediaeval Studies* 72 (2010), 197–244; Ludwig HÖDL – Rolf PEPPERMÜLLER – Heinrich J. F. REINHARDT, Anselm von Laon und seine Schule, in *Theologische Realenzyklopädie*,
Bd. 3, Berlin-New York: Walter de Gruyter, 1978, 1–2; Beryl SMALLEY, Glossa ordinaria, in
Theologische Realenzyklopädie, Bd. 13, Berlin-New York: Walter de Gruyter, 1984, 453.
23 *Biblia cum glossa ordinaria* (ad Lc 15,4.8), pars IV, Straßburg: Adolf Rusch, 1480/1481, [201]:
"Centum oves. Quia centenarius numerus perfectus est. Deus centum oves, i. perfectum numerum habuit, cum angelorum et hominum substantiam creavit, sed una periit, quando homo
pascua vitae peccando derelinquit, ergo quia rationalis creaturae numerus pereunte homine
erat diminutus, quaerit in terra hominem ut summa integretur. [...] Habens drachmas decem.
Angelorum et hominum naturam, quam ad aeternitatem Dominus constituere voluit, ad suam
similitudinem creavit. Decem ergo drachmas mulier habuit, eum novem ordinibus angelorum
additus est homo, ut compleretur decimus electorum numerus. Qui nec post culpam a Creatore
perrit, quia eum sapientia Dei per carnem miraculis coruscans ex lumine testem reparavit."
24 *Biblia cum glossa ordinaria* (ad Eph 1,10), pars IV, [375–376]: "Instaurare. Aug. Instaurantur
quippe quae in caelis sunt, cum id quod inde cecidit in angelis redditur ex hominibus; instaurantur autem quae in terris, cum ipsi homines qui praedestinati sunt in aeternam vitam
a corruptionis vetustate renovantur. Omnia, quae in caelis. Id est angelos. Vel Instaurare, id
est supplere. Quae in caelis. Id est numerum angelorum diminutum implere. Quae in caelis.
Augustinus in Enchiridion. Non pro angelis mortuus est Christus, sed ideo pro angelis fit
quidquid hominum per eius mortem redimitur: quia cum redit homo in gratiam post inimicitias quas inter homines et sanctos angelos, et ruinae angelicae damnum reparantur. Et utique
noverunt angeli sancti docti a Deo cuius veritatis aeterna contemplatione beati sunt, quanti
numeri supplementum de genere humano integritas illius civitatis exspectat."
25 *Biblia cum glossa ordinaria* (ad Ap 11,13), pars IV, [569]: "Et decima pars. Id est homo qui ad
hoc constitutus videtur ut decimus ordo restauretur."
26 [ANSELMUS LAUDUNENSIS?], *Enarrationes in Apocalypsin* 11 (PL 162,1541): "...decima pars
civitatis, id est mali, licet ad hoc sint constituti, ut decimus ordo ex hominibus restitueretur."

witness to the fact that the statements of both fathers were known to the school of Laon.

Other writings connected with the name Anselm of Laon and his school include a number of "sentences," short writings in which a biblical starting point is developed into a systematic theological thesis. They are contained in the florilegio *Liber pancrisis*[27] and in other collections of sentences.[28]

A more detailed investigation reveals that the school of Laon responded in greater measure to Augustine's statement in *De Genesi ad litteram* 9,6,11–9,7,12, according to which God created man as male and female so that from their conjugal union as many human beings would be born as were necessary to complete the predetermined number of holy citizens of the heavenly city. God's plan assumed human procreation before the original sin, but it was to be carried out with all purity and without passion. All begotten human beings would then by the grace of God proceed straight to their final state. After the first sin, the intention to complete the number of heavenly citizens through the union of man and woman remained unchanged. What is necessary now, however, is also conversion and resurrection from the dead. Augustine added that if God holds virginity and continence in such high regard then it must mean that a sufficient number of human beings have already been begotten.[29]

---

27 See for example Cédric GIRAUD, *Per verba magistri*, 185–326.

28 There are several of these. The editions are of variable quality, not always easily accesible, and difficult to orient oneself within (See Rolf SCHÖNBERGER et alii, *Repertorium edierter Texte des Mittelalters aus dem Bereich der Philosophie und angrenzender Gebiete*, Bd. 1, Berlin: Akademie Verlag, 2011, 529–534). We will hold to the results achieved by Cédric GIRAUD, *Per verba magistri*, 339–388, who identified

(a) the eight most important collections, which provide the basic evidence for the theology of the school of Laon, from which four attained wide circulation: *Deus non habet* and its successor *Deus itaque summe; Deus de cujus* and its successor *Deus principium et; Principium et causa* = *Sententiae Anselmi;* and *De sententia divine* = *Sententie divine pagine;* and four with a smaller circulation: *Divina essentia teste* = *Sententiae Atrebatenses; Quid de sancta* = *Sententiae Berolinenses; Potest queri quid; Deus est sine* = *De conditione angelica et humana*

(b) ten incomplete collections, although still connected with the school of Laon: *Augustinus. Semel immolatus est Christus; Deus hominem fecit perfectum; Tribus ex causis; Dubitatur a quibusdam; Decretum Dei fuit; Origo et principium; Antequam quicquam fieret; Filius a Patre gigni; Voluntas Dei relata;* and *De novissimis;*

(c) two insufficiently representative collections: *Prima rerum origo;* and *Sententiae Klagenfurtes* = *Deus est sine;*

(d) three collections which bear little similarity to the teaching and language of the school of Laon: *Pater iste familias; Sententiae magistri A.;* and *Sententiae Varsavienses.*

Our study will be working the collections noted in (a) and (b).

29 See AUGUSTINUS, *De Genesi ad litteram libri duodecim* 9,7,12 (CSEL 28/1,275; PL 34,397).

This idea does not itself contain the theme we are interested in, so the corresponding sentences do not always represent it clearly[30] and often settle for a direct quotation from Augustine,[31] as is the case with *Glossa*.[32] At other times, however, we will find the idea in connection with the assertion that man was created in order to replace fallen angels, thus in the sense of Augustine's *Sermo* 229/H,2 and *De civitate Dei* 14,26, as we find in the incomplete collection of sentences *Origo et principium*,[33] and in the sentences of William of Champeaux.[34] The assertion that is most worthy of note, however, is in the collection *Quid de sancta* = *Sententiae Berolinenses*, which represents an explicit polemic with the thesis and with the authorities that support it: the church fathers agree that man was created in order that his offspring might replace the apostate genus of angels (*ut eorum immaculata sobole apostaticum suppleretur genus angelorum*); "We, however, say that God created man in order that he [God]

---

30 *Liber pancrisis* (L 41, n. 45); *Deus non habet* (John C. WEI, The Sentence Collection: Devs Non Habet Initivm Vel Terminvm and Its Reworking, Devs Itaqve Svmme atqve Ineffabiliter Bonvs, *Mediaeval Studies* 73 (2011), 65); *Quid de sancta* = *Sententiae Berolinenses* (Friedrich STEGMÜLLER, Sententiae Berolinenses. Eine neugefundene Sentenzensammlung aus der Schule des Anselm von Laon, *Recherches de théologie ancienne et médiévale* 11 (1939), 48); *Voluntas Dei relata* (L 346, n. 523); *In primis hominibus* (Bernd MATECKI, *Der Traktat In primis hominibus: eine theologie- und kirchengeschichtliche Untersuchung zu einem Ehetext der Schule von Laon aus dem 12. Jahrhundert*, Frankfurt am Main: Lang, 2001, 1*).

31 *Principium et causa* = *Sententiae Anselmi* (Franz BLIEMETZRIEDER (ed.), *Anselms von Laon systematische Sentenzen*, Münster: Verlag der Aschendorffschen Verlagsbuchhandlung, 1919, 130); *Decretum Dei fuit* (Heinrich WEISWEILER, *Das Schrifttum der Schule Anselms von Laon und Wilhelms von Champeaux in Deutschen Bibliotheken: ein Beitrag zur Geschichte der Verbreitung der ältesten scholastischen Schule in Deutschen Landen*, Münster i. W.: Verlag der Aschendorffschen Verlagsbuchhandlung, 1936, 363); *Sententiae Magistri A* n. 22 (Heinrich J. F. REINHARDT, *Die Ehelehre der Schule des Anselms von Laon. Eine theologie- und kirchenrechtsgeschichtliche Untersuchung zu den Ehetexten der frühen pariser Schule des 12. Jahrhunderts. Anhang: Edition des Ehetraktates der Sententie Magistri A*. Münster: Aschendorff, 1974, 171).

32 *Biblia cum glossa ordinaria* (ad Gn 2,18), pars I, Straßburg: Adolf Rusch, 1480/1481, [27].

33 *Origo et principium* (L 331, n. 520): "... postea vero providens rerum unitatem competenter futuram, disposuerat enim per hominem, rem scilicet fragilioris nature, spiritualem ordinem iam deiectum se reparaturum, ne nimis [nimirum] ex diversis crearentur homines, fecit Deus obdormire Adam et subtraxit ei costam unam, fecit ei Evam et inspiravit ei animam fragilioris tamen nature quam viro."

34 GUILLELMUS DE CONCHIS, *Sententiae* (L 202, n. 246): "Plantavit et lignum vite quo senium et mortem vitaret; sic ergo vivendo, sine aliqua carnis molestia, sine libidinis ardore, filios et filias procrearet donec, praedestinatorum numero completo, ad veram immortalitatem transferretur, ubi nullo ligni usu indigeret"; L 204, n. 248: "Cum autem Adam in obedientia permanens sine concupiscentia esset, tamen coiret cum uxore quia sciebat se ideo factos esse ut ex illis restitueretur angelicus ordo..."; L 207, n. 254: "Sciens enim se a Deo ideo creatum ut per eum numerus perditorum restaureretur, sina aliqua carnali delectatione coiret cum uxore, ut si aliquis digitum suum imponeret in aliquid sine aliqua delectatione."

may receive entirely sufficient praise." (*Nos vero dicimus, idcirco hominem creasse, ut eius laus esset omnino sufficiens.*) God was to be praised by all kinds of creature imaginable, which is why in addition to creatures of a spiritual nature – angels – he created creatures of a physical nature, and man as a being who was both physical and spiritual.[35]

This critique relies upon a typical and fundamental theological perspective of the school of Laon inspired by the church fathers,[36] through whom it interprets Plato's dialogue *Timaios* (29E–30A), which was known from Calcidius's Latin translation.[37] Thus in Laon they reached a formula that provided some kind of a synthesis: God in himself is supremely and infinitely perfect and blessed, and is not dependent on anything outside of himself; but in this he is also free of all envy and self-centredness. For this reason, out of his goodness and love, he wished for beings to exist that would participate in his blessedness. But since God is a

35 *Quid de sancta = Sententiae Berolinenses* (Friedrich STEGMÜLLER, Sententiae Berolinenses, 45): "Sed quaeritur: Quare homo factus sit. Sancti Patres inveniuntur in hoc esse concordes, dicentes scilicet, Deum idcirco masculum et feminam fecisse ut eorum immaculata sobole apostaticum suppleretur genus angelorum. Alias quoque reddunt causas. Dicit enim beatus Hieronymus: Deus in ruina malignorum spirituum petentem iustitiam et latentem exercuit misericordiam. Sed non decebat tantum patrem familias, in quo patens erat iustitia, patente carere misericordia. Fecit igitur hominem in quo non modo iustitiam sed etiam patentem exerceri misericordiam. Nos vero dicimus, idcirco hominem creasse, ut eius laus esset omnino sufficiens. Quia enim a solis incorporeis laudabatur creaturis. Si esset vel esse posset aliud genus creaturae, a quo posset laudari et non laudaretur, non esset laus eius omnino sufficiens. Fecit igitur Deus hominem ut qui ab invisibilibus et incorporeis ladabatur creaturis, a visibilibus quoque et corporeis dignae et plenae laudis sucsciperet famulatum."

36 Cédric GIRAUD, *Per verba magistri*, 261 points, via *Liber pancrisis* 140, to GREGORIUS MAGNUS, *Moralia in Iob* 4,3,8 and 4,7,12 (CCSL 143,168–169.171; PL 75,641–642.643–644). No less significant is AUGUSTINUS, *De civitate Dei* XI,24 (CCSL 48,343–344; PL 41,338); ID., *Enchiridion de fide et spe et caritate* 3,9 (CCSL 46,53; PL 40,236).

37 PLATO, *Timaeus a Calcidio translatus commentariosque instructus*, ed. Jan Hendrik Waszink, London: The Warburg Institute – Leiden: Brill, 1962, 22–23 (Corpus Platonicum Medii Aevi: Plato Latinus 4): "Timaeus: Dicendum igitur, cur rerum conditor fabricator que geniturae omne hoc instituendum putaverit. Optimus erat, ab optimo porro invidia longe relegata est. Itaque consequenter cuncta sui similia, prout cuiusque natura capax beatitudinis esse poterat, effici voluit; quam quidem voluntatem dei originem rerum certissimam si quis ponat, recte eum putare consentiam. Volens siquidem deus bona quidem omnia provenire, mali porro nullius, prout eorum quae nascuntur natura fert, relinqui propaginem, omne visibile corporeum que motu importuno fluctuans neque umquam quiescens ex inordinata iactatione redegit in ordinem sciens ordinatorum fortunam confusis inordinatis que praestare. Nec vero fas erat bonitati praestanti quicquam facere nisi pulchrum erat que certum tantae divinitati nihil eorum quae sentiuntur, hebes dumtaxat nec intellegens, esse melius intellegente, intellectum porro nisi animae non provenire. Hac igitur reputatione intellectu in porro anima in corpore locata, totum animantis mundi ambitum cum veneranda illustratione composuit. Ex quo apparet sensibilem mundum animal intellegens esse divinae providentiae sanctione."

spirit, such participation is possible only for creatures that are capable of knowing and willing. For this reason God created angels, beings of a purely intellectual nature. At this stage, however, all kinds of beings capable of participating in his blessedness were yet to be created, and the praise of God was as yet incomplete. This is the precise reason God also created the material world and in it placed man, a being who was both physical and spiritual. Everything that is purely material is made for man, and through man matter gives praise to God. Thereby, through angels and men, in whom the material world is also contained, a city is established, the heavenly Jerusalem, in which he is given to wonder at and celebrate God, and this way, in his knowing, loving, and praising, to participate in God's eternal bliss: *Beatitudo enim vera et summa est Deum amare et videre*. The creation of rational beings, men and angels, for God's glory and the tasting of eternal life is, however, committed to their freedom and thus also to their merits: from here unfolds the drama of salvation.[38]

This perspective is so fundamental for the school of Laon that we will find it not only in all of the principal and widely disseminated collections of sentences[39] but also in those collections that gained a more restricted

---

38 *Potest queri* (Heinrich WEISWEILER, *Das Schrifttum der Schule Anselms von Laon*, 260): "Deus enim creans hominem ad gloriam sui, scilicet ut frueretur eterna vita, sicut et angelica natura ad hoc quoque condita est, voluit ex magna bonitate sua, ut hoc quoque promereretur, ut in exhibitione illius eterne vite sicut bonitas Dei ita quoque eius iusticia existeret, quia omnes vie Domini misericordia et veritas."

39 *Deus non habet* (John C. WEI, The Sentence Collection, 39): "Deus non habet initium vel terminum, et ipse qui tantus est voluit cognosci, sicque amari atque laudari, et hoc ideo ut aliqui essent participes sue beatitudinis, que est ineffabilis. Unde creavit rationalem creaturam et incorpoream, scilicet angelos, et corpoream, ut hominem." *Deus de cujus* (Heinrich WEIS-WEILER, Le recueil de sentences Deus de cujus principio et fine tacetur et son remaniement, *Recherches de théologie ancienne et médiévale* 5 (1933), 254): "Deus de cuius principio et fine taceretur voluit agnosci et cognoscendo laudari et laudando amari ut cognoscendo, laudando, amando aliquis efficeretur particeps glorie sue." Ibid., 258: "Laus divina nondum fuit perfecta ab incorporea creatura. Fecit igitur et corpoream non ex angelica natura sed ex diversa materia hominem scilicet ex terra et animam ad imaginem et similitudinem suam." Ibid., 265: "Queritur, quare creavit, quem casurum previdit. Voluit Deus cognosci et cognoscendo laudari et laudando hominem et angelum sue glorie participes fieri." *Principium et causa* = *Sententiae Anselmi* (Franz BLIEMETZRIEDER (ed.), *Anselms von Laon systematische Sentenzen*, 48–49): "Creavit autem hec omnia non, ut sue beatitudini, que plena semper et perfecta in se et per se fuit, aliquid adderet, sed ut aliquos sue beatitudinis participes faceret. Sed quia huius beatitudinis capax esse nichil potest, nisi quod et eam intelligit et discernit, creaturam fecit rationalem, angelum et hominem, quibus intellectum dedit et rationem, ut cognoscerent Creatorem suum, et cognoscendo laudarent et laudando amarent, ut cognoscendo, amando, laudando sue immense beatitudinis participes fierent. Beatitudo enim vera est Deum amare et videre." *De sententia divine* = *Sententie divine pagine* (Franz BLIEMETZRIEDER (ed.), *Anselms von Laon systematische Sentenzen*, 10–11): "Cum divina essentia sit summe bona et ab ea teste

circulation,[40] or that are incomplete, or that are connected with the school of Laon somewhat more loosely.[41] We will also find them in the school's most prominent students, primarily in the sentences of William of Champeaux,[42] who may also have been the person who discovered on Laon's behalf the relevant interpretation of Plato.[43] The interpretation also

Augustino etiam omnis invidia relegata esset, essetque in ea plenitudo caritatis, necessitas erat non exigens, sed decens, ut quod caritatis erat exequeratur. Sed quia caritas non vult sola esse, non sola frui suis rebus, ideo decuit eum velle aliquos fieri participes sue glorie. Excogitavit ergo penes ipsum Deus, quod constitueret quandam civitatem, id est, celestem Iherusalem, que et eum admiraretur et glorificaret, et glorificando fieret participes sue beatitudinis. Decrevit autem facere civitatem non unius parietis, sed duorum, id est, corpoream substantiam, scilicet hominem, et incorpoream, scilicet angelum, quia in ore unius non est tam perfecta laus, sicut in ore duorum. Unde dicit apostolus: In ore duorum vel trium testium stet omne verbum. Corpoream autem substantiam non fecit hebetem, sed animatam et rationalem, et hoc non ex se, sed ex admixtione incorporee substantie, id est anime."

40 *Divina essentia teste* = *Sententiae Atrebatenses* (L 405, n. 531): "Cum vero a divina essentia, teste Augustino super Genesim, omnis invidia relegata, id est remota esset, et in ea esset plenitudo caritatis, voluit Deus facere aliquos participes sue beatitudinis, non ut sue beatitudinis que plena et perfecta semper fuit, aliquid adderet, sed quia huius beatitudinis capax esse nichil potest nisi quod eam et intelligit et discernit, creaturam fecit rationalem, angelum scilicet et hominem, quibus intellectum et rationem dedit ut creatorem suum cognoscerent et cognoscendo laudarent et laudando amarent, ut cognoscendo, laudando, amando, sue immense beatitudinis participes fierent: beatitudo enim summa et vera est Deum videre et amare." *Quid de sancta* = *Sententiae Berolinenses* (Friedrich STEGMÜLLER, Sententiae Berolinenses, 43): "Ille qui tantus erat, noluit esse solus. Sed voluit cognosci atque laudari et aliquos suae beatitudinis participes fieri. Fecit itaque duo genera creaturarum, corpoream scilicet et incorporeum. Corporeum, videlicet hominem. Incorporeum vero angelos." *Deus est sine* = *De conditione angelica et humana* (Yves LEFÈVRE, Le De conditione angelica et humana et les Sententiae Anselmi, *Archives d'histoire doctrinale et littéraire du moyen âge* 26 (1959), 256): "Deus est sine principio et sine fine et ipse qui tantus est voluit se cognosci ut ameretur. Et ideo voluit se cognosci et amari ut per cognitionem et amorem sui aliqui essent participes suae immensae beatitudinis. Creavit igitur rationalem creaturam incorpoream et rationalem creaturam corpoream."

41 *Antequam quicquam fieret* (L 335, n. 521); *Voluntas Dei relata* (L 343, n. 523).

42 GUILLELMUS DE CONCHIS, *Sententiae* (L 198, n. 240): "Deus igitur, cum esset bonus et felix, voluit aliquos sue bonitatis ac felicitatis esse participes, constituitque rationales creaturas, angelos scilicet et homines, ex quibus civitatem suam componeret."

43 In *De sententia divine* = *Sententie divine pagine* a *Divina essentia teste* = *Sententiae Atrebatenses,* cited above, Plato's motif is actually attributed to St. Augustine, in whom it is not present, however. Explicitly in connection with Plato: GUILLELMUS DE CONCHIS, *Glossae super Platonem* 1, 48 (CCCM 203,85–86): "OPTIMUS ERAT. Incipit ostendere finalem causam mundi scilicet divinam bonitatem. Cum enim certum esset divinae sapientiae omne bonum cum participatione plurium in commune deductum pulcrius elucescere, talem facere creaturam voluit quae ratione et intellectu illam inquireret, inquirendo inveniret, inventam diligeret, dilectam imitaretur. Et quoniam duo genera creaturarum sunt, corporea et incorporea, ut in utroque esset aliquid rationale, angelum et hominem creavit. Sed angelo, quia spiritus est, caelum, homini ut ponderoso terram habitationi permisit. Sed quia homo diversorum est indigens, propter hominis indigentiam cetera creavit. Ut ergo sola bonitas fuit hominem creare, sic et necessaria homini praeparare. Ergo sola bonitas divina est omnium finalis causa. Et hoc est: OPTIMUS

appears in the works of Peter Abelard (1079–42),[44] and in hints – connected with the teachings of the school of Laon – in the works of Gilbert
de la Porrée (1076–1154).[45]
It was from these suppositions that Anselm of Laon and his school
arrived at the assertion we have noted from the collection of sentences
Quid de sancta = Sententiae Berolinenses: man was not created in order that
he may beget offspring to replace fallen angels but simply in order
that through knowing, loving, and praising he may participate in God's
blessedness; man was necesary for the praise of God to be complete. Every creature is an individual voice in the choir that glorifies its Creator,
and each is necessary for what the school of Laon called *laus perfecta*. The

ERAT Creator, quia nichil est melius ipso vel aequaliter bonum. Sed ne aliquis putaret quod
optimus esset sed invidia tardaretur, addit: PORRO id est certe INVIDIA RELEGATA EST id
est retro legata scilicet remota AB OPTIMO id est a Creatore. Quod per diffinitionem invidi
probari potest. Est enim invidi alienis bonis affligi: quod in Creatore convenire non potest a
quo et in quo est omne bonum nec aliquid alienum. Ergo, cum omnia et sciret et posset nec
invidia retardaretur, omnia bona creavit."

44 PETRUS ABAELARDUS, *Theologia christiana* 1,3 (CCCM 12,73): "Ex summa itaque illa bonitate sua Deus, qua iuxta Moysen cuncta valde bona condidit, et iuxta etiam Platonis asser-
tionem „optimus" ipse omnium conditor, „a quo invidia relegata longe est, cuncta sui similia,
prout cuiusque natura capax beatitudinis esse poterat, effici voluit, – volens siquidem Deus
bona quidem omnia provenire, mali porro nullius, prout eorum quae nascuntur natura fert,
reliquit propaginem nec fas sit bonitati praestanti quidquam facere nisi pulcherrimum", – ex
hac, inquam, tanta bonitate sua Deus, qua singula, quantum potest aut decet, bona efficit ac
bene disponit etiam mala altissimo suo et incomprehensibili nobis consilio, Spiritus Sanctus,
ut supra meminimus, ipse est appellatus." PETRUS ABAELARDUS, *Sententiae magistri Petri
Abaelardi* 167 (CCCM 14,85): "Deus, ut diximus, benignus est et misericors et miserator, huius
benignitatis effectum, cum ipse in se nichilo indigeat – utpote qui sibi per omnia sufficiens
est – in creaturis suis exercet. Cum igitur in se solo sit affectu benignus, in creaturis solis efficit
quod bonitate tali constat efficiendum. At vero qui summe bonus est ab eo porro omnis invidia
relegata est, omnis itidem ira, omnis furor ab eo longe remotus est."

45 GILBERTUS PORRETANUS, *Sententiae* XIII,7: Nicholas M. HÄRING, Die Sententiae
magistri Gisleberti episcopi Pictavensis, *Archives d'histoire doctrinale et littéraire du moyen âge* 45
(1978), 162–163: "Queritur quare creavit duo genera spirituum rationalium, scilicet hominum
et angelorum. Unde talis causa redditur quia Deus ante rerum creationem solus summe bonus
et qui nulli invidebat volens aliqua facere que participarent sua bonitate et hoc non poterat
facere sine intellectu. Ideo creavit angelos et animas hominum qui participarent sua bonitate."
See Nicholas M. HÄRING, Die Sententiae magistri Gisleberti episcopi Pictavensis, *Archives
d'histoire doctrinale et littéraire du moyen âge* 46 (1979), 96. [GILBERTUS PORRETANUS],
Sententiae divinitatis, in Bernhard GEYER, *Die Sententiae divinitatis: Ein Sentenzenbuch der
gilbertschen Schule aus den Handschriften zum ersten Male herausgegeben und historisch untersucht*,
Münster: Aschendorffische Buchhandlung, 1909, 7*–8*: "Creavit igitur Deus rationalem
creaturam, angelum scilicet et hominem, ut Deum cognoscerent, cognoscendo laudarent,
laudando diligerent. [...] facturus erat Deus hominem ad se laudandum et glorificandum,
qui loco indiget; ideoque mundum creavit quasi domum, in qua hominem poneret, cuius
consideratione in eius cognitione et dilectione homo proficeret."

idea that is implied here is very clear: man was created for his own sake. It is not declared formally in these texts but is nonetheless clearly present. The school of Laon was not, however, content only to critique the assertion that man was created as a replacement for fallen angels. They went further, to assert that man would have been saved even had no angel fallen, and to claim that if man had not been saved, the creation of the world would have been in vain. The passage that is relevant to our enquiry is taken from a commentary on Heb 2:10, which states: "For it was fitting that he, for whom and by whom all things exist, in bringing many sons to glory, should make the pioneer of their salvation perfect through suffering." (*Decebat enim eum propter quem omnia et per quem omnia, qui multos filios in gloriam adduxerat, auctorem salutis eorum per passionem consummare.*) *Glossa,* therefore, contains the core of the sentence[46] that *Liber pancrisis* attributes to Anselm of Laon, and which may also be the source for all of the works mentioned above.

In this sentence, Anselm stated that the supremely blessed God, out of his supreme goodness, wished for creatures to participate in his blessedness. This is possible only through knowing and loving, which is why he created angels who can praise him. But so that this praise should not be imperfect (*ut laus imperfecta non esset*), he also created material creatures with whom he desired to share his blessedness. He therefore joined a body to a rational soul and created man to praise God, with body and soul, so that God was fully praised by all creatures (*et ita laus Dei ab omni creatura plena esset*). All creatures offer praise to God when rational beings, angels and man, recognize in themselves and all other creatures God's power and goodness and give him praise. As the author of the epistle to the Hebrews stated, everything is created for him and through him (Anselm reads, for God), and nothing is superfluous (*nihil scilicet superflue*).[47]

---

46   *Biblia cum glossa ordinaria* (ad Heb 2,10), pars IV, [432].

47   *Liber pancrisis* (L 50, n. 54): "Idem secundum magistrum Anselmum super versum illum: Deus enim eum propter quem omnia et per quem omnia. Deus omnipotens si nullam penitus creaturam fecisset, in seipso plene beatus esse potuisset, quippe nullo indigens, sed sibimet usquequaque sufficiens. Volens autem ex summa bonitate creaturam beatificari, quod ipsius tantum cognitione et amore fruiturum erat, angelicas fecit creaturas a quibus laudaretur, non ut ei aliquid de laude eorum accresceret, sed ipsis. Porro eadem bonitate, ut laus imperfecta non esset, corpoream creaturam condidit et beatificare voluit; hac de causa spiritum rationalem corpori indidit, quatenus bene regendo ipsum simul cum corpore in Deo beatificaretur et ita laus Dei ab omni creatura plena esset. Inde est quod omnia dicuntur Deum laudare, dum rationales creaturae, angeli scilicet et homines, miram Dei potentiam et bonitatem tam in se quam in ceteris creaturis mirantur et laudant. Sic ergo, ut Apostolus ait, propter eum omnia scilicet laudandum et glorificandum et per eum omnia, nihil scilicet superflue."

Anselm follows the writer of the letter to the Hebrews and moves from the order of creation to the order of redemption. If what has been said is true, it was necessary for man to be brought to the glory of re-demption. When man fell into sin, he ceased to praise God. He and all of the physical-material creation was therefore created in vain (*otiose igitur facta est*). Furthermore, the angels also ceased to fully praise God as their number had been depleted (*nec ipsi angeli plane laudant, cum numerus eorum diminutus sit*). From here follows the necessity for redemption – a necessity that has its source exclusively in God's highest goodness.[48]

A line of argument follows by which Anselm attempts to prove that neither God by himself, nor any man or angel, or any kind of incarnate angel, but only God-who-became-man was able to effect this redemption. By his sin, man put himself at the mercy of the devil. If the devil was to be stripped of his rights (*ius diaboli*), this had to be done justly, which is precisely why man needed to be released from the power of the devil by the incarnate God, who as God *could* do it and as a man *had* to do it (*oportet ergo ut auctor ille salutis Deus in homine sit, qui ex hoc quod Deus est possit, ex hoc quod homo debeat*). It had to happen through the suffering of the God-man, as it was by the devil's slaying of this innocent, a slaying by which he transgressed the boundaries of his entitlements, that he rightly lost all of his power over men.[49]

---

48 *Liber pancrisis* (L 50, n. 54): "Quod si verum est, immo quia verum est, hominem duci ad gloriam necesse est, que tamen necessitas non aliunde quam ex maxima Dei quam prediximus bonitate descendit. Homo peccato suo perditus est; ergo ad gloriam non ducitur, ergo ipse non laudat, consequenter ergo corporea creatura non laudat; otiose igitur facta est. Quod si ita est, ergo nec ipsi angeli plane laudant, cum numerus eorum diminutus sit. Ut autem omnia hec inconvenientia ab ipso quo procedunt fonte suprimamus, hominem perditum ad gloriam duci constituamus, cuius gloriose salvationis ordinem ipso auctore adiuvante videamus."

49 *Liber pancrisis* (L 50, n. 54). The patristic thesis relating to *ius diaboli* was clearly of great interest within the school of Laon. See for example *Biblia cum glossa ordinaria* (ad Heb 2,11), pars IV, [432]; the sentences of Anselm (L 44–47, n. 47–48) and the sentences of Ralph, two of which again relate to Heb 2:10: RADULPHUS LAUDUNENSIS, *Sententiae* (L 184–186, n. 231–232, 187–188, n. 234); the collection *De sententia divine = Sententie divine pagine* (Franz BLIEMETZRIEDER (ed.), *Anselms von Laon systematische Sentenzen*, 37–38, 40–42). It is clear that Anselm of Laon established a similar subject to Anselm of Canterbury in *Cur Deus homo*. It should be noted that when the archbishop of Canterbury argued, in *Cur Deus homo* I,7, against the theory concerning *ius diaboli* (S. Anselmi Cantuariensis Opera omnia II,55–59), he was distancing himself from Ralph of Laon's definition (L 186, n. 232). See Cédric GIRAUD, *Per verba magistri*, 264–266; R. W. SOUTHERN, *Saint Anselm and his Biographer: A Study of Monastic Life and Thought 1059–c. 1130*, Cambridge: Cambridge University Press, 1963, 357–361; C. W. MARX, *The Devil's Rights and the Redemption in the Literature of Medieval England*, Cambridge: D. S. Brewer, 1995; Judith Rachel DUNTHORNE, *Anselm of Canterbury and the Development of Theological Thought, c. 1070–1141* (Durham theses – submitted for examination for PhD), Durham: Durham University, 2012, passim <http://etheses.dur.ac.uk/6360/> [2013-05-21].

The conclusion to the sentence provides the following summary: God the Father created everything so that he may be praised and glorified. For this to be realised, however, it was necessary that through the incarnation, surrender, and suffering of the pioneer of salvation a number of God's sons from among the ranks of men were brought to eternal glory. From this it follows that man would have had to be saved even if the angels had not sinned (*quem ordinem si diligenter attendis, videbis hominem debuisse salvari, etsi nullus angelus cecidisset*).[50] The implication is that *laus perfecta* is possible only through man, a spiritual and physical being without whose salvation everything would have been created in vain. This claim appears not only in this sentence of Anselm's but also in the work of his brother Ralph, whose phrase *aliter omnia frusta essent facta*[51] recalls the commentary on Heb 2:10: *frustra omnia facta essent*.[52] It also appears in the collection of sentences contained in the manuscript Paris, BNF, n.a.l. 181, in which Anselm and Ralph's idea raises angelological implications: the angels praise God through man, not because they require a visible creature for their praise, but because they rejoice in man's conversion and so praise God for this, all the more because they know that the world would have been created in vain if man had not been saved (*scit enim mundi fabricam in cassum factam nisi homo salvandus sit*).[53]

---

50 *Liber pancrisis* (L 50, n. 54): "Singulos nota passus: Decebat multos filios in gloriam adducere eum, scilicet Patrem, propter quem scilicet laudandum et glorificandum facta sunt omnia et per quem facta sunt omnia et hoc dando auctorem salutis, et hunc dando passioni et sic consummando. Quem ordinem si diligenter attendis, videbis hominem debuisse salvari, etsi nullus angelus cecidisset."

51 RADULPHUS LAUDUNENSIS, *Sententiae* (L 187, n. 234): "Cum ergo hinc sub iure eius cui spontanee se addixerat esset, tamen locum venie apud Deum habebat, hinc etiam nec [necessarium? VN] esset salvari hominem, quia aliter omnia frusta essent facta; omnia enim Deus fecerat [sibi] nec possent laudare Deum nisi per hominem et sic laudant per hominem, quia dum homo utpote rationalis mirificentia Dei considerans in creaturis et propter usus suos esse factas laudat Deum propter creaturas et ita creature per hominem laudant Deum, ecce necesse est salvari hominem."

52 *Biblia cum glossa ordinaria* (ad Heb 2,10), pars IV, [432]: "Per passionem. Quia aliter homo redemptus periret, quod si esset, frustra omnia facta essent. Cetera enim homini serviunt, homo Deo. Nec in aliquibus Deus glorificetur, cum ad hoc omnia facta sunt, falsa esset predestinatio de adducendis filiis."

53 Cédric GIRAUD, Théologie et Pédagogie au XIIe siècle: les sentences d'Anselme de Laon et de son école dans le manuscrit Paris, BNF, n.a.l. 181, *Archives d'histoire doctrinale et littéraire du Moyen Âge* 1 (2012), 270, n. 153: "Laudare dicitur quelibet creatura Deum quando incitat hominem ad laudandum. Propter hominem enim omnia visibilia facta sunt. Quare non etiam propter angelum queret aliquis. Nonquid enim angeli non laudant Deum commoti per visibilia? Sed sciendum quoniam spiritualis natura spiritualiter videt nec eget ut a visibilibus excitetur, sed de homine converso gaudet et laudat. Scit enim mundi fabricam in cassum factam

The sentence we have quoted widely does not contain any explicit reference to the thesis that man was created as a replacement for fallen angels, but neither does it argue directly against it. It did, however, fundamentally go beyond that idea as it assumes that man is a being who was made for his own sake, that is, for his irreplaceable contribution to the work for which everything was created, namely the perfect praise of God, by which, through knowing and loving, creation participates in God's blessedness. This praise is so indispensable that in his infinite goodness, God the Father was somehow obliged to save sinful man through the incarnation and suffering of his Son, regardless of what happened to the angels (according to Anselm of Laon, even if the angels had not sinned).

In the light of these assertions, those statements in which the school of Laon commented on the patristic thesis become easier to comprehend. What is being suggested is not that man would not have been created if the angels had not fallen, but that he simply takes their place in eternal glory.[54] The collection of sentences *De sententia divine = Sententie divine pagine* goes so far as to assert that man was not created primarily in order to make up the number of angels: although this goal was in actual fact fulfilled, man would have been created even if the angels had not sinned (*non ideo factus est homo principaliter, ut restitueretur numerus angelorum; consecutus est quidem ille effectus, scilicet restauratio, sed etiamsi angelus non cecidisset, tamen homo fieret*).[55]

---

nisi homo salvandus sit." See n. 11: "Fecit etiam corporalia que nulla ratione vigerent nec Dei contemplatione beata fierent. Videtur ergo aliquid superfluere in magna Dei rei publica, nisi illa bruta animalia alicui prodessent ad beatitudinem. Spiritus enim his non vescebatur nec in aliquo his egebat. Factus est itaque ex rationali e spiritu et corpore homo qui ex natura corporali his opus habebat, ex rationali autem spiritu Deum contemplaretur et sic se et corpus cui unitum fuit simul beatificaret."

54 *Divina essentia teste = Sententiae Atrebatenses* (L 411, n. 531): "Qui homo propter restaurationem predictorum angelorum factus dicitur; non quin factus esset etsi illi non cecidissent, sed quia in gloriam quam illi perdiderunt homo suscipitur, quasi locum illorum subintrare videtur; et ideo propter eorum restaurationem factus dicitur." *Principium et causa = Sententiae Anselmi* (Franz BLIEMETZRIEDER (ed.), *Anselms von Laon systematische Sentenzen*, 55): "Hinc homo loco perditorum angelorum factus dicitur, non quin factus esset etiam, si illi non cecidissent, sed cum in gloriam, quam illi perdiderunt, homo suscipitur, quasi locum illorum subintrare videtur."

55 *De sententia divine = Sententie divine pagine* (Franz BLIEMETZRIEDER (ed.), *Anselms von Laon systematische Sentenzen*, 15): "Si quis autem querat, cum Deus sciret casurum, quare ergo peccavit? Penes ipsum sit. Intelligendum est autem, quod de omnibus illis ordinibus ceciderunt, et plures remanserunt, quam cecidissent. Unde, cum dicat auctoritas, quod tot ascensuri sunt quot ceciderunt, dicimus, quod non ideo factus est homo principaliter, ut restitueretur numerus angelorum; consecutus est quidem ille effectus, scilicet restauratio, sed etiamsi angelus non cecidisset, tamen homo fieret."

This last statement is proffered in the context of reflections upon the assertion that as many people will be admitted into heaven as there were angels who fell. As we have already stated, this is a subject that interested Augustine, Gregory, and Eriugena. In Laon, they clearly knew the patristic authors, and with them asked whether as many people will be admitted into the heavenly country as there were angels who remained there, or as many as who fell, or still more.[56] They were also acquainted with how Anselm of Canterbury commented on the matter in *Cur Deus homo* 18. Together with him, they asked themselves why the company of angels was not restored from among other angels but from among people, which they answered simply by pointing to *beneplacitum Dei*.[57] They also asked whether man was created only for this purpose or also for his own sake (*an etiam propter se*),[58] but here this question remained more

---

56 See *Deus non habet* (John C. WEI, The Sentence Collection, 48–49): "Queritur etiam quot de hominibus sint ascensuri ad celestem patriam: vel quot remanserunt spiritus, vel quot ceciderunt, an plures," and the following collection of the relevant texts from Gregory and Augustine. See also the various sentences that touch on the subject: L 83, n. 99, l. 14–16: "Novem autem tantum fuerunt ordines angelorum et de singulis dignior pars cecidit. Quot autem remanserunt tot homines ascendunt." L 125, n. 173: "Erant qui dicunt tot fideles ad vitam intraturos quot angeli ceciderunt, cum sancti multis rationibus affirment tot homines salvandos quot angeli permanserunt. Et si plures salventur a nullo diffinitur." L 126, n. 175: "Erant etiam qui dicunt unum solum chorum et illum totum cecidisse, cum potius aliqui de singulis choris ceciderint, quia adhuc tot sunt chori angelorum quot primum a Deo sunt ordinanti." L 343, n. 523.

57 *De sententia divine* = *Sententie divine pagine* (Franz BLIEMETZRIEDER (ed.), *Anselms von Laon systematische Sentenzen*, 18): "Solet queri, quare non ex angelis restaurandi alii angeli, sed ex hominibus. Et est summa causa beneplacitum Dei. Cur autem sic ei placuerit, penes ipsum sit. In libro tamen qui intitulatur: Cur Deus homo, habentur inde due coniecture, quarum prima est talis. Si Deus restauraret numerum angelorum ex angelis, hoc videretur contrarium priori creationi rerum. Quod nec ipse evidenter explanat, nec nos aliud percipimus, nisi quod Deus omnia in perfectione creavit, et ita angelum qui cecidit. Ille autem qui restauraret locum eius, maioris dignitatis videretur esse quam qui cecidit, in hoc scilicet, quod nec caderet sicut et ille. Sed hec coniectura debilis est, cum idem de homine coniectari possit. Alia coniectura est talis, quod qui in locum illius restitueretur, deberet esse illius beatitudinis, ad quam ille, si stetisset, pervenisset; sed ille, si stetisset, esset beatus sine exemplo vel terrore precedentis casus; et ita non esset eiusdem beatitudinis, et ita non ex angelis debuit restitui locus ille. Sed eadem oppositio fieri de homine potest."

58 *De sententia divine* = *Sententie divine pagine* (Franz BLIEMETZRIEDER (ed.), *Anselms von Laon systematische Sentenzen*, 18–19): "Cum autem ex hominibus restaurentur angeli, potest queri an propter restaurationem angeli tantum factus sit homo, an etiam propter se. Si autem angelus et homo simul creati sunt, secundum auctoritatem Qui manet [in eternum, creavit omnia simul], non est ratio quod homo pro restauratione illa sit factus, cum ante casum angeli fuerit creatus. Dicunt quidam quod fuit quaedam preparatio, cum previdisset casurum. Si autem post formatus est, tunc est verisimile, sed non cogens. Item sunt alie coniecture, quod non ideo tantum. Si enim ideo tantum homo factus esset, homo sciens se non pervenisse ad beatitudinem, nisi ille cecidisset, gauderet de casu angeli, et ita non maneret in dilectione proximi, et ita Deus non bene consuluisset creature sue, cum sibi tam difficile posset cavere."

or less unanswered, which corresponds fairly closely to the state of affairs with Anselm of Canterbury, who although inclined to the conviction that each nature (including human nature) was willed and created for its own sake, eventually returned to the original thesis about the creation of man as a replacement for fallen angels.

However, in other texts, led by the theological principle of *laus perfecta*, the school of Laon was more assertive. It was aware of the patristic thesis and made reference to it, but reached the clear and unambiguous conclusion that above all man was made for his own sake, that is, in order that he may offer the praise to God that only he can give, and which is also necessary as within this praise resounds the voice of all other physical creatures: for the purpose of creation to be fulfilled, man must praise God. Hence the work of redemption, for which the angels give praise to God, was to a certain degree also necessary. The number of angels was diminished by the fall, and so too was their praise. Redeemed man, however, makes up for the praise of these fallen angels even though man would have been created and redeemed even if the angels had not fallen. What remains undecided, however, is the ratio of angels to men assumed by this substitution.

We should add that among the other prominent students of the school – aside from William of Champeaux – there was little interest in the question as to whether man was created as a replacement for fallen angels or for his own sake. Peter Abelard mentioned it only in direct quotation from St. Gregory;[59] Gilbert de la Porrée did so when he took an interest in the ratio of the number of angels who remained – or who fell – to the number of men who are to take their place in heaven.[60]

Item cum plures angeli remanserint quam ceciderint, et tot sint ascensuri de hominibus quod remanserunt, apparet quod non tantum pro restauratione; quia si tantum pro restauratione, tunc non plures ascenderunt, quam ceciderant."

59 He does so in *Sic et non* 49,1 (ed. Blanche B. Boyer – Richard McKeon, Chicago: The University of Chicago Press, 1976, 222), where he does not take issue with it. We have not found the theme at all in Gilbert de la Porrée and his school.

60 GISLEBERTUS PORRETANUS, *Sententiae* XIII,27–29: Nicholas M. HÄRING, Die Sententiae magistri Gisleberti episcopi Pictavensis, *Archives d'histoire doctrinale et littéraire du moyen âge* 45 (1978), 166: "27. Modo queritur utrum sint tot ascensuri quot cecidere. Cum enim inveniatur quod homo ad hoc creatus est ut restauraret angelorum casus videtur quod tot sint ascensuri quot cecidere. 28. Sed alia auctoritas est quod tot sint ascensuri quot remansere. Ibi statuit terminos gencium iuxta numerum filiorum Dei. Et si tot ascensuri sunt quot cecidere vel quot remansere, ergo tot ceciderunt quot remanserunt. Sed hoc nescimus utrum sint tot ascensuri quot cecidere. Sed scimus tot ascendent quot remanserunt. 29. Item queritur utrum VIIII ordines tantum creat sunt. Dicimus quod novem tantum. Si autem inveniatur decimus ordo cecidit, diversis modis exponitur. Decimus ordo i.e. tot fuerunt qui ceciderunt ex VIIII

Despite this, it is certainly legitimate to suggest that the school of Laon made an essential contribution to the fact that our theme went on to be addressed with considerable innovation by some of the authors who followed.

3. Rupert of Deutz

One of the most significant authors in this category was Rupert of Deutz (1075/80–c. 1129). Rupert was born in Liège, entered the monastery there, and after a clash with theological adversaries sheltering under the authority of Anselm of Laon, retreated – from 1114 to 1117 and again in 1119 – to the monastery in Siegburg; in 1120 he became abbot of the monastery in Deutz. His polemic with the school of Laon related to three fundamental themes: the place assigned to sin in God's purposes for the world, and thus the question as to whether or not God willed sin (*an Deus velit mala fieri*); the place of Christ in this plan, and the question as to whether or not sin was the only reason for the incarnation, which would not otherwise have happened (*cur Deus homo*); and the place taken by man in this plan, that is, the question as to whether man would have been created if the angels had not sinned (*cur homo*).[61]

When Magrassi was exploring the third of these questions, he relied on the analysis in *De sancta Trinitate et operibus eius, Commentaria in evangelium sancti Iohannis,* and *De glorificatione Trinitatis et processione Spiritus sancti.* He established the presence of our theme in *De sancta,* but stated that it is only there by implication in *Commentaria* (where it should in fact no longer be), and that it is subjected to critique in *De glorificatione.* He wanted to demonstrate, therefore, that in the works of Rupert of Deutz the subject of man's creation as a replacement for fallen angels first recedes into the background and is then openly criticized through Rupert's development of his Christocentric understanding of the history of salvation. In his presentation, however, Magrassi lost sight of the dating

ordinibus quod posset fieri ex illis unus ordo i.e. multitudo convenientium in aliquo, scilicet in superbia. Si autem inveniatur quod decem ordines creati sunt, dicamus quod novem ordines boni. Illis autem qui ceciderunt fuerunt quasi ordo decimus." See Nicholas M. HÄRING, Die Sententiae magistri Gisleberti episcopi Pictavensis, *Archives d'histoire doctrinale et littéraire du moyen âge* 46 (1979), 98–99.

61 On the relationship between Rupert and the school of Laon, see Mariano MAGRASSI, *Teologia e storia nel pensiero di Ruperto di Deutz,* 263–271; Maria Lodovica ARDUINI, Anselmo di Laon, Ruperto, sant'Agostino, *Aevum* 2 (2006), 377–387; Cédric GIRAUD, *Per verba magistri,* 162–177.

of individual works. He did not, moreover, consider all of the works in which the theme occurs.[62] Our subject first appears, for the time being in hints only, in *De divinis officiis* from 1111, in which the topoi of Luke 2:14 and Luke 15:8–10 are inserted into a commentary on the holy mass.[63] Rupert wrote two further works, *Commentaria in evangelium sancti Iohannis* and *De sancta Trinitate et operibus eius*, concurrently. The former was written between 1115 and 1116; the latter between 1114 and 1117. The final redaction of *Commentaria in evangelium sancti Iohannis* predates the redaction of *De sancta Trinitate et operibus eius*. However, Magrassi, who established the date of this work,[64] offered a presentation of these writings in reverse order, doing so in order to support his existing thesis.

In service of his thesis, Magrassi laid great stress on Rupert's commentary on John 1:4, in which it is suggested that just as an architect carries in his mind the entire form of the future building, so God's intention for the world was, from the beginning, directed towards the Word, in which existed the order and nature of God's plan for everything that was to be made. In it God foreknew the fall of creation and also held the intention of re-establishing his glory. The incarnation of the Word does not represent an addition to God's decision but an idea the Father liked to such a degree that he decided upon it even before the devil began his destructive work; it is akin to a playful act of God's wisdom; an expression of the joy of God's goodness (Prov 8:30–31).[65]

---

62 Mariano MAGRASSI, *Teologia e storia nel pensiero di Ruperto di Deutz*, 25–26. For a list of Rupert's works and their dates, see Ibid., 23–35; Rolf SCHÖNBERGER et alii, *Repertorium edierter Texte des Mittelalters aus dem Bereich der Philosophie und angrenzender Gebiete*, Bd. 3, Berlin: Akademie Verlag, 2011, 3548–3554; Jean GRIBOMONT, Introduction, 40–43; Maria Lodovica ARDUINI, Rupert von Deutz, *Theologische Realenzyklopädie*, Bd. 29, Berlin-New York: Walter de Gruyter, 1998, 474–483.

63 RUPERTUS TUITIENSIS, *De divinis officiis* 30 (PL 170,27).

64 He proceeded in a similar vein in the chapter devoted to the place of Christ in God's plan of salvation, doing so in order to prove a linear development of Rupert's ideas. See Mariano MAGRASSI, *Teologia e storia nel pensiero di Ruperto di Deutz*, 221–244.

65 RUPERTUS TUITIENSIS, *Commentaria in evangelium sancti Iohannis* I (CCCM 9,14–15; PL 169,211): "Plane incomparabiliter constantius atque perfectius omnium quae facienda erant in hoc Verbo vivebat ordo vel natura. Nec solum noverat ab initio quae vel qualiter omnia conderet suo que statu singula disponeret sed etiam quaedam perdita qualiter ad suam gloriam recuperaret. Inde est quod suum certe servat omnis natura cursum nihil que fit sub sole novum. Quia videlicet semel de immutabili voluntate posuit praeceptum semel et simul omnia creavit qui vivit in aeternum. Sic omnino insuperabilis manet altitudo divini consilii quod habuit super salutem generis humani. Nec enim electos alios vocavit iustificavit et magnificavit quam quos ante saecula praescivit et praeordinavit. Neque tamquam praeventus aut circumventus a diabolo novum aliquid excogitavit quando hoc Verbum misit

According to Magrassi, even though our theme does not appear explicitly in this context, it does shine through from time to time, for example when Rupert uses the phrases *lux est hominum, scilicet optimae partis omnium facta sunt*, and *nec enim propter angelos, sed propter homines tantum venit Christus*.[66] This restraint of Rupert, and his understanding of the unity of God's plan of salvation, led Magrassi to state that *"Difficile spiegarsi come mai Rupert non prenda espressamente posizione contro una dottrina che ha certamente presente e che tutto lo sviluppo delle idee tende a scalzare."* His explanation for this was that due to his polemic with the school of Laon, Rupert had already had problem enough.[67]

The way in which Magrassi's argument progresses is not entirely convincing, however. The first statement he quotes is too general and does not relate to our theme. The second is an echo of Augustine's *Enchiridion* 16,61, in which the subject is indeed mentioned, but Rupert does not develop the idea in that direction. Neither statement, therefore, directly relates to our theme. We can read clearer hints to it in the assertion that God knew from the beginning what he would create and how he would create it, and how he would direct it and regain it for his glory, which is also why he created everything simultaneously (Sir 18:1). The idea of any additional intention to create man as a replacement for fallen angels is thus implicitly rejected. For the time being, however, there is no implication of an explicit refutation of the patristic thesis and Rupert's work can still be interpreted in a number of different ways.

What could rather have been quoted from *Commentaria in evangelium sancti Iohannis* was the commentary on John 17:5: "And now, Father, glorify thou me in thy own presence with the glory which I had with thee before the world was made." This is because Rupert understood the glorification of the Word as meaning a new creation of man through his immersion into the death of the incarnate Son, adding that by this the tenth order of fallen angels is restored (*unde angelorum qui cecidit*

---

incarnari. Sed sicut praefinitum est sic omnino quia pulchrum et speciosum erat ante Patrem complacitum est ut inter inimicitias adversantis diaboli semper in melius saluti nostrae prospiciens usque ad summum suae dispositionis beneficientia divina perveniret quid ergo impotentiae vel temeritatis Deum arguis haeretica temeritas. Quod factum est hic subdistingue ac deinde subinfer: in ipso scilicet Verbo vita erat. Vel certe ut iam secundum Scripturam aliam loquar: quod factum est spectabilis atque deliciosus coram Deo sapientiae suae ludus erat."

66 RUPERTUS TUITIENSIS, *Commentaria in evangelium sancti Iohannis* I (CCCM 9,16; PL 169,212); Mariano MAGRASSI, *Teologia e storia nel pensiero di Ruperto di Deutz*, 264.

67 Mariano MAGRASSI, *Teologia e storia nel pensiero di Ruperto di Deutz*, 267.

decimus ordo restauretur).[68] This is a direct echo of Gregory's *Homiliae in evangelia* II,34.

It appears that Rupert betrayed no hint of having any kind of problem with our theme; on the contrary, he quietly integrated it into his exegesis. This then problematizes the interpretation offered by Magrassi, but what suddenly seems more comprehensible is the fact that our theme appears uncritically in *De sancta Trinitate et operibus eius*, which was completed a year later than *Commentaria in evangelium sancti Iohannis*.

In *De sancta Trinitate et operibus eius* 2, *In Genesim* II,15, Rupert addresses the creation of the angels along the lines of the interpretation of the parable of the lost drachma in Gregory's *Homiliae in evangelia* II,34. From this he inferred that the division of the angels into ten choirs took place only after some of them had fallen, and that these fallen angels had been foreknown and predestined by God to be one of the choirs, the tenth, thus referring to our subject indirectly. It is laid out fully, however, in chapter II,20, in which Rupert focuses on the creation of man, and in this context recalls Rom 9:20–21. With respect to the verses that follow he then stated that what is so important is not why God made man (*cur ita fecerit*), a fragile earthen vessel, but that man does not fall apart in God's hands and is not replaced by a different vessel that the Creator would like better. Nonetheless, this primarily spiritual attempt is accompanied by a quiet sense of awe at why God – who could have restored the angelic ruins by creating and elevating into heaven as many new angels as had fallen so that the citizens of the heavenly city would have been of one kind only – proceeded in such a way as to create men of a different nature and put them in the place of the angels, and, moreover, in such a way that he created only one being from whom others would be multiplied. Rupert suggests that investigation into these and other matters should be carried out soberly: it should not be a sign of superiority, but a humble drawing near to God; we should be content with what he wished to reveal about his plan.[69]

---

68 RUPERTUS TUITIENSIS, *Commentaria in evangelium sancti Iohannis* XII (CCCM 9,696; PL 169,753): "Aliter: et nunc clarifica me tu Pater apud temetipsum claritate quam habui priusquam mundus esset apud te videlicet ut sicut Spiritus tuus Spiritus meus in principio ferebatur super aquas ut angelica natura per me Verbum tuum crearetur te dicente: fiat lux ita et nunc idem Spiritus super aquas feratur ut per me Filium tuum nova hominum creatura nascatur dum in morte mea baptizantur unde angelorum qui cecidit decimus ordo restauretur. Nam hoc etiam modo clarificatio qua ego tunc clarui nunc iterabitur."

69 RUPERTUS TUITIENSIS, *De sancta Trinitate et operibus eius* 2, *In Genesim* II,20 (CCCM 21,207; PL 167,265): "Itaque et nos cum legimus quia formavit Dominus hominem de limo terrae non discutiendum nobis est cur ita fecerit sed potius illud timendum cuique nostrum

Chronologically, the fourth occurrence of our theme is in *Commentarium in Apocalypsim* (1117–1120; or 1119–1121), which focuses on the topoi of Eph 1:10 and Rev 11:13.[70] The fifth text in which Rupert returns to our question is *De victoria Verbi Dei* from 1124, and this text brings a fundamental shift. Rupert still accepts the idea that man was created as a replacement for fallen angels, but for the first time incorporates it into the context he had set out in *Commentaria in evangelium sancti Iohannis* I: God foresaw all of this in his Word, in whom was life and through whom he made all that is (John 1:4). In this Word he had already seen what he was going to do for the glory and praise of his name. The Word became flesh, and because of this men and angels knew what God resolved to do.[71]

de se ipso ne vas quod facit ipse dissipetur in manibus eius et hoc abiecto faciat aliud vas sicut placuit in oculis eius ut faceret. Attamen sobrie quaerere id est mirari licet cur Deus cum posset ruinas angelorum novis angelis reaedificare et totidem quot ceciderunt simul creare et in caelum levare ut unius generis esset plebs cuncta omnis que nobilitas caelestis patriae cur homines alterius naturae vel conditionis fecit quos reponeret pro angelis et non cunctos aut multos simul sed unum tantummodo plasmavit de quo propagarentur ceteri. Hoc ut praedictum est et similia sobrie quaerentibus nobis non congruit neque propter nos facta vel dicta est illa apostoli obiectio: o homo tu quis es qui respondeas Deo nec illa sententia Domini qua propter irrisores dictum est apostolis: nolite margaritas vestras mittere ante porcos. Quaerimus enim non alta sapientes ut Deo respondeamus aut iudicia comprehendere praesumamus sed ut appropinquantes pedibus eius de doctrina illius accipiamus. Unde et in hoc praesenti responsum accipimus quo dignum est ut contenti simus quia quod habuit hoc de thesauro cordis sui protulit omnium artifex deus. Dicit nobis evangelista de Verbo eius quia quod factum est in ipso vita erat. Nonne ergo qualis in ipso vita erat talia foris opera fieri oportebat."

70 RUPERTUS TUITIENSIS, *Commentarium in Apocalypsim Iohannis apostoli* 6,7.11 (PL 169,967.1033): "Sicut turbae magnae ex omnibus gentibus, tribubus, et populis, et linguis, numerus nemini comprehensibilis est, ita et hic, et superius, ubi primum Agnus librum accepit, angelorum numerus definitus non est, de istis iam illic dictum est, quia et si non per ipsum redempti sunt, quia non perierant, attamen per divinitatem eius conditi sunt, et per sanguinem eius, ut apostolus quoque testis est, nobis conciliati, sive pacificati sunt, et instauratus est hominibus [coetus] numerus ipsorum, qui diminutus fuerat per ruinam angelorum apostatarum. [...] Porro, quod supra civitatem magnam dixit, quam et spiritualiter Sodomam et Aegyptum vocari asseruit, id nunc non civitatem, sed decimam appellat partem civitatis, quam et cecidisse, vel casuram esse dixit. Et revera quae dicitur civitas diaboli, non civitas est, sed ruinae sunt magnae et sanctae civitatis Ierusalem coelestis, cuius novem sunt angelorum ordines, et idcirco qui inde ceciderunt, et homines, qui de illorum sorte sunt, recte dicuntur decima pars, ruinosa pars eiusdem civitatis."

71 RUPERTUS TUITIENSIS, *De victoria Verbi Dei* II,4 (MGH Quellen zur Geistesgeschichte des Mittelalters 5,49–50): "De prescientia Creatoris, quod illi solum notum et cunctis angelis tunc erat absconditum pietatis sacramentum, unde vel quomodo recuperaretur diminutio, quę acciderat civium supernorum. – Et quidem sancti angeli detrimentum (ut iam dictum est) suę multitudinis plangere poterant in spiritu pietatis; Deus autem apud se in Verbo suo, in quo vita erat, quidquid factum est, iamdudum habebat et videbat, quid esset facturus ad gloriam et laudem nominis sui. Solus ipse noverat et cunctis angelis absconditum erat, quemadmo-

Up to this time, Rupert had worked with our thesis as a matter of course, admonishing only its sober use and connecting it to the intention God has, in his Word, for creation.

Although a subsequent work, *De gloria et honore filii hominis super Matthaeum* (1124–1126), did not address our subject, it nonetheless clarified the context established by *Commentaria in evangelium sancti Iohannis* I and *De victoria Verbi Dei* II,4 by finding a connection between the cause of creation and the cause of the incarnation in the predestination of the Word. The cause of the creation of all things – including, therefore, angels and men – was the Son of Man, who through the Father's will was to enjoy communion with all creatures and was, through suffering, to attain among them unutterable glory (*propter istum Filium hominis, gloria et honore coronandum, Deus omnia creavit*). The cause of creation was the incarnation, or more precisely the loving decision of the Father that his Word would – as a man amongst angels and men – rejoice with men (*caritatis propositum, quo proposuerat Deus Dei Verbum deliciari cum filiis hominum, formam habendo circumscriptam ex natura humana in medio angelorum et hominum*). For this reason it is not possible to say that the cause of the incarnation was the sin of the angels or of men, even though it is certainly true that the nature of the communion between men and the incarnate Son of God is established by the Father's intention to reconcile with himself, through Christ's death on the cross, a world fallen into sin.[72]

The key moment in the development of Rupert's approach towards the subject of man as a replacement angel comes in *De glorificatione Trinitatis et processione Spiritus sancti* (1127–1128).

The third book addresses the matter of angels and their creation. In this context, in chapters 16 and 17, Rupert criticizes some of the interpretations of Gregory's thesis that by their own virtue men become like particular angelic orders and even become in some manner part

---

dum apostolus cum dixisset, quę sit dispensatio sacramenti, addidit: absconditi a saeculis in Deo, qui omnia creavit, ut innotescat principatibus et potestatibus in cęlestibus per ecclesiam multiformis sapientia Dei. Quid erat absconditum vel quale erat illud sacramentum? Nimirum ut summę benevolentię largitas, largissima Creatoris benevolentia, de inope et abiecta terrę materia, quę tunc sub aquis latebat, gloriosam et angelicę claritati consimilem ederet creaturam et uni personę ex multitudine eiusdem creaturę suam daret potestatem et honorem et regnum, nihilque minus haberet creatura quam ipse Creator omnium, totumque rei publicę eius obtineret imperium. Vere magnum pietatis sacramentum, quod tunc quidem (ut iam dictum est) erat absconditum, nunc autem manifestum est in carne, iustificatum est in spiritu, praedicatum est gentibus, creditum est mundo, assumptum est in gloria. Nota est persona illa, quia non solummodo creatura, sed etiam Creator est, id est, non solummodo homo, sed etiam Deus est."

72 See RUPERTUS TUITIENSIS, *De gloria et honore Filii hominis super Matheum* 13 (CCCM 29,409–416; PL 168,1624–1630).

of them (*Homiliae in evangelia* II,34,11). According to Rupert, some authors (*nonnulli*) inferred from this that the fall of the angels applied to all angelic orders, which is why all of these ruined orders are to be restored from among men.[73] Rupert objected that nothing of the sort can be shown from Scripture, and pointed out that if the angels had already been established in particular orders then it is not clear how certain of them could have fallen. How, for example, could a seraph, the one who is burning with love, fall? It would be more probable and more reasonable to assume that angels were established into particular orders only in reward for not having sinned; thus returns the theme from *De Trinitate et operibus eius* II,15.

In chapters 20 and 21, Rupert then directly addresses Gregory's interpretation of the parable of the lost drachma, which reaches its climax with the words *sed ut compleretur electorum numerus, homo decimus est creatus* (*Homiliae in evangelia* II,34,6).[74] Rupert noted that there were many (*plerique*) who deduce from Gregory's words that if the angels had not sinned, and their ranks had not been damaged, man would not have been created and neither would there have been a reason for this to happen.[75] To this, however, in an echo of the above quoted *Commentaria in evangelium sancti Iohannis* I, Rupert replies that we should not imagine things in such a childish way, as if it were true that before the angels fell God had no intention of creating man, and that after the angels' fall it occurred to him that he could create the human race in order that from among it he could restore the depleted number of citizens of his house.[76] What's

---

73 RUPERTUS TUITIENSIS, *De glorificatione Trinitatis et processione Spiritus sancti* III,17 (PL 169,68): "Dum haec dicit, scilicet ex hominibus alios in angelorum, alios in archangelorum numero deputari, alios inter supernas virtutes, alios inter coelestes potestates, alios inter principatus, alios inter dominationes, alios inter thronos, alios inter cherubim, alios inter seraphim accipere sortem suae vocationis, nonnulli solent asserere, quod de singulis ordinibus multitudines ceciderint quod itidem in singulis ordinibus ruinae debeant ex hominibus reparari."

74 In Gregory, this point is followed by the assertion that the heavenly city consists of angels, and we believe as many men are to enter it as there are angels who remained there, which he substantiates from Deut 32:8 (LXX): *Constituit terminos gentium, iuxta numerum angelorum Dei.* Rupert remarked, however, that arguing in such a way from this verse of Scripture does not seem appropriate for confirming such a conclusion as in this place the LXX does not correspond to the Hebrew version. RUPERTUS TUITIENSIS, *De glorificatione Trinitatis et processione Spiritus sancti* III,20 (PL 169,72).

75 RUPERTUS TUITIENSIS, *De glorificatione Trinitatis et processione Spiritus sancti* III,20 (PL 169,72): "Solent plerique arbitrari quod si omnes angeli perstitissent, nullaque ruina facta fuisset ex eis, non crearetur neque fuisset causa cur deberet homo creari."

76 RUPERTUS TUITIENSIS, *De glorificatione Trinitatis et processione Spiritus sancti* III,20 (PL 169,72): "Quod si conceditur, cavendum est ne ita pueri simus, ut existememus Deum nullum ante ruinam angelorum de homine creando habuisse propositum, sed postquam casus ille

more, it should be emphasized that man was not made for angels, but angels, and everything else, for man, which means that man whom the Word was to accept into the unity of his person, and about whom Heb 2:10 says: *Decebat enim propter quem omnia, et per quem omnia....*[77] Who are those "many"? There is very little on which to base a definitive answer, but we can at least suggest a hypothesis. Rupert identified them as proponents of the belief that after the fall of the angels, God decided to create the human race *ob recuperandam multitudinem domus seu familiae suae quae cecidit.* As we have already shown, this assertion can be found in Augustine (*Sermo* 229/H,2; *De civitate Dei* 14,26), who had been the common point of reference for all theologians. Nonetheless, the assertion occurs repeatedly during Rupert's time, especially in the works of the school of Laon and its wider circle, in which Rupert had a keen interest. Perhaps, therefore, it is these theologians he had in mind.[78] It is not totally clear, however. There are texts other than those Rupert indicated where a similar set of ideas is expressed, for example *Epistola de praevaricatione Adae* (and *Liber de quattuor quaestionum*) from the first half of the twelfth century.[79] Here, an unknown author[80] expressed certain

---

contigit, tunc demum illi venisse in mentem consilium huiusmodi, scilicet facere genus nostrum ob recuperandam multitudinem domus seu familiae suae quae cecidit."

77 RUPERTUS TUITIENSIS, *De glorificatione Trinitatis et processione Spiritus sancti* III,20 (PL 169,72): "Rectius ergo dicitur quia non homo propter angelos, immo propter hominem quemdam angeli quoque facti sunt sicut et caetera omnia, testante apostolo cum dicit: Decebat enim propter quem omnia, et per quem omnia."

78 It is worth noting that immediately after describing it as such, he made an argument from Heb 2:10, which also played a crucial role for Anselm and Ralph of Laon at the time they were considering God's intentions for the world. It was the same with Rupert, who usually, however, also quoted John 1:3–4 and Prov 8:30–31. This is the case not only in *De glorificatione Trinitatis et processione Spiritus sancti* III,20, but also in *De gloria et honore Filii hominis super Matheum* 13, and, furthermore, in *Commentaria in evangelium sancti Iohannis* III (CCCM 9,167–169; PL 169,330–332) where the author asks *cur Deus pro mundi dilectione [...] non legatum neque angelum sed ipsum unigenitum suum dederit,* answering using Heb 2:10 and with a similar line of argument to that used by the school of Laon.

79 Quotations are from [ANONYMOUS], *Epistola Hugonis a Sancto Victore* (Paris, Bibliothèque nationale de France, latin 14366, fol. 8v–23r, *Gallica: Bibliothèque numérique.* <http://gallica.bnf.fr>).

80 "Quia igitur sola vasa in contumeliam facta et super numerum electorum multiplicata et nullum electorum praevaricatio possidet, nihil omnino nocet. Si non nocet, mala non est; si mala non est, plus mala quam Christi passio bona non est. [...] Electis enim multum profuit, quos turpiter amissura ad tempus tenuit. Nam si non tenuisset, Deus homo non fieret. Si Deus homo non fieret, homo angelos non transcenderet. Nunc autem Deo gratias, quia praevaricatio suos cum suis non usurpavit; Deus homo factus illam captivavit; quia vero Deus supra sit hominem: angelis illum superposuit. [...] Si ergo ubi Deus, ibi homo; quia Deus homo; praevaricatio qua suos tenens nihil obfuit, non suos usurpans multum profuit. Si autem profuit,

ideas against which Rupert and – as will become clear – Honorius of Autun argued. The anonymous writer asserted that sin provided a certain benefit to man since without it God would not have become a man and man would not therefore have transcended the angels (*homo angelos non transcenderet*); as a consequence of the incarnation, however, man is indeed elevated above the angels.[81] *Epistola* also claims that the prelapsarian task of the first man was to beget offspring in paradise and from among them to restore the celestial damage (*ex his coelestia damna restaurare*); the more he tried, the more he would have been loved by his Creator.[82] What is more, man was created precisely in order to repair the damage in heaven by filling up the celestial dwelling places that belonged to them (*homo ad hoc factus est ut mansiones quas isti in coelo habuerunt possidendo coelestia damna repararet*). At the same time it holds that through Adam's sin, all of his progeny became sinners, while through personal sin each acquires a different degree of guilt. Similarly, Adam's obedience would have brought all of his progeny sanctification, while each could have attained in paradise, by greater or lesser devotion to God, differing levels of sanctity. Precisely through this diversity in merit, men could fill all of the places that the fallen angels vacated.[83]

---

bona fuit; si vero nihil profuit, mala non fuit: si autem bona et mala non fuit: plus ergo passio Christi est bona qua multis profuit, quam illa praevaricatio mala qua iuxta aliquid bona, et non iuxta aliquid mala fuit." (fol. 9r–10v)

81 "Quia igitur sola vasa in contumeliam facta et super numerum electorum multiplicata et nullum electorum praevaricatio possidet, nihil omnino nocet. Si non nocet, mala non est; si mala non est, plus mala quam Christi passio bona non est. [...] Electis enim multum profuit, quos turpiter amissura ad tempus tenuit. Nam si non tenuisset, Deus homo non fieret. Si Deus homo non fieret, homo angelos non transcenderet. Nunc autem Deo gratias, quia praevaricatio suos cum suis non usurpavit; Deus homo factus illam captivavit; quia vero Deus supra sit hominem: angelis illum superposuit. [...] Si ergo ubi Deus, ibi homo; quia Deus homo; praevaricatio qua suos tenens nihil obfuit, non suos usurpans multum profuit. Si autem profuit, bona fuit; si vero nihil profuit, mala non fuit: si autem bona et mala non fuit: plus ergo passio Christi est bona qua multis profuit, quam illa praevaricatio mala qua iuxta aliquid bona, et non iuxta aliquid mala fuit." (fol. 9r–10v)

82 "Hoc ergo opus erat filios propagare in paradiso et ex his coelestia damna restaurare, in quo opere, quia homo aliquantisper laboret, utpote cui omnis voluptatis delectatio abessent, quanto alter altero in illo opere fieret studiosior, tanto fieret suo Creatori carior." (fol. 18r)

83 "Pessima autem omnium est superbia qua de his omnibus angelicis olim spiritibus daemones fecit. Sed homo ad hoc factus est ut mansiones quas isti in coelo habuerunt possidendo coelestia damna repararet. Non ergo omnes erant unius et eiusdem meriti futuri, licet omnes boni. Nam si quia omnes sancti essent, ideo omnes unius meriti essent: igitur omnes in eadem mansione recipiendi essent. Si vero omnes in eadem mansione manerent: certe mansiones omnes praeter illam vacua remanerent. Si autem aliqua mansio vacua remaneret, homo non omnia coelestia damna repararet. Hoc autem est impossibile, Scriptura teste qua dicit: Constituisti terminos populorum iuxta numerum filiorum Israel. Si autem verum est, imo quia verum est,

It is clear that the ideas Rupert was addressing were alive and well in the theology of the day. As a counter to these ideas, Rupert asserted that God's entire plan concerning men and angels has its focus in the Word, through whom everything came into being and without whom nothing that is came into being; in him was life, and that life was the light of men. This Word is identical with the Wisdom of God, whose delight is in playful communion with mankind. In the beginning, before God had made anything, and on making it, he intended that the Word of God should become flesh and dwell among men with great love and the utmost humility.[84] It appears more likely, therefore, that rather than man having been created in order to replace the number of fallen angels, men and angels were made for the one man Jesus Christ (*non tam homo propter supplendum angelorum numerum, quam et angeli et homines propter unum hominem Iesum Christum facti sunt*), and that it was for him for whom a family was to be prepared from both manners of creature: for God a family of angels, and for man a family of men. Above them all he, as the Lord, was to reign and be pre-eminent.[85]

In these words is Rupert's final answer to the question *cur homo*. Man was not created for angels (that is, as a replacement for those who fell

---

teste beata memoria viro beato Gregorio, tot homines illuc esse futuros quot contigit ibi angelos remanere. Impossibile est non tot quot ceciderunt angeli homines redire. Si tot redeunt, aut in illorum mansionibus aut alibi manebunt. Sed alibi non erunt, in illorum igitur locis erunt: Si in illorum locis erunt, mansio nulla remanebit vacua. Ergo non omnes erunt unius meriti, sed diversi; aliquin in diversis mansionibus non manerent amplius." (fol. 19v-r)

84 RUPERTUS TUITIENSIS, *De glorificatione Trinitatis et processione Spiritus sancti* III,20 (PL 169,72): "Si enim verum dicit imo quia verum dicit evangelista: Quod factum est in ipso, vita erat, nihil excipiens, praemiserat enim: Omnia per ipsum facta sunt, et sine ipso factum est nihil; quanto magis homo iste decorus, ab ipso Verbo in unitatem personae assumendus angeli, qua antequam angeli fierent, in ipso vita erat? Testatur et hoc ipsa Sapientia, quae non est aliud quam ipsum Verbum, dum dicit: Dominus possedit me ab initio viarum suarum, et caetera usque quando appendebat fundamenta terrae, cum eo eram cuncta componens, et ludens coram eo omni tempore, ludens in orbe terrarum. Statimque subiungit: Et deliciae meae esse cum filiis hominum. Quidnam hoc est, nisi ac si dixisset: Antequam Deus quidquem faceret a principio, et quando haec vel illa faciebat, hoc erat in proposito, et ego Verbum Dei, Verbum Deus caro fierem, et in hominibus habitarem magna charitate et summa humilitate, quae verae deliciae sunt."

85 RUPERTUS TUITIENSIS, *De glorificatione Trinitatis et processione Spiritus sancti* III,21 (PL 169,72–73): "Igitur probabilius hoc dicimus, quod non tam homo propter supplendum angelorum numerum, quam et angeli et homines propter unum hominem Iesum Christum facti sunt, ut quoniam unus idemque et Deus ex Deo natus erat, et homo nasciturus erat, haberet praeparatam ex utroque latere familiam, hinc angelorum, hinc hominum, et ipse Deus, et homo, Dominus et creator angelorum, Dominus et Creator et Salvator emineret hominum sanctorum, Dominus, inquam, in eis sicut in domo sua, Rex in gente sua, Deus in maiestate sua. Quia, sicut dictum iam est, et propter ipsum, et per ipsum omnia."

so that the number of those who persevered was completed); rather, the truth is that angels and all other creatures, including men, were created for man, meaning for Jesus Christ, the incarnate Word of God, through whom they are to become alike unto God, just as sons are like their fathers.[86]

4. Honorius of Autun

Chenu, who first drew attention to our subject, believed that "the most intriguing witness"[87] to the argument we are following here is the *inclusus, solitarius, presbyter,* and *scholasticus* Honorius of Autun. Very little is known about this man's life story and most of the details connected with him have been established only tentatively, beginning with his birth, which is usually placed between the years 1060 and 1080, up to his death, dated between 1125 and 1160.[88] Honorius began his intellectual and spir-

---

86 See RUPERTUS TUITIENSIS, *De glorificatione Trinitatis et processione Spiritus sancti* IV,2 (PL 169,75–76): "Faciamus hominem ad imaginem et similitudinem nostram. [...] Quaenam erat intentio vel quid erat in intentione eius [= Trinitatis], nisi is qui nunc sedet ad dexteram Patris mediator Dei et hominum, homo Christus Iesus? Si enim, quod saepe dictum, semperque sciendum est, non solum per ipsum, verum etiam, ut apostolus ait, propter ipsum omnia, quanto magis humana propter ipsum facta est creatura! Cum ergo dicit: Faciamus hominem ad imaginem et similitudinem nostram, parum est ad consummationem propositi Dei hoc attendere, quod omnes electi, qui secundum propositum vocati sunt sancti, et rationales creati, et similes Deo sunt futuri, tanquam patri suo filii, iuxta illud: Charissimi nunc filii Dei sumus, sed nondum apparuit quid erimus; scimus quia, cum apparuerit, similes ei erimus, quoniam videbimus eum sicuti est, parum, inquam, hoc est, nisi hunc hominem attendas qui ipse est, ut apostolus ait, imago Dei invisibilis, et sicut idem alibi loquitur: Splendor gloriae et figura substantiae eius. Nunquid enim cum haec diceret beata Trinitas. Faciamus hominem, et caetera, de homine isto nihil cogitaverat aut proposuerat, sed postquam peccavit Adam, tunc demum istud cogitavit Deus, ut homo fieret Dei Filius, ob redimendum humanum genus. Diximus de hoc in praecedentibus, cum de angelis loqueremur, quia si verum dicit, imo quia verum dicit evangelista: Quod factum est in ipso vita erat, nihil excipiens, praemiserat enim: Omnia enim per ipsum facta sunt, et sine ipso factum est nihil, multo magis homo iste ab ipso Verbo in unitatem personae assumendus, antequam angeli fierent, in ipso vita erat, et hoc erat propositum eius deliciosum, sicut Sapientia loquitur, quae non est aliud quam ipse Dei Filius: Dominus possedit me initio viarum suarum, antequam quidquam faceret, a principio, et caetera quae ita concludit, et deliciae meae esse cum filiis hominum."

87 Marie-Dominique CHENU, *La théologie au douzième siècle*, 55.

88 For a basic bibliography and a summary of what is known, see Walter A. HANNAM, *The Inevitabile of Honorius Augustodunensis: A Study in the Textures of Early Twelfth-Century Augustianisms: a dissertation*, Boston College: The Graduate School of Arts and Sciences: Department of Theology, 2013, 2–40 <http://gradworks.umi.com/35/60/3560655.html> [2013-08-01]; Fabian SCHWARZBAUER, *Geschichtszeit: über Zeitvorstellungen in den Universalchroniken Frutolfs von Michelsberg, Honorius' Augustodunensis und Ottos von Freising*, Berlin: Akademie Verlag, 2005,

84

itual formation in England, perhaps in Worcester and Canterbury, where he was directly or indirectly a student of St. Anselm. Around 1102 (and certainly before 1115), he set off for the Continent, perhaps accompanied by Princess Matilda of England (1102–1167), who in 1108 was under the care of Anselm of Canterbury and as early as 1110 became betrothed to King Henry V of Germany (1081/1086–1125). Around 1126, Honorius arrived in Regensburg and lived nearby as an *inclusus*. His writings are yet to be reliably dated.

His earliest work is certainly *Elucidarium,* the first edition of which was written between 1098 and 1101 (at the latest).[89] The theme we are following is indicated here when the author claims that God determined a fixed number of beings for his heavenly kingdom, who are to form nine choirs of angels (a symbol of God's Trinity) and one choir of men (a symbol of God's unity);[90] man was created as the tenth order when the number of the elect was depleted by the fall.[91] God's plan was for man to remain in paradise and multiply until such time as the number of angels who fell, or the number of angels that needed to be completed if the angels had not fallen, was completed.[92]

39–47; R. AUBERT, Honorius Augustodunensis, *Dictionnaire d'histoire et de géographie ecclésias-tiques,* Paris: Letouzey et Ané, 1993, tome 24, 1056–1058. Further, for our purposes, especially: E. Matthews SANFORD, Honorius, Presbyter and Scholasticus, *Speculum* 3 (1948), 397–425; Hermann MENHARDT, Der Nachlass des Honorius Augustodunensis, *Zeitschrift für deutsches Altertum* 89 (1958–1959), 23–69; Valerie I. J. FLINT, The chronology of the works of Honorius Augustodunensis, *Revue bénédictine* 82 (1972), 215–242; ID., Honorius Augustodunensis of Regensburg, in Patrick J. GEARY (ed.), *Authors of the Middle Ages: Historical and Religious Writers of the Latin West,* vol. II, Aldershot: Variorum, 1995, 89–183; Marie-Odile GARRIGUES, L'œuvre d'Honorius Augustodunensis: Inventaire critique, *Abhandlungen der Braunschweigischen Wissen-schaftlichen Gesellschaft* 38 (1986), 7–136; 39 (1987), 123–228; 40 (1988), 129–190; Robert LUFF, *Wissensvermittlung im europäischen Mittelalter: »Imago mundi«-Werke und ihre Prologe,* Tübingen: Niemeyer 1999, 20–57 (Das Elucidarium des Honorius Augustodunensis – ein Handbuch des Glaubens); Loris STURLESE, Zwischen Anselm und Johannes Scotus Eriugena: der seltsame Fall des Honorius, des Mönchs von Regensburg, in Burkhard MOJSISCH – Olaf PLUTA, *Historia philosophiae Medii Aevi: Studien zur Geschichte der Philosophie des Mittelalters,* Bd. 2, Amsterdam; Philadelphia: B. R. Grüner, 1991, 927–951; Rolf SCHÖNBERGER et alii, *Repertorium edierter Texte des Mittelalters aus dem Bereich der Philosophie und angrenzender Gebiete,* Bd. 2, Berlin: Akademie Verlag GmbH, 2011, 1995–2003.
89 The possibility of an earlier date is discussed by Judith Rachel DUNTHORNE, *Anselm of Canterbury and the Development of Theological Thought, c. 1070–1141,* 45–56.
90 HONORIUS AUGUSTODUNENSIS, *Elucidarium* I,6 (PL 172,1113; Yves LEFÈVRE, *L'Elucidarium et les Lucidaires,* 365–366).
91 HONORIUS AUGUSTODUNENSIS, *Elucidarium* I,11 (PL 172,1116; Yves LEFÈVRE, *L'Elucidarium et les Lucidaires,* 371): "D. Nonne casus malorum minuit numerum bonorum? – M. Sed, ut impleretur electorum numerus, homo decimus est creatus."
92 HONORIUS AUGUSTODUNENSIS, *Elucidarium* I,14 (PL 172,1118; Yves LEFÈVRE,

The same idea appeared in another early work, a dialogue called *Inevitabile*, which concerned predestination and free will. The first edition originated between 1098 and 1108, and the second after 1108. Our theme does not appear in the first edition,[93] but in the second the author moves towards the classical conclusion of the completion of the number of fallen angels from among the ranks of men.[94] The same concept appears in a brief remark in a Christmas homily included in the collection of homilies *Speculum Ecclesiae* from between 1100 and 1110.[95]

None of these early works recalls the question as to whether men were in fact created for their own sake, and few of Honorius's other writings either mention or question the patristic thesis. This is not the case, however, with three texts in which it appears extensively and assertively: *Liber duodecim quaestionum*, *Liber octo quaestionum*, and *Expositio in Cantica*

L'Elucidarium et les Lucidaires, 375): "D. Quamdiu debuerunt esse in paradiso? – M. Usquequo impleretur numerus angelorum qui ceciderant et ille numerus electorum qui erat implendus si angeli non cecidissent."

93   See Johann KELLE, Untersuchungen über des Honorius Inevitabile sive de praedestinatione et libero arbitrio dialogus, *Sitzungsberichte der Akademie der Wissenschaften in Wien. Philosophisch-historische Klasse* 150/3 (1905), 9–33, here especially 19–20. See also Franz BÄUMKER, *Das Inevitabile des Honorius Augustodunensis und dessen Lehre über das Zusammenwirken von Wille und Gnade*, Münster: Aschendorffschen Verlagsbuchhandlung, 1914, 16–18; Loris STURLESE, Zwischen Anselm und Johannes Scotus Eriugena: der seltsame Fall des Honorius, des Mönchs von Regensburg, in Burkhard MOJSISCH – Olaf PLUTA (eds.), *Historia philosophiae Medii Aevi: Studien zur Geschichte der Philosophie des Mittelalters*, Bd. 2, Amsterdam-Philadelphia: B. R. Grüner, 1991, 937.

94   HONORIUS AUGUSTODUNENSIS, *Inevitabile* (PL 172,1211–1212): "Antequam Deus conderet mundum, praescivit et angeli et hominis casum: quem ideo fieri permisit, quia bonum malo illustrari censuit. Praescivit etiam, qui et quot secum essent permansuri, qui et quot essent recessuri, qui et quot ad se reversuri. Si enim hoc ignorasset, praescius futurorum non esset. Et si certus numerus electorum non esset, tunc regnum Dei, non ordinata dispositione, sed fortuito casu constaret, ad quod incerti numeri frequenta conflueret. Sed cum apud Deum sit certus numerus capillorum, multo magis est apud Deum praefixus numerus electorum. Quot autem sunt in hoc numero a Deo praescripti hi ante mundi constitutionem sunt ad beatitudinem electi. De his nullus peribit, sed ad praedestinatam gloriam toto conamine quisque festinabit. Qui autem super hunc numerum multiplicantur, inter oves Christi non numerantur. Et quia hic numerus angelis cadentibus est imminutus, hominibus nascentibus est restitutus. Et ideo sicut ab uno numerare incipimus, sic ab uno homine numerus est incoeptus. Et, sicut numerus crescit ad perfectionem, ita propago humana successit usque ad electorum completionem. Hic ergo sacer numerus, soli Deo cognitus, et ab eo, aeterna certitudine praefixus, est quasi cuiusdam civitatis ambitus, intra quem necesse sit omnes contineri, cui huius civitatis cives ab aeterno sunt praecogniti." See HONORIUS AUGUSTODUNENSIS, *Inevitabile*, in Walter A. HANNAM, *The Inevitabile of Honorius Augustodunensis*, 433–436.

95   HONORIUS AUGUSTODUNENSIS, *Speculum Ecclesiae – De nativitate Domini* (PL 172,815): "Hodie namque rex coelorum terras sua praesentia visitare et damnum in coelo per ruinam angelorum factum per homines voluit reparare."

canticorum. The date of these works – and therefore the order in which they were written – is a matter of some debate as any obvious clues are lacking. The opinion clearly prevails, however, that none of these works was written until the final period of Honorius's life, after 1130.

Exceptions we should mention are the hypotheses of Flint, who put the two *Libri* into the earlier English period of Honorius's life and *Expositio* after 1132, and Garrigues, who put the *Libri* between 1111 and 1115 (1116) and *Expositio* between 1153 and 1156. Both of these hypotheses operate with the idea that Rupert of Deutz adopted the notion that man would have been created even if the angels had not sinned from the *Libri* of Honorius, and not the other way around. They therefore reject the conclusion reached by Magrassi that with respect to our question Honorius was, in comparison to Rupert, merely "an intelligent popularizer."[96]

Flint arrived at her early date of the two *Libri* on the basis of their textual similarity to certain passages in *Elucidarium* and *Inevitabile*, suggesting that *Liber octo quaestionum* reflects the early interest of Honorius in the relative merits of canonical and monastic life, and that *Liber duodecim quaestionum* is an "ill-organized work" and a "collection of somewhat hastily constructed questions and answers on quite random topics." The lack of quality in the two writings is said to explain why the *Libri* do not appear in the list of Honorius's writings in *De luminaribus*.[97]

It should be noted, however, that the similarity between the writings is due to their original sources rather than to any specific conclusions they reach or modes of argumentation they employ. An interest in status evidently accompanied Honorius until the end of his life, and the fact that *Liber duodecim quaestionum* consists of a catalogue of various subjects proves nothing at all. It is simply a free collection of questions about angels and men. Problems concerning the listing in *De luminaribus* are, as is well known, extremely complicated. It is clear, however, that the list of Honorius's works reflects an expansion of the author's knowledge; an author who is not, however, in all probability, Honorius alone. This may explain why the list does not contain a number of his other works, especially partial questions that have been preserved in various manuscripts. Flint's arguments therefore lack conviction.

Magrassi saw a certain similarity between Rupert's *Commentaria in evangelium sancti Iohannis* I and Honorius's *Liber duodecim quaestionum* I. He attempted to demonstrate that this similarity manifests itself in a

---

96 Mariano MAGRASSI, *Teologia e storia nel pensiero di Ruperto di Deutz*, 272–276.
97 Valerie I. J. FLINT, The Chronology of the Works of Honorius Augustodunensis, 239–240.

number of ways: in their use of passages of Scripture (John 1:4; Sir 18:1); in the analogy between God who in the Word anticipates the entirety of his later work, and a man who has his work fully formed in his mind before realizing it (the architect and musician in Rupert; the writer and the motif of the zither in Honorius); and finally in the whole "guarding of ideas."[98] Based on the very same ideas, however, Garrigues was seeking to prove that, on the contrary, Rupert took his inspiration from Honorius, as Honorius had already worked with the relevant biblical texts in *Elucidarium*. Moreover, Rupert was said to have taken from Honorius a particular idea that came from Eriugena. Garrigues had to add, however, that earlier sources of inspiration exist on which both authors could have drawn independently of each other.[99]

This suggestion has greater validity than she herself realized: if Honorius and Rupert worked with the same biblical texts, it was because Christian tradition had connected them with the theology of creation. From this theology, also independently of each other, they adopted their basic interpretative paradigm and related images, including the image of a man (for example a craftsman, an architect, a musician) who first has his work fully formed in his mind and then gradually realizes it. From this then follows the concordance in their choice of passages of Scripture. The same conclusion is also supported by the fact that each of these two thinkers worked with this common tradition in his own way.

In *Commentaria in evangelium sancti Iohannis* I, Rupert saw in the incarnate Word the unity in the intention that God the Father has for creation, and on this basis refuted the notion of the gradual development of God's plans for the world; in *De victoria Verbi Dei* II,4, he connected the same idea with the motif of man as a replacement angel; in *De gloria et honore Filii hominis super Matheum* 13, he deepened the connection between creation and the incarnation; and in *De glorificatione Trinitatis et processione Spiritus sancti* III,20, he employed it when working with Gregory's *Homiliae in evangelia* II,34 as evidence of the fact that everything – men and angels – is created for the man Jesus Christ. There is therefore no sense in speaking of the replacement of angels by men.

On the basis of the same biblical texts, Honorius expressed, in *Liber duodecim quaestionum,* the idea that the unchanging nature of God's plan

---

98   Mariano MAGRASSI, *Teologia e storia nel pensiero di Ruperto di Deutz,* 272–274.

99   Marie-Odile GARRIGUES, L'œuvre d'Honorius Augustodunensis: Inventaire critique, *Abhandlungen der Braunschweigischen Wissenschaftlichen Gesellschaft* 39 (1987), 137.153–166; ID., Utrum Honorius ubique sit totus? *Abhandlungen der Braunschweigischen Wissenschaftlichen Gesellschaft* 35 (1983), 38–39.

for creation is firmly established in the eternal (not the incarnate) Word of God, and in this plan there is no place for the arbitrary dependence of the creation of man on the free actions of angels. From this follows the necessity of rejecting the thesis of man being created as a replacement for fallen angels. Honorius repeated the argument in *Liber octo quaestionum* and in *Expositio in Cantica canticorum*, in which, however, he connected those biblical passages with the term "predestination," doing so in a way that is known from other writings of his.[100]

It is therefore unlikely that Honorius, when choosing biblical texts and interpretative paradigms or images, drew inspiration from Rupert; or indeed vice versa. We are ruling out, therefore, that *Commentaria in evangelium sancti Iohannis* could have directly influenced *Liber duodecim quaestionum*. We are of the opinion that while writing *Liber duodecim quaestionum,* Honorius was looking to *De glorificatione Trinitatis et processione Spiritus sancti*. Later, in *Liber octo quaestionum,* he drew on his earlier work, which he later summarized in *Expositio in Cantica canticorum*.

The most significant evidence for the dependence of Honorius's *Libri* and *Expositio* on Rupert's *De glorificatione Trinitatis et processione Spiritus sancti* – evidence neglected by both Flint and Garrigues – is their accordance with the then somewhat unusual supra-lapsarian understanding of the primary purpose of the incarnation. This concept is developed theologically in Rupert's works, and away from the context of reflections upon the creation of man as a replacement for fallen angels.[101] It is from the logic of his understanding of the primary purpose of creation and the

---

100 HONORIUS AUGUSTODUNENSIS, *Elucidarium* I,4 (PL 172,1112; Yves LEFÈVRE, *L'Elucidarium et les Lucidaires*, 363): "Scriptum est: Quod factum est, in ipso vita erat. In quo patet omnem creaturam semper fuisse visibilem in Dei praedestinatione, quae postea visibilis ipsi creaturae apparuit in creatione: ut artifex, qui vult construere domum, prius tractat quomodo velit quaeque disponere, et machina quae post surgit in aedificio, eadem est quae prius stabat in ingenio. Unde Deus dicitur non esse antiquior sua creatura, tempore, sed dignitate." ID., *Hexaemeron [De Neocosmo]* (PL 172,260): "In principio creavit Deus coelum et terram. Hoc est, in Filio suo, scilicet in Sapientia sua, Deus Pater creavit omnia simul spiritualia et corporalia; sicut scriptum est: Qui manet in aeternum, creavit omnia simul. Et iterum: Omnia per ipsum facta sunt, et sine ipso factum est nihil, quod factum est; in ipso vita erat. Hoc est dicere: Omne quod postmodum factum est, materialiter ac formabiliter, semper in Verbo Dei fuit causaliter ac praedestinaliter. Unde scriptum est, qui fecit quae futura sunt. Coeli autem ac terrae nomine universaliter omnis creatura comprehenditur. Non est autem aestimandum aliud insensibile a Deo ante angelos creatum: omne enim sensibile dignius insensibili praedicatur. Angelica itaque natura, quae est intellectualis, in primis conditur, ubi Deus in principio coelum creasse legitur. Sicut de primo angelo scribitur: Ipse est principium viarum Dei. Quae idcirco coelum appellatur, quia Deus in ea habitat, et divina secreta in ea celantur: et haec coelum coeli dicitur."
101 See Mariano MAGRASSI, *Teologia e storia nel pensiero di Ruperto di Deutz*, 219–255.

incarnation that Rupert organically arrived at his critique of the thesis of man as a replacement angel (perhaps in discussion with the school of Laon). Honorius, on the other hand, only ever mentions the concept in the context of our theme, while in others of his writings this emphasis is entirely absent. Furthermore, as we are yet to show, he holds onto the full meaning of Rupert's suggestion.[102] The theological affinity and primacy of Rupert's ideas appears to provide the most obvious indication as to whom we should attribute the origins of this filiation.

Further evidence can be seen in the similarity of the sequence of ideas and in the degree of lexical affinity. From the synopsis included at the end of this chapter, it is clear that in *De glorificatione Trinitatis et processione Spiritus sancti,* Rupert first recalled Gregory's assertion (1), then referred to the sentence that was formulated in relation to the recalled theme (2), submitted it to critique (3), formulated his own sentence (4), substantiated it by argument from Scripture (5), and returned again to his sentence (6). In *Liber duodecim quaestionum,* Honorius followed Rupert's process from points (2) to (6), while using different content, particularly in exchanging the idea that everything was created for the man Jesus Christ with everything being created for man, so that if he had not been created, then nothing at all would exist.

Honorius adopted the same procedure in *Liber octo quaestionum* and *Expositio in Cantica canticorum,* adding in each a further step, step (7), in which he addressed Rupert's question from *De gloria et honore Filii hominis super Matheum* 13: *utrum iste Filius Dei [...] etiam si peccatum, propter quod omnes morimur, non intercessisset, homo fieret, an non.*

His answer in the affirmative is taken from Rupert; his argument is slightly different, however, as Honorius uses the term "deification," which he most likely adopted from his favoured Eriugena. As far as we are aware it appears explicitly only in *Liber octo quaestionum* 2 and in *Expositio in Cantica canticorum* I,1 v. 1; II,5, v. 1,2, therefore, with only one exception, precisely in the places we have explored.[103]

---

102 It is worth noting that when Honorius addressed the fall of the angels and the creation of man in other contexts drawn directly from the work of St. Augustine, he did not introduce our theme. See for example HONORIUS AUGUSTODUNENSIS, *De anima et de Deo*, in Marie--Odile GARRIGUES, Honorius Augustodunensis: De anima et de Deo, quaedam ex Augustino excerpta, sub dialogo exarata, *Recherches augustiniennes et patristiques* 12 (1977), 265–268; [HONOROIUS AUGUSTODUNENSIS], *De cognitione verae vitae* (PL 40,1005–1032).

103 What Honorius understood by this term nonetheless appears elsewhere. According to evidence gathered by Joseph Anton ENDRES, *Honorius Augustodunensis: Beitrag zur Geschichte des geistigen Lebens im 12. Jahrhundert*, Kempten-München: Verlag der Josef Kösel'schen Buchhandlung, 1906, 121–126, Honorius's understanding of deification caused Gilbert de la Porrée to suspect

For all of these reasons we are therefore of the opinion that there is strong evidence to support the assumption that Honorius, in the texts we are interested in (and not only these), took his inspiration from Rupert.[104] The link between the two theologians could have been Chuno, Rupert's former abbot in Siegburg, who became bishop of Regensburg (1126–1132) and took with him a number of Rupert's writings. Let us not forget, however, that in their reflections on the question as to whether man was created as a replacement for fallen angels or for his own sake, both Rupert and Honorius were applying themselves to a problem that had already been introduced and discussed elsewhere, that is, by Anselm of Canterbury and especially in the school of Laon. It is no accident, therefore, that they both approach it with reference to the discussions taking place in the theological discourse of the day.[105]

If it is true that the writings of Honorius are an echo of Rupert's *De glorificatione Trinitatis et processione Spiritus sancti* from 1127–1128, then they must originate after this date. The fact that there are clear similarities between the argument of *Liber octo quaestionum* and that of *Expositio in Cantica canticorum*, written after 1132,[106] leads us to believe that the date for these two works could be similar, but that *Liber octo quaestionum* precedes *Expositio*, which summarizes its ideas. We assume, therefore, that *Libri* originated after 1128 and *Expositio* after 1132, thus yielding the sequence *Liber duodecim quaestionum*, *Liber octo quaestionum* and *Expositio in Cantica canticorum*.[107]

---

him of heresy. See GILBERTUS PORRETANUS, *Commentaria in librum De duabus naturis et una persona Christi* (PL 64,1397).

104 See Wolfgang BEINERT, *Die Kirche-Gottes Heil in der Welt: die Lehre von der Kirche nach den Schriften des Rupert von Deutz, Honorius Augustodunensis und Gerhoch von Reichersberg: ein Beitrag zur Ekklesiologie des 12. Jahrhunderts*, Münster: Aschendorffsche Verlagsbuchhandlung, 1973, 69–72; Maria Lodovica ARDUINI, Di alcune analogie testuali tra il Liber Tertius del De apologeticis suis di Ruperto di Deutz e il Quid vasa honoris et quid vasa contumeliae di Onorio di Ratisbona (Augustodunensis), *Aevum* 64/2 (1990), 203–226.

105 Rupert had already stated his thesis in *De glorificatione Trinitatis et processione Spiritus sancti* III,20 in the words, "Solent plerique arbitrari quod si omnes angeli perstitissent, nullaque ruina facta fuisset ex eis, non crearetur neque fuisset causa cur deberet homo creari." In *Liber octo quaestionum,* Honorius first asks the question "utrum homo crearetur, si angelus in coelo perstitisset," and then the question "utrum Christus incarnaretur, si homo in paradiso perstitisset." In *Expositio in Cantica canticorum,* he asks "Solet quaeri a quibusdam utrum homo esset conditus, si angelus non fuisset lapsus," and "Item quaeritur utrum Filius Dei esset incarnatus, si homo non fuisset lapsus." In *Liber duodecim quaestionum,* he introduces the subject: "Plerique arbitrantur hominem hac sola causa conditum, ut per eum instauretur lapsus angelorum."

106 See Maria Lodovica ARDUINI, Di alcune analogie testuali, 223–226.

107 Chenu and Garrigues place *Liber duodecim quaestionum* before *Liber octo quaestionum* by referring to the words in *Liber duodecim quaestionum,* "Sed quia hoc durius quibusdam dictum videtur

Now we come to the thesis of man as a replacement angel. *Liber duodecim quaestionum* is presented as a development of the dialogue, in written form, in which Honorius answers the question (*evangelia quaestio*) as to who enjoys the primacy: a canon, whose patron is St. Peter (*canonicus dixit se esse beati Petri*), Prince of the Apostles and keeper of the keys of heaven; or a monk, whose patron is the Archangel Michael (*monachus vero dixit se esse sancti Michaelis archangeli*), angel and commander of the heavens. There is authority behind both opinions so Honorius sought a resolution by rational argument.[108]

The course taken by his treatise shows us that the introduction primarily forms a literarily sophisticated preface to a theological exposition on the relationship between men and angels, which is the main subject of the treatise, which follows a three-fold structure: origins in the theology of creation (chapters 1–3);[109] an eschatological perspective and ecclesiological application (chapters 4–8);[110] and the spiritual nature of angels and the physical nature of man (chapters 9–12).[111] The initial question, taken

tota Scriptura clamante, numerus angelorum electis hominibus redintegrandus, enucleatius ratione duce elucidetur," (PL 172,1184) which they understand as Honorius announcing his intention to write a further treatise on the subject, which would have been *Liber octo quaestionum*. But this is a mistake as in reality these words simply introduce an exposition in which the author, at the end of *Liber duodecim quaestionum,* returns once more to the previous subject. See Marie-Dominique CHENU, *La théologie au douzième siècle*, 58; Marie-Odile GARRIGUES, L'œuvre d'Honorius Augustodunensis, 158.

108 HONORIUS AUGUSTODUNENSIS, *Liber XII quaestionum* 1 (PL 172,1177).

109 I. Quod Deus Pater omnia simul in Filio fecit, et quod hic mundus sensibilis illius archetypi umbra sit. II. Quod universitas in modum citharae sit disposita, in qua diversa rerum genera in modum chordarum sint consonantia. III. Quod sicut nullum genus pro altero, sed pro seipso sit conditum: ita homo non pro apostata angelo, sed pro seipso sit conditus; et ideo si nullus angelus cecidisset, homo tamen suum locum in universitate habuisset.

110 IV. Est quod electi homines non pro apostatis angelis sed pro seipsis in coelum assumantur; reprobi autem, vel angeli vel homines ut dissonae chordae apto loco ad consonantiam ponantur. V. Quod de singulis angelorum ordinibus aliqui ceciderint; et quod electi homines stantibus angelis pro meritis associandi sint, similiter et reprobi singulis ordinibus lapsorum pro meritis aggregandi sint. VI. Quod chorus apostolorum seraphim associandus sit; et ideo Petrus superior Michaele sit in coelo, quem Christus Deus homo principem Ecclesiae constituit, et cui Roma, quae est caput mundi, primatum obtulit. VII. Quod homo sit angelo dignior, sed angelus homine felicior: eo quod angeli adorent hominem Deum, non homines angelum Deum. VIII. Quod in Ecclesia sint novem ordines iustorum secundum novem ordines angelorum.

111 IX. Quod Deus et angeli et animae non habeant corpora, sicut iustitia et sapientia; et quod sola mente videantur. X. Quod corporalia corporeo visu, imagines spiritu, voluntates intellectu discernantur, et hoc modo per angelorum mentem discernantur. XI. Quod angeli aetherea, daemones aeria; homines terrena corpora habeant: et sicut nos vestes mutare possumus, ita daemones sua corpora in varias figuras transformare, et angeli sua, prout velint, valeant per-

from discussions then taking place in the church community, is merely a pretext. The author also addressed it here, however, and in such a way as to create more than a few difficulties for historians.[112] The introduction could have been seen as particularly sensitive in Regensburg, as Chuno, once abbot of St. Michael's monastery in Siegburg, had been promoted to the bishop's seat at St. Peter's, alongside which there was also, naturally, a cathedral chapter.[113]

Honorius started from the assertion of numerous thinkers that man was created only so that through him the fall of the angels would be repaired (*plerique arbitrantur hominem hac sola causa conditum, ut per eum instauretur lapsus angelorum*). This would imply, however, that if the angels had remained in heaven, man would never have been created, nor would there be a material world, which was created for man and of which he is a lord.[114]

In God's mind the world is simple, unchanging, and eternal: God the Father eternally begets his Son, the Word, in whom is contained in all

---

mutare. XII. Quod animabus corpore exutis forma corporis adhaereat: et quod Dominus post resurrectionem suam suum corpus prout voluit, exhibuerit.

112 This work was understood as the only one of Honorius's treatises in which primacy is ascribed to a canon over a monk. This gave cause to the assumption that perhaps *Liber duodecim quaestionum* does not reflect the reality that Honorius, after arriving on the Continent, first became a canon and later somehow turned to the more demanding and noble status of a monk. See, for example, Julius Dieterich's introductory study to an edition of portions of these writings: *Libelli de lite Imperatorum et Pontificum saeculi XI. et XII. conscripti*, tomus III, Hannoverae: Impensis Bibliopolii Hahniani, 1897, 29–38 (MGH Ldl).

113 *Liber duodecim quaestionum* does not clarify whether the term *canonicus* is to mean a member of a cathedral chapter or a monastic order. Elsewhere, however, Honorius defined and graded the categories as follows: *canonici – regulares – monachi*. The question remains whether this should also be applied to the works here. See HONORIUS AUGUSTODUNENSIS, *Quod monachis liceat predicare*, in Joseph Anton ENDRES, *Honorius Augustodunensis*, 149–150: "... notandum, quod ex clericali officio hi proprie dicuntur canonici, qui sub preposito et aliqua regula sunt constituti. Hii vero acephali, qui nullo magistro [magisterio] sunt subditi. Porro hi regulares nominati sunt, qui communem vitam sub regula sancti Augustini in cenobiis ducunt. Que regula his primitus dicitur instituta, qui in civitatibus degunt. Monachi autem hi dicti sunt, qui a mundo segregati seculo mortui sunt, soli Deo vivunt. Regularium itaque vita quanto a canonica est districtior, tanto a monachica remissior, et quanto ab illa altior, tanto ab ista inferior ac seculari vicinior [...]. Unde sicut a canonica licet cuique ad regularium vitam, ita licet a regulari cuique ascendere ad monachicam, nulli autem licet a monachica ad regularem sicut nec de regulari ad canonicam."

114 HONORIUS AUGUSTODUNENSIS, *Liber XII quaestionum* 1 (PL 172,1178): "Plerique arbitrantur hominem hac sola causa conditum, ut per eum instauretur lapsus angelorum. Quod si ita est, necessario sequitur, hominem nunquam fuisse conditum, si perstitisset in coelo numerositas angelorum. Et si homo non fuisset conditus, nec hic mundus creatus, cuius ipse dominus est constitutus, et qui propter eum creditur institutus."

originality, simultaneously, all of that which is in time created gradually, just as a writer has in mind a whole text that then gradually appears on paper (John 1:4; Gen 1:1; Sir 18:1). This simplicity is multi-faceted, however. Just as a zither's strings play a variety of notes that together form a single melody, so also the plurality and unity of angelic choirs resound in a single harmony when they give praise to their Creator together, while each of them is satisfied with his own glory and does not covet the gifts of the other (*dum concorditer suum factorem amando laudant; et singulis propria gloria sufficit, nec quis alterius donum concupiscit*);[115] so it is also with physical, that is, material creatures – and with all creatures – in their plurality.[116]

To each belongs his own place: it does not exist for anyone else (*unusquisque in proprio loco fundatur, nec ullum pro alio locatur*). It is the same with men as it is with angels (*ita et homo in universitate habet suum proprium locum, sicut et angelus suum proprium*): God made the world in such a way that there is a heaven, a dwelling place for angels, and an earth, a dwelling place for men. Man is not, therefore, created as a function of

---

115 Honorius is perhaps inspired by the motif of *laus perfecta* from the school of Laon, which is also clearly reflected in HONORIUS AUGUSTODUNENSIS, *De cognitione verae vitae* I (PL 40,1005): "Constat profecto naturam rationalem ad hoc solum factam, ut factorem suum verum Deum intelligat, intelligendo diligat, diligendo in eo, qui est aeterna vita, aeternaliter beate vivat." The relationship between Honorius and the school of Laon has not yet been adequately researched; comparison between the sentences of this school and *Elucidarium* is inconclusive and chronologically questionable: See Franz BLIEMETZRIEDER, L'oeuvre d'Anselme de Laon et la littérature théologique contemporaine, *Recherches de théologie ancienne et médiévale* 5 (1933), 275–291.

116 HONORIUS AUGUSTODUNENSIS, *Liber XII quaestionum* 2 (PL 172,1179): "Summus namque opifex universitatem quasi magnam citharam condidit, in qua veluti varias chordas ad multiplices sonos reddendos posuit: dum universum suum opus in duo, vel duo sibi contraria distinxit. [...] Ipsi ordines spirituum reddunt discrimina vocum, dum archangeli angelos in gloria praecellunt, illos autem virtutes honore transcendunt, has vero potestates dignitate vincunt, et his Principatus superiores existunt. Horum gloriam Dominationes superant, ipsaeque thronos in claritate non aequiparant; et hos Cherubim in scientia, Seraphim in sapientia obscurant. Qui omnes dulci harmonia consonant, dum concorditer suum factorem amando laudant; et singulis propria gloria sufficit, nec quis alterius donum concupiscit. Similiter corporalia vocum discrimina imitantur, dum in varia genera, in varias species, in individua, in formas, in numeros separantur: quae omnia concorditer consonant, dum legem sibi insitam quasi tinnulos modulis servant. Reciprocum sonum reddunt spiritus et corpus, angelus et diabolus, coelum et infernus, ignis et aqua, aer et terra, dulce et amarum, molle et durum, et sic caetera in hunc modum."

the angels (*homo non est pro angelo, sed pro seipso creatus*),[117] otherwise a worm would be better placed than a man![118]

After establishing this basic principle, Honorius proceeds to the eschatological perspective, which also represents a transition to an ecclesiological application of our theme. First he recaps existing theses that discuss the issue of whether and how the replacement of angels by men takes place. According to one such thesis there is no such replacement of fallen angels by men. Righteous men were, through begetting, to assume their own place with God. When, after the fall of angels and men, the great zither of creation began to resound discordantly, God moved them from the higher place to the lower, thus erasing the disharmony.[119] Others say that into the heavens will enter as many men as there were angels who fell. Some, using Rev 12:4, specify this number as being one third,[120] while others hold that in the beginning there were ten orders of angels and that one entire order, the tenth, fell. This they substantiate from the parable of the lost drachma (Luke 15:8–10).[121] Honorius himself, however, was of the opinion that there were only nine orders of angels and that the fall affected some from each order (*nos autem sacrae Scripturae*

---

117 HONORIUS AUGUSTODUNENSIS, *Liber XII quaestionum* 3 (PL 172,1179–1180): "Et notandum quod unusquisque in proprio loco fundatur, nec ullum pro alio locatur. In generibus quippe nec avis pro pisce nec piscis pro bestia, nec lapis pro arbore surgit, nec arbor pro lapide succedit. Similiter in speciebus nec aquila pro ciconia, nec palma pro oliva, nec topazius pro chrysolitho surgit: ita et homo in universitate habet suum proprium locum, sicut et angelus suum proprium. Igitur homo non est pro angelo, sed pro seipso creatus, alioquin maioris dignitatis vermis esset, qui proprium haberet, quam homo, qui proprio loco careret; et alterius locum occuparet sicque dissonantia in universitate fieret. Sed et Deus improvidus esset, qui aliquid in loco alterius poneret. Et quia hoc veritati repugnat vera ratio probat: si omnes angeli in coelo permansissent, homo in coelo proprium locum pleniter habuisset. Post lapsum quorumdam angelorum tot homines assumuntur in consortium persistentium, quot assumendi essent, si omnes permansissent; insuper tot, quot inde lapsi sunt: qui tamen non locum angelorum occupabunt, sed proprium locum implebunt."

118 See above, ANSELMUS CANTUARIENSIS, *Cur Deus homo* I,18 (S. Anselmi Cantuariensis Opera omnia II,77–78).

119 HONORIUS AUGUSTODUNENSIS, *Liber VIII quaestionum* 4 (PL 172,1180): "Quidam namque affirmant, quod pro apostatis angelis nec alii angeli nec homines reponantur: sicut nec pro damnatis hominibus, in Ecclesia alii homines vel angeli redonantur; sed stantes angeli in charitate firmati in sua numerositate permaneant: et homines iusti in sua multiplicatione proprium locum impleant. Deus enim, qui creavit omnia, ut sint, et nihil de creaturis suis patitur redigi in nihilum, ut non sit, cum sit melius esse, quam non esse: angelum et hominem per liberum arbitrium a summo bono ad minus bonum declinantes, quasi chordas in magna cithara dissonantes, de loco excellentium tulit, et in locum gravium posuit: in quo nullam dissonantiam faciant, sed universitati apte concinant."

120 HONORIUS AUGUSTODUNENSIS, *Liber XII quaestionum* 4 (PL 172,1180).

121 HONORIUS AUGUSTODUNENSIS, *Liber XII quaestionum* 5 (PL 172,1180).

auctoritate dicimus novem ordines angelorum fuisse, et esse, et de singulis or-dinibus aliquos corruisse). He substantiated this by the set of biblical texts that mention the fall of particular angelic orders.[122]

He concluded his exposition by recalling Gregory's belief (*Homiliae in evangelia* II,34,11) that men will be assigned to particular choirs according to their merits (*eisdem nominibus perditi homines secundum merita associandi erunt: electi autem homines secundum merita sanctorum angelorum ordinibus associandi erunt*).[123]

This is also why, in the Gospel, the nine angelic orders correspond to the nine orders chosen from among men (*sicut ergo leguntur novem ordines angelorum, ita in Evangelio a Domino ponuntur novem ordines electorum*), each of which is defined by a particular beatitude. The highest order, the ninth, which corresponds to the seraphim, consists of those who are reviled, persecuted and maligned: these are the apostles. From this it follows, Honorius concluded, that the degree by which the order of the seraphim surpasses the order of archangels, is the same as that by which the chief among the apostles, Peter, surpasses the Archangel Michael. It is also why to Rome is accorded the primacy of the apostle Peter not of Michael, and why in major towns the bishops' sees are dedicated to St. Peter,[124] just as it was, as we have seen, in Regensburg.

From here, Honorius drew the question as to whether man, who is so greatly exalted, will therefore surpass the angels in dignity. To this he gave his answer in the affirmative: man will undoubtedly surpass the angels in dignity because in Christ God became a man, which is why – as Honorius had already stated in *Liber octo quaestionum* – the angels bow to the God-man, not men to the angels. The angels will, however, surpass men in joy (*homo est dignior, licet angelus sit felicior*), as they have remained in a blessed state, which by God's grace they never left by their sin, while sinful man must earn his blessedness through his battle with vices and demons. This is also why salvation is mediated by angels – salvation which is given to men in Christ – and angels are called ministers of the

---

122 HONORIUS AUGUSTODUNENSIS, *Liber XII quaestionum* 5 (PL 172,1180–1181).
123 HONORIUS AUGUSTODUNENSIS, *Liber XII quaestionum* 5 (PL 172,1180–1181).
124 HONORIUS AUGUSTODUNENSIS, *Liber XII quaestionum* 6 (PL 172,1181–1182): "Apostoli autem quos summus Dominus de hominibus elegit, et Ecclesiae sponsae suae praefecit, summum chorum angelorum scilicet seraphim intrabunt; quia ipsi pro nomine Iesu flagellati, contumeliamque passi, gavisi sunt. Igitur quantum ordo seraphim praecellit dignitate ordinem archangelorum, tantum praecellit Petrus princeps apostolorum Michaelem unum de ordine archangelorum. Hinc est, quod Roma caput mundi Petro apostolo, non Michaeli archangelo primatum regiminis obtulit; et universa Ecclesia per orbem non solum in privatis locis, sed etiam in praecipuis urbibus episcopalem sedem Petro contulit."

Spirit; they are also the criterion according to which the church divided the faithful into nine orders (patriarchs, prophets, apostles, martyrs, worshippers, monks, virgins, widows, and married people) and nine ministries (laity, ostiaries, readers, exorcists, acolytes, sub-deacons, deacons, presbyters and bishops).[125] So it is then that through Christ, men will surpass the angels in dignity, but that through God, the angels will surpass men in joy (*igitur homo per Christum praecellit angelum dignitate; ast angelus per Deum praecellit hominem felicitate*).[126]

By such an argument, Honorius answered not only the question concerning the relationship between men and angels but also the question that he submitted in the introduction to his treatise. The whole dispute between canons and monks is unnecessary as both men (canons) and angels (monks) have, in the light of the purposes God has in Christ for the world, their original and incommutable place in glory, just like the strings on a zither. Man will surpass the angels in the dignity that he attained by God himself having become man. But angels will surpass man by the enduring nature of their blessedness, by their innocence, by their nearness to God, and by their service of salvation and of the Spirit. It is irrelevant to look for primacy here. But if in a symbolic continuation of this reflection, the question is introduced as to whether a canon will surpass a monk, or vice versa, then Honorius offers the following suggestion: a canon will surpass a monk in his dignity, but a monk will surpass a canon in the blessedness that results from his nearness to God. Behind this serious act of conciliation we can detect a kind of playful irony, and it is in this sense that *Liber duodecim quaestionum* places itself among the treatises through which Honorius commented on the question of the relationship between monastic and other statuses within the church.[127]

---

125 HONORIUS AUGUSTODUNENSIS, *Liber XII quaestionum* 8 (PL 172,1182).
126 HONORIUS AUGUSTODUNENSIS, *Liber XII quaestionum* 7 (PL 172,1182): "Et cum homo tanta gloria per hominem sit exaltatus, quaeritur: quis dignior sit, homo an angelus? Resp. Absque dubio: homo est dignior, licet angelus sit felicior; quia homo in Christo est Deus, quod non est angelus; et angeli adorant supra se hominem Deum, non homines angelum. Angelus est felicior, quia semper in beatitudine mansit; homo autem dignior, quia in miseria positus, contra vitia et daemones pugnans, virtute beatitudinem promeruit, quam angelus per gratiam Dei non amisit. Et angeli administratorii Spiritus dicuntur quia salus aeterna hominibus per Christum danda, per eos administratur: sicut lex per ministerium angelorum scripta traditur, et oracula prophetarum per eos administrata creduntur. Hi non solum homini Christo sed et apostolis ministrabant, cum eos de vinculis vel de carcere solvebant. Igitur homo per Christum praecellit angelum dignitate; ast angelus per Deum praecellit hominem felicitate."
127 See Valerie I. J. FLINT, The place and purpose of the works of Honorius Augustodunensis, *Revue bénédictine* 87 (1977), 97–127, where the subject forms the basis of an interpretation of

At the end of *Liber duodecim quaestionum,* Honorius returns to the idea attributed in the fourth question to the more loosely defined *quibusdam,* who held that the place of the fallen angels is assumed neither by other angels nor by men, just as the place of reprobate men is assumed neither by other men nor by angels. The number of angels who persevered in love will be completed by just men who will take their own place alongside them (*homines iusti in sua multiplicatione proprium locum impleant*). In the twelfth question, Honorius offered the following summary: man does not replace fallen angels but is admitted into heaven, into blessedness, on his own behalf. He adds that for some this idea seems difficult to accept as the whole of Scripture (by which he means Tradition) speaks of the number of angels being completed from among elect men. Because of this he aims to clarify the matter yet further.[128]

He thus indicated that he was taking the position of the *quibusdam* for his own and considered it to be a correct interpretation of the thesis offered by Scripture (Tradition). Honorius states this explicitly in *Liber octo quaestionum,* where he suggests that Gregory's homily presupposes that the whole – perfect – number of the elect consists of the nine orders of angels as well as a tenth order of men, with no reference to any form of substitution.[129] The fact that Honorius identified himself with the position taken by the *quibusdam* is theologically coherent as it added to his initial suggestion concerning the fact that man was, like all other creatures, created for his own sake, with a postscript that he will be admitted as such into the heavens.

Honorius elucidated his position with a simple analogy: if all men look at the sun, then all of them see it, but each for himself. If, however, somebody closes his eyes or loses his sight, then he will be deprived of the sun while the others will still see it as before. And if a sighted person was born of a blind person then each of them will have their own, original

---

the whole of Honorius's life's work; there is more on this in Wanda CIZEWSKI, Interpreting the Hexaemeron: Honorius Augustodunensis De Neocosmo, *Florilegium* 7 (1985), 84–108.

128 HONORIUS AUGUSTODUNENSIS, *Liber XII quaestionum* 8 (PL 172,1184): "Superius dictum est, quod homo pro apostata angelo non reponatur, sed pro seipso in coelum, id est, in beatitudinem assumatur. Sed quia hoc durius quibusdam dictum videtur tota Scriptura clamante, numerus angelorum electis hominibus redintegrandus, enucleatius ratione duce elucidetur."

129 HONORIUS AUGUSTODUNENSIS, *Liber VIII quaestionum* 1 (PL 172,1185): "Et huic sententiae auctoritas illius magni viri, scilicet Gregorii, non refragatur, sed potius suffragatur: quia nimirum electorum numerus non in solis constitit angelis, sed in angelis simul et hominibus, et quia in novem ordinibus angelorum non erat perfectus numerus electorum, ut hic impleretur numerus, est homo decimus ordo creatus."

place in the world: the sighted person will see the sun for himself, not for the blind, and the blind person will not see it also for himself (*sed cum caecus suum locum in universitate, sicut videns suum, possideat, manifestum est, quod videns pro eo locum non teneat, sed iste in loco, id est in numero non videntium.*).[130]

By analogy, God is light, in which there is no darkness; he is the sun of justice. Angels beheld this light each for themselves, each in their own way. Some closed the eyes of their mind when they turned away from the light of truth. Elect men, who are given to behold the light of which the fallen angels deprived themselves, will behold it for themselves in the same way they would have beheld it even if the angels had not deprived themselves of the light (*electi homines, qui ipsum gaudium percepturi sunt, id est qui illud lumen visuri sunt, quo ipsi privati sunt, non pro apostatis angelis, sed pro seipsis illud videbunt*). So, when it is said that elect men assume their place, it means that they taste the joy and light of which the fallen angels deprived themselves (*ideo autem electi homines pro eis reponi dicuntur, quia illo gaudio, vel illa luce fruuntur, qua illi privantur*).[131]

In terms of material things, it holds that what one person has another cannot have. It is not like this, however, with spiritual things: many people can know the same thing and each will know it for himself. This is why angels and men will both be able to experience God, and the only ones who will not be able to do so are those who avert their mind's eye from him. Men will not therefore replace angels but will enjoy God, eternal light, eternal life, and eternal joy for themselves (*igitur homines non pro angelis restituuntur, sed pro seipsis Deo, aeterna luce, aeterna vita, ac aeterno gaudio perfruuntur*).[132]

So much for *Liber duodecim quaestionum*, the most comprehensive treatise Honorius wrote on our theme.

The second work, *Liber octo quaestionum*, is presented as a dialogue between a teacher and a student, in which the latter asks the former eight loosely connected questions. The first question concerns whether man would have been created even if all the angels had remained in heaven (*utrum homo crearetur, si angelus in coelo perstitisset*). The student explains the reasons for this question of his by referring to the authority

---

130 HONORIUS AUGUSTODUNENSIS, *Liber XII quaestionum* 8 (PL 172,1184).
131 HONORIUS AUGUSTODUNENSIS, *Liber XII quaestionum* 8 (PL 172,1184).
132 HONORIUS AUGUSTODUNENSIS, *Liber XII quaestionum* 8 (PL 172,1185): "Sic Deum, qui est lux, vita et gaudium angeli et homines similiter habere poterunt; quem soli non habebunt, qui visum mentis ab eo avertunt. Igitur homines non pro angelis restituuntur, sed pro seipsis Deo, aeterna luce, aeterna vita, ac aeterno gaudio perfruuntur."

of St. Gregory, according to whom man was created tenth in order to complete the number of the elect. From this it would appear to follow that some people were made only so that the diminished number of angels would be completed, which means that the cause of the creation of man was in fact the fall of the angels.[133]

The teacher replied that the authority both of Scripture and of reason attest to the fact that man and his offspring would certainly have been created even if all of the angels had remained in heaven (*si omnes angeli in coelo permansissent, tamen homo cum omni posteritate sua creatus fuisset*). God made the world – heaven and earth and everything in it – for man. It would therefore be truly absurd to suggest that if the angels had not fallen, the one for whom, according to Scripture, everything was created would not have been created (*valde absurdum credi videtur, ut stantibus angelis is non crearetur, propter quem universitas creata legitur*).[134]

This statement is supported by reference to the fact that God made everything simultaneously through a single act of creation (Sir 18:1), both heaven and earth (Gen 1:1), thus a totality in which heaven is the dwelling place of angels and the earth is the dwelling place of men. In the same way, man was created together with the angels (*homo cum angelo sit creatus*) in the sense of predestination (*creatione praedestinationis*). While in terms of the actual order of creation (*creatione formationis*) purely spiritual angels precede man, created from the soil of the earth, in terms of the order of predestination they are created together, in such a way, however, that begins with the angels and ends with man, who is created in the image and likeness of God, and to whom everything is subordinated (*hinc per illum inchoatio, per istum vero consummatio operum Dei innuitur: cui omnis creatura reliqua subicitur*).[135]

---

133 HONORIUS AUGUSTODUNENSIS, *Liber VIII quaestionum* 1 (PL 172,1185): "DISCIPU-LUS. Vellem mihi certa auctoritate monstrari, ac firma ratione probari, utrum homo crearetur, si angelus in coelo perstitisset? Cum enim auctoritas cuiusdam magni dicat, ut impleretur electorum numerus, homo decimus creatur: videtur ad hoc solum facta multiplicitas hominum, ut impleretur imminuta numerositas angelorum, et sic consequenter ruina angeli fuit causa conditionis hominis."

134 HONORIUS AUGUSTODUNENSIS, *Liber VIII quaestionum* 1 (PL 172,1185): "MAGIS-TER. Nihil est aliud auctoritas, quam per rationem probata veritas: et quod auctoritas docet credendum, hoc ratio probat tenendum. Evidens scripturae auctoritas clamat, et perspicax ratio probat: si omnes angeli in coelo permansissent, tamen homo cum omni posteritate sua creatus fuisset. Iste quippe mundus propter hominem est factus; mundus autem est coelum et terra, et universa quae ambitu continentur; et valde absurdum credi videtur, ut stantibus angelis is non crearetur, propter quem universitas creata legitur."

135 HONORIUS AUGUSTODUNENSIS, *Liber VIII quaestionum* 1 (PL 172,1185–1186). See also the above-cited ID., *Elucidarium* I,4 (PL 172,1112; Yves LEFÈVRE, *L'Elucidarium et les Luci-*

This is why angels were not, therefore, created for condemned men, neither were men created for fallen angels: they each have their own place in glory and this is how they complete the tenth order of creation (*sicut nec angeli pro perditis hominibus creantur, ita nec homines pro lapsis angelis creati creduntur, sed proprio loco gloriae possidendo et decimum ordinem electorum implendo*). If we say that men were made in the place of the angels who fell, it is only because they are admitted into the glory from which the angels had fallen; this would have happened, however, even without the angels' fall. Furthermore, people do not bow to angels, but angels bow to the God-man, who restored everything in heaven and on earth when on the earth he released man from the power of the devil and joined him to the angels in heaven.[136]

The student's second question arises from the assumption, as had just been rationally proven, that the cause of creation was not the fall of the angels and that man was not created in the angels' stead but for his own sake (*rationabiliter est probatum, ruinam angeli non fuisse causam creationis hominis, nec hominem pro angelo, sed pro semetipso creatum*). It relates to whether Christ would have been incarnated if man had remained in paradise (*utrum Christus incarnaretur, si homo in paradiso perstitisset*). If human sin was the reason why God became man and thus also why man became God, then this sin was not an evil but a great good![137] The teacher responds: the cause of Christ's incarnation was the predestination of man to deification (*causa autem Christi incarnationis fuit praedestinatio humanae*

---

daires, 363); ID., *Hexaemeron* [*De Neocosmo*] (PL 172,260). Honorius works here with Gregory's interpretation of Job 40:10,19 (*Moralia in Iob* 32,12.23–24), which makes a stable topos (see *Biblia cum glossa ordinaria* (ad Iob 40,10.19), pars II, Straßburg: Adolf Rusch, 1480/1481, [454.455]), and then shifts it by means of the doctrine of double creation (Gen 1:6–2:7), the origins of which lie in Philo of Alexandria (c. 20 BC–c. AD 50) and some church fathers.

136 HONORIUS AUGUSTODUNENSIS, *Liber VIII quaestionum* 1 (PL 172,1185–1187): "Igitur sicut nec angeli pro perditis hominibus creantur, ita nec homines pro lapsis angelis creati creduntur, sed proprio loco gloriae possidendo et decimum ordinem electorum implendo. Ideo autem pro perditis angelis dicuntur facti, quia in gloriam, de qua ipsi ceciderant, sunt assumendi: quod nihilominus fieret, si nullus angelorum corruisset. Et ecce nullus hominum adorat angelum, multitudo autem angelorum adorat super se hominem Deum, qui omnia in coelis et in terris restauravit: dum hominem de potestate diaboli in terris liberavit, et in coelis angelis associavit."

137 HONORIUS AUGUSTODUNENSIS, *Liber VIII quaestionum* 2 (PL 172,1187): "DISCIPULUS. Quia rationabiliter est probatum, ruinam angeli non fuisse causam creationis hominis, nec hominem pro angelo, sed pro semetipso creatum, vellem item eadem auctoritate, comitante ratione, doceri, utrum Christus incarnaretur, si homo in paradiso perstitisset? Cum enim tota Scriptura clamat, Christum pro humana redemptione in carne venisse; putatur nunquam in carne venisse, si homo non peccasset quem redimeret: et sic videtur peccatum hominis causa fuisse Christi incarnationis."

deificationis), which was to happen according to the Father's plan precisely through Christ. This is why the Son would have become man even
if man had not sinned, because the very goal of his incarnation, on which
sin had no effect, was the deification of man.[138]

Theoretically, Christ could have come to man before man's fall, or not
until after man had attained his final state; in either case man would have
been immediately deified and, as the tenth order, joined to the angels.
Because, however, Christ foreknew human sin, he came to him in such
a way as to deliver him from this state and grant him deification.[139] Sin
therefore influenced the *manner* of the incarnation and the way in which
its goal, human deification, was fulfilled, but it was not the *cause*.

Further progress in the debate is not relevant to our study, with the
exception of where Honorius evokes the theory of *ius diaboli* and connects it with the assertion that because of his disobedience man deserved
death and so brought dissonance into creation, whereas Christ, through
his obedience, returned consonance to creation.[140] This musical termino-
logy provides a point of concurrence with the motif of the zither in *Liber
duodecim quaestionum*.

The final text we need to mention is *Expositio in Cantica canticorum* II,5. Here, Honorius inserts into an interpretation of the Song of
Solomon two questions that follow a classical form of scholastic theological disputation: *Solet quaeri a quibusdam utrum homo esset conditus, si
angelus non fuisset lapsus... Item quaeritur utrum Filius Dei esset incarnatus,*

---

138 HONORIUS AUGUSTODUNENSIS, *Liber VIII quaestionum* 2 (PL 172,1187): "MAGISTER.
[...] Causa autem Christi incarnationis fuit praedestinatio humanae deificationis: ab aeterno
quippe a Deo erat praedestinatum, ut homo deificaretur, dicente Domino: Pater, dilexisti eos
ante constitutionem mundi, subaudi, per me deificandos. [...] Et ideo non sequitur, peccatum
fuisse causam eius incarnationis; sed hoc magis sequitur, peccatum non potuisse propositum
Dei immutare de deificatione hominis. Siquidem auctoritas sacrae Scripturae et manifesta ratio
declarat, Deum hominem assumpsisse, etiamsi homo nunquam peccasset."
139 HONORIUS AUGUSTODUNENSIS, *Liber VIII quaestionum* 2 (PL 172,1188): "Quod autem
Christus mortuus est, qui est vita omnium, tres status sunt hominis: unus ante peccatum, in
quo mori, et non mori potuit; alter post peccatum in quo mori necesse habuit: tertius, qui erat
ei futurus, si tentatus non peccasset, et adhuc post resurrectionem speratur, in quo mori non
potuit. Si ergo Christus in primo statu venisset, nec ipse nec homo unquam moreretur, sed iam
deificatus completo numero ordinis decimi angelis associaretur: quod utique factum ita esset,
si homo tentatus non peccasset. Sed Christus hominem peccaturum, et per hoc moriturum
praescius, ideo in secundo statu venire et mori voluit: ut hominem de morte redimeret, et
ad statum vitae reduceret. Et ideo dicitur pro humana redemptione venisse, quia nisi ipse
moriendo mortem nostram destrueret, nunquam homo post culpam statum vitae reciperet.
Igitur Christi incarnatio fuit humanae naturae deificatio, eius mors nostrae mortis destructio,
eius resurrectio vitae nostrae reparatio."
140 HONORIUS AUGUSTODUNENSIS, *Liber VIII quaestionum* 5 (PL 172,1190).

si homo non fuisset lapsus. In their content, and in the way they are formulated, both questions provide a clear echo of the question from *Liber
octo quaestionum*.[141]

So Honorius asks again whether man would have been created even
if the angels had not fallen. He replies that the number of men would
have been created on earth even if the whole number of angels had remained in heaven. Scripture says that the world was created for man, so
if there had been no man there would have been no world, and this is
totally absurd (*quod absurdissimum est*). In the beginning, God created
the heavens and the earth, the dwelling place of angels and of men, who
were created simultaneously (Gen 1:1; Job 40:10; Sir 18:1). The conclusion is that *homo non propter angelum, sed propter seipsum factus est: mundus
autem propter ipsum factus est*. And yes, the angelic fall was corrected by
man as the fathers said, but in such a way that God became man and as
a consequence of this man then became God.[142] Herein lies the answer to

---

141 Similarly, three formal questions appear in *Expositio in Cantica canticorum*. The first immediately
follows the two just cited: "Adhuc quaeritur: Si homo in paradiso perstitisset, utrum mali ex
eo nascerentur" (PL 172,433). Others appear later: "Quaeritur, quomodo Deus dicatur abire
vel adire [...] Item quaeritur cum Deus ubique sit totus, quomodo dicatur esse totus alicubi;
quod enim est totum alicubi, illius pars nulla est alibi." (PL 172,445) By all appearances it
represents a resumé of Honorius's previous texts that circulated individually. This is attested
to, for example, by manuscripts from the final third of the twelfth century, which contain
various partial questions from Honorius. BSB Clm 22225 (fol. 46): "Utrum Deus sit in loco, qui
praedicatur ubique esse [...] Item quaeritur utrum Deus ubique totus sit [...] Item quaeritur
utrum anima in loco sit." Bodleian Library, Lyell 56 (fol. 205): "Queritur utrum Deus sit in loco
qui predicatur ubique esse"; "Item queritur utrum Deus ubique totus sit"; "Iterum queritur
utrum Deus in omnibus sit"; "Item queritur utrum anima in loco sit, que corpori includi."
Klosterneuburg, Cod. 931 (fol. 59–60): "Quaestio utrum anima localis sit." See Karl HALM –
Georg von LAUBMANN – Wilhelm MEYER, *Catalogus codicum latinorum Bibliothecae Regiae
Monacensis*, Bd. 2,4, *Codices num. 21406 – 27268 complectens*, secundum Andreae Schmelleri
indices composuerunt Carolus Halm et Gulielmus Meyer, Monachii, 1881, 31, n. 253; Albinia
de la MARE, *Catalogue of the collection of medieval manuscripts bequeathed to the Bodleian Library*,
Oxford, by James P. R. Lyell, Oxford: At the Clarendon Press, 1971, 171; *Mittelalterliche Handschriften in österreichischen Bibliotheken*. <http://manuscripta.at/>.

142 HONORIUS AUGUSTODUNENSIS, *Expositio in Cantica canticorum* II,5, v. 1,2 (PL 172,432–
433): "Solet quaeri a quibusdam utrum homo esset conditus, si angelus non fuisset lapsus.
Putant enim lapsum angelorum causam fuisse creationis hominum; sed hi falluntur. Ratione
quippe docente, et sacra auctoritate consentiente, si tota numerositas angelorum in coelo
perstitisset, tamen multitudo hominum in terra creata esset. Et sicut angelus in universitate
habet suum locum, ita homo in universitate habet suum. Si quidem tota Scriptura clamat
hunc mundum propter hominem factum; quod si homo non esset creatus, consequenter et hic
mundus non esset conditus. Quod absurdissimum est. [...] Igitur homo non propter angelum,
sed propter seipsum factus est: mundus autem propter ipsum factus est. Et lapsus angelorum
per hominem reparatus est, quia Deus creator homo factus est, consequentes et homo Deus
factus est."

a further question, which is whether the Son would have become incarnate if man had not sinned: the incarnation as a "means to the end" of the deification of man was part of God's predestination from the ages before human sin, but the manner of redemption is dependent on that sin.[143]

It is clear that through the two *Libri* and in *Expositio,* Honorius took a very strong stand on the question as to whether man was created as a replacement for the fallen angels or for his own sake. The question itself, and the answer to it, came to him from elsewhere: perhaps from Anselm of Canterbury or from the school of Laon, but more probably from Rupert of Deutz. But it piqued his interest to such a degree that he paid more attention to it than did any other medieval author. He also expressed himself more strongly and attempted to find his own arguments by which he could support the idea that man was created for his own sake and as such will be admitted as the tenth choir into heaven, where he will, in proportion to his own merits, be made like the nine angelic choirs. Honorius admits that his position appeared difficult to some as it was not in accordance with how, following the prevailing interpretation of Scripture, they understood that the number of angels would be completed from among elect men; in his early works he himself had shared their opinion.

It appears that the key to the transformation of Honorius's opinions was his reading of Rupert's *De glorificatione Trinitatis et processione Spiritus sancti* (1127–1128). Honorius follows a similar line of thought to that set out by Rupert, but there are significant differences that reflect the fact that Honorius did not reach the same theological conclusions: Rupert linked the unity of God's intentions for the world with the relationship between the Father and the Son by suggesting that when he was creating the world, the Father already had in mind his incarnate Son; it was according to him, and for him, that he created the world so that through suffering his incarnate Son obtains glory and delights in the communion with men and angels. The abbot from Deutz therefore had in mind the predestination of Jesus Christ, and from here deduced that men are not created as a replacement for fallen angels, as everything – including men and angels – was created for the man Jesus Christ, the incarnate Son of God.

Honorius also set the question *cur homo* alongside the question *cur Deus homo* but purely in terms of juxtaposition, rather than by thinking

---

143 HONORIUS AUGUSTODUNENSIS, *Expositio in Cantica canticorum* II,5, v. 1,2 (PL 172, 433–434). On the scribes' disagreement with this theological position, see Joseph Anton EN-DRES, *Honorius Augustodunensis,* 119.

them through together. But like Rupert he linked the unity of God's intention for the world with the relationship between the Father and the Son by suggesting that when creating the world the Father has in mind his eternal Son, but by which the unchangeable fact that the world was created for man is secured. This predetermined fact is not, therefore, conditional upon the arbitrary actions of the angels, and the assertion that man was created only so that through him the fall of the angels would be corrected is absurd (*valde absurdum, absurdissimum*). Rather, it holds that each kind of being was created for its own sake and to each, in the order of creation, belongs its own incommutable place. This place is to belong to man forever. Men will not replace angels in heaven, but will be there on their own behalf – by the angels' side – enjoying God. God predestined man for deification and determined that this should take place through the medium of Christ. This is why the Son would have become incarnate even if man had not sinned, as the very goal of his incarnation, upon which sin had no effect whatever, was the deification of man.

Such is the particular emphasis of the mysterious Honorius.

Synopsis of the works of Rupert of Deutz and Honorius of Autun

	RUPERT: *De glorificatione Trinitatis*	HONORIUS: *Liber XII quaestionum*	HONORIUS: *Liber VIII quaestionum*	HONORIUS: *Expositio in Cantica canticorum*
(1)	*Nunc illud dicere praestat quia propter illa verba quae dixit: sed ut compleretur electorum numerus homo decimus est creatus.*		*DISCIPULUS. Vellem mihi certa auctoritate monstrari, ac firma ratione probari, utrum homo crearetur, si angelus in coelo perstitisset? Cum enim auctoritas cuiusdam magni dicat, ut impleretur electorum numerus, homo decimus creatur:*	
(2)	*Solent plerique arbitrari quod si omnes angeli perstitissent, nullaque ruina facta fuisset ex eis, non crearetur neque fuisset causa cur deberet homo creari.*	*Plerique arbitrantur hominem hac sola causa conditum, ut per eum instauretur lapsus angelorum.*	*videtur ad hoc solum facta multiplicitas hominum, ut impleretur imminuta numerositas angelorum, et sic consequenter ruina angeli fuit causa conditionis hominis.*	*Solet quaeri a quibusdam utrum homo esset conditus, si angelus non fuisset lapsus. Putant enim lapsum angelorum causam fuisse creationis hominum; sed hi falluntur.*
(3)	*Quod si conceditur; cavendum est ne ita pueri simus, ut existememus Deum nullum ante ruinam angelorum de homine creando habuisse propositum, sed postquam casus ille contigit, tunc demum illi venisse in mentem consilium huiusmodi, scilicet facere genus nostrum ob recuperandam multitudinem*	*Quod si ita est, necessario sequitur; hominem nunquam fuisse conditum, si perstitisset in coelo numerositas angelorum.*	*Evidens scripturae auctoritas clamat, et perspicax ratio probat: si omnes angeli in coelo permansissent, tamen homo cum omni posteritate sua creatus fuisset.*	*Ratione quippe docente, et sacra auctoritate consentiente, si tota numerositas angelorum in coelo perstitisset, tamen multitudo hominum in terra creata esset.*

(3)	*domus seu familiae suae quae cecidit.*			*Et sicut angelus in universitate habet suum locum, ita homo in universitate habet suum. Si quidem tota Scriptura clamat hunc mundum propter hominem factum; quod si homo non esset creatus, consequenter et hic mundus non esset conditus. Quod absurdissimum est.*
(4)	*Rectius ergo dicitur quia non homo propter angelos, immo propter hominem quemdam angeli quoque facti sunt sicut et caetera omnia, testante apostolo cum dicit: Decebat enim propter quem omnia, et per quem omnia [...].*	*Et si homo non fuisset conditus, nec hic mundus creatus, cuius ipse Dominus est constitutus, et qui propter eum creditur institutus. Quod si hic mundus factus non fuisset, consequenter nec infernus esset, qui utique in hoc mundo est positus et in quem trusus est diabolus, mox ut a coelo est pulsus; sive aer iste, qui est pars mundi, in quo adhuc dicitur servari usque in diem iudicii.*	*Iste quippe mundus propter hominem est factus; mundus autem est coelum et terra, et universa quae ambitu continentur; et valde absurdum credi videtur, ut stantibus angelis is non crearetur; propter quem universitas creata legitur. [...]*	
(5)	testante Apostolo cum dicit: Decebat enim eum propter quem omnia, et per quem omnia, cuius capituli memoria nos non praeterivit in primo libello praesentis operis, cum de principio loqueremur, *in quo creavit Deus coelum et terram.* Si enim verum dicit imo quia verum dicit Evangelista: Quod factum est in ipso, vita erat, nihil excipiens,	Si hoc verum esset, tunc falsum esset, quod ait evangelista: Quod factum est in ipso, vita erat. Vita in Deo est Deus, dicente Filio Deo: Ego sum vita et veritas. Quod si omne quod factum est, in Christo vita et veritas est, et vita et veritas est Deus; igitur omnis ista creatura est umbra vitae et veritatis: et sicut semper fuit vita et veritas, ita semper	AD HUNC ERROREM REMOVENDUM SACRA SCRIPTURA, FUTURORUM PRAESCIA, ANTE CREATIONEM ANGELI ET CREATIONEM HOMINIS EXORSA EST DICENS: *In principio creavit Deus coelum et terram.* **Utquid coelum? Ut esset utique habitatio angelorum. Utquid terram? Ut videlicet esset habitatio hominum.** Et huic sententiae auctoritas illius magni viri,	QUEM ERROREM SPIRITUS SANCTUS PRAEVIDENS, ET PER SCRIPTURAM PRAECAVENS QUOD ANTE CREATIONEM ANGELI VEL HOMINIS CREATUS SIT PRONUNTIAT, CLAMANS: *in principio creavit Deus coelum et terram*: coelum autem et terra est mundus. **Ad quid fecit coelum? Ut esset habitatio angelorum. Ad quid terram? Ut esset habitatio hominum.**

(5)			
praemiserat enim: Omnia per ipsum facta sunt, et sine ipso factum est nihil; quanto magis homo iste decorus, ab ipso Verbo in unitatem personae assumendus angeli, qua antequam angeli fierent, in ipso vita erat? Testatur et hoc ipsa Sapientia, quae non est aliud quam ipsum Verbum, dum dicit: Dominus possedit me ab initio viarum suarum, et caetera usque quando appendebat fundamenta terrae, cum eo eram cuncta componens, et ludens coram eo omni tempore, ludens in orbe terrarum. Statimque subiungit: Et deliciae meae esse cum filiis hominum. Quidnam hoc est, nisi ac si dixisset: Antequam Deus quidquam faceret a principio, et quando haec vel illa faciebat, hoc erat in proposito, ut ego Verbum Dei, Verbum Deus caro fierem, et in hominibus habitarem magna charitate et	fuit umbra eius. Verbi gratia: Dictamen a me compositum, et adhuc non scriptum, quodammodo in me vivit, quod quasi exemplar inspicio, dum illud in tabulis scribo: et illud, quod foris scriptum apparet, est umbra illius non scripti, quod intus latet. Et exterius quidem potest redigi in nihilum, interius autem manet incorruptum; sed intrinsecus est simplex et uniforme, forinsecus multiplex et varium, scilicet in litteris et in dictionibus, et in syllabis et in casibus, in temporibus, in schematibus, in figuris. Sic universa creatura in divina mente concepta est simplex, invariabilis et aeterna, in seipsa autem multiplex, variabilis, transitoria videlicet in generibus, in speciebus, in individuis. *Manet autem in aeternum qui creavit omnia simul*; quasi diceret: Deus Pater Filium, id est, sapientiam	scilicet Gregorii, non refragatur, sed potius suffragatur: quia nimirum electorum numerus non in solis constitit angelis, sed in angelis simul et hominibus, et quia in novem ordinibus angelorum non erat perfectus numerus electorum, ut hic impleretur numerus, est homo decimus ordo creatus. *Quod autem homo cum angelo sit creatus, testatur ipse creator Deus loquens ad Iob: Ecce Behemoth, quem feci tecum, quod est dicere: Quando feci hominem, feci et angelum.* Est autem dualis creatio hominis, una in aeternitate per praedestinationem, altera sub temporalitate per formationem. De creatione praedestinationis scribitur: Faciamus hominem ad imaginem et similitudinem nostram. Et fecit Deus hominem ad imaginem et similitudinem suam. De creatione formationis scriptum est: Formavit Deus hominem	***Domino autem attestante angelus et homo simul facti sunt, dicens ad Iob: Ecce Behemoth quem feci tecum, quod est dicere: Quando feci angelum, feci et hominem.*** Sacra autem Scriptura omnia simul facta clamat dicens; *Qui manet in aeternum creavit omnia simul.*

(5)	summa humilitate, quae verae deliciae sunt.	de limo terrae et inspiravit in faciem eius spiraculum vitae; et factus est in animam viventem. *Qui enim manet in aeternum*, ait Scriptura, *creavit omnia simul*. Omnia creavit simul per materiam, distinxit vero sex diebus per genera, per species, per formas, per numeros. Illi autem sex dies non sunt, ut isti volubiles, intelligendi, sed in aeternitate fixi, ad quorum exemplar isti sunt facti. [...] Quod autem angelus sit principium viarum Dei, scribitur in Iob: homo vero ultima factura Dei legitur. Hinc per illum inchoatio, per istum vero consummatio operum Dei innuitur: cui omnis creatura reliqua subiicitur.	suam ex se aeternaliter genuit, in quo omnia simul fecit. [...]	
(6)	*Igitur probabilius hoc dicimus, quod non tam homo propter supplendum angelorum numerum, quam et angeli et homines, propter unum hominem Iesum Christum facti sunt, ut quoniam*	*Igitur homo non est pro angelo, sed pro seipso creatus, alioquin maioris dignitatis vermis esset, qui proprium haberet, quam homo, qui proprio loco careret; et alterius locum occuparet*	*Igitur sicut nec angeli pro perditis hominibus creantur, ita nec homines pro lapsis angelis creati creduntur, sed proprio loco gloriae possidendo et decimum ordinem electorum implendo.*	*Igitur homo non propter angelum, sed propter seipsum factus est: mundus autem propter ipsum factus est. Et lapsus angelorum per hominem reparatus est, quia* **Deus creator homo factus**

(6)	unus idemque et Deus ex Deo natus erat, et homo nasciturus erat, haberet praeparatam ex utroque latere familiam, hinc angelorum, hinc hominum, et ipse Deus, et homo, Dominus et creator angelorum, Dominus et Creator atque Salvator emineret hominum sanctorum, Dominus, inquam, in eis sicut in domo sua, Rex in gente sua, Deus in maiestate sua.	sicque dissonantia in universitate fieret. Sed et Deus improvidus esset, qui aliquid in loco alterius poneret. Et quia hoc veritati repugnat vera ratio probat: si omnes angeli in coelo permansissent, homo in coelo proprium locum pleniter habuisset.	*Ideo autem pro perditis angelis dicuntur facti, quia in gloriam, de qua ipsi ceciderant, sunt assumendi: quod nihilominus fieret, si nullus angelorum corruisset. Et ecce nullus hominum adorat angelum, multitudo autem angelorum adorat super se hominem Deum, qui omnia in coelis et in terris restauravit: dum hominem de potestate diaboli in terris liberavit, et in coelis angelis associavit.*	**est, consequentes et homo Deus factus est.**
(7)			DISCIPULUS. Quia rationabiliter est probatum, ruinam angeli non fuisse causam creationis hominis, nec hominem pro angelo, sed pro semetipso creatum, vellem item eadem auctoritate, comitante ratione, doceri, utrum Christus incarnaretur, si homo in paradiso perstitisset? **Cum enim tota Scriptura clamat, Christum pro humana redemptione in carne venisse; putatur nunquam in carne venisse,**	*Item quaeritur utrum Filius Dei esset incarnatus, si homo non fuisset lapsus. Putant enim casum hominis causam fuisse Christi incarnationis; sed hi non falluntur.* **Ratio enim manifeste clamat, et sacrae Scripturae auctoritas consonat, quod, quia homo in paradiso peccavit, propterea Deus hominem assumpserit.** *Ab aeterno quippe erat apud Deum praedestinatum quod homo deificaretur. Sicut enim Deus est*

si homo non peccasset quem redimeret: et sic videtur peccatum hominis causa fuisse Christi incarnationis. Quod si ita est, tunc illud peccatum non fuit malum, imo magnum bonum, cuius causa **Deus factus est homo, consequenter et homo Deus.** MAG. Peccatum hominis non bonum, sed maximum malum fuisse, clamat totus mundus, cum multis miseriis suis. Unde enim mors cum tot cladibus regnat in mundo, nisi de peccato hominis? et ideo peccatum primi hominis non fuit, causa Christi incarnationis, sed potius fuit causa mortis et damnationis. **Causa autem Christi incarnationis fuit praedestinatio humanae deificationis: ab aeterno quippe a Deo erat praedestinatum, ut homo deificaretur,** dicente Domino: Pater, dilexisti eos ante constitutionem mundi, subaudi, per me

immutabilis, ita et praedestinatio eius est immutabilis. **Et si Deus non incarnaretur, homo non deificaretur. Et sic praedestinatio Dei immutaretur, quod erat impossibile. Igitur oportuit Deum incarnari, ut posset homo deificari.** Huic rationi videtur auctoritas astipulari. Siquidem antequam Adam peccaret, Deus per Adam praedixit Christum de carne Adam incarnandum, et Ecclesiam ei coniungendam, ita dicens: Erunt duo in carne una, hoc Apostolus ita exponit dicens: Sacramentum hoc magnum est, ego autem dico in Christo et in Ecclesia. Ecce ante peccatum hominis praedicta est incarnatio Dei, quia ergo homo peccavit, propterea Christus immortalis factus est mortalis. Qui si in statu immortalitatis nasceretur, nunquam moreretur, et homo sine interpositione mortis

(7)

eius deificaretur. Quod fieri non potuit. Quia ergo Christus in illo statu natus est quo mori posset, ideo mori voluit; quia vero ad vitam resurrexit, mortem homini abstulit, et vitam amissam reddidit. Et sicut in illo statu mortis omnes moriuntur, sic in isto statu vitae omnes in Christo vivificabuntur, et secundum immutabilem praedestinationem Dei deificabuntur. Unde dicit apostolus: Elegit nos in Christo ante mundi constitutionem; quasi dicat: **antequam mundus esset, statuit Deus Filium suum incarnari, et nos homines in ipso deificari.** Hunc dum fugit apostata angelus in coelo in Patris claritate regnantem, invenit eum in matris terrae gremio latentem, sese quandoque iudicantem.

deificandos. Sicut autem Deus est immutabilis, ita et praedestinatio eius est immutabilis: **oportuit ergo hunc incarnari, ut homo posset deificari.** Et ideo **non sequitur, peccatum fuisse causam eius incarnationis; sed hoc magis sequitur, peccatum non potuisse propositum Dei immutare de deificatione hominis.** Siquidem auctoritas sacrae Scripturae et manifesta ratio declarat, Deum hominem assumpsisse, etiamsi homo nunquam peccasset.

(7)

IV. Decline: the twelfth and thirteenth centuries

The authors to whom the previous chapter was devoted not only addressed but to a large degree answered the question as to whether man was created only as a replacement for fallen angels or also – and especially – for his own sake. Because of this, the debate around the subject – already far from being either stormy or extensive – now quietens still further as these authors' successors largely fail to enter into it with any degree of passion. But echoes of it do remain, and at least in the discipline of systematic theology referring to it has become almost a duty, especially as the subject found its way into Hugh of St. Victor's *Summa sententiarum* and Peter Lombard's *Sententiae in IV libris distinctae*. We will show how the theology of the twelfth and thirteenth centuries approached the patristic thesis and its associated discussion with reference to a number of significant theologians, including Albert the Great, Bonaventure of Bagnoregio, and Thomas Aquinas. Before that, however, we will note that in those who cannot be counted among the scholastic theologians but who belong rather to the realm of monastic theology, the discussion fails to register and the motif of the replacement angel continues to be used merely to describe man's situation and role in the world. We will demonstrate this by exploring the works of a number of these authors, including Bernard of Clairvaux and other Cistercians, Eckebert of Schönau, Alain of Lille, and Hildegard of Bingen.

1. Authors from the monastic tradition

Although St. Bernard of Clairvaux (1090–1153), founder of the Cistercian order, frequently refers to the theme of man as a "replacement angel," he does not use it to explore the question as to whether man was willed as an "original" being.[1] The statement that man was created to fill the empty spaces in the heavenly Jerusalem (*propter hoc enim et ipse creavit homines ab initio, ut repleantur ex his loca vacua et ruinae Ierusalem restaurentur*) serve him rather as a means for drawing lessons for the spiritual life of his listeners, such as warnings against pride or exhortations to love, and pointing out that communion in the heavenly city is expressed by the mutual help provided by angels for people and people for angels in healing each other's wounds.[2] At other times, however, he does not connect references to our theme with the subject of creation, but simply settles on its spiritual content, amplified by the wider context in which monastic life is understood as an anticipation of angelic life (*bios angelikos*).[3] Perhaps the most explicit use of our theme appears in Bernard's exposition of the Song of Solomon, in which he suggests that the great mystery of the church, the bride of Christ, is a function of the three-way co-operation between God, the angels, and man. God is surely concerned about the marriage of his beloved Son, and even though he would be able to take care of everything himself he also leaves space for the freedom of others and enables men to love angels, and angels to love men – so much the more as the angels know that it is men who will restore the ancient damage to their city.[4]

---

1   Antonio ORAZZO, Il mistero della Sposa nei Sermones sul Cantico dei Cantici di san Bernardo, 245–246; Yves-Marie-Joseph CONGAR, Église et Cité de Dieu chez quelques auteurs cisterciens, 174–181; Dominik TERSTRIEP, *Weisheit und Denken: Stilformen sapientialer Theologie*, Roma: Editrice Pontificia Università Gregoriana, 2001, 198.

2   BERNARDUS CLARAEVALLENSIS, *Sermones in adventu Domini* 1,5 (Bernardi opera 4,164; PL 183,37): "Propter hoc enim et ipse creavit homines ab initio, ut repleantur ex his loca vacua et ruinae Ierusalem restaurentur. Sciebat enim nullam angelis patere redeundi viam. Nempe novit superbiam Moab, quod superbus est valde, et superbia eius remedium paenitentiae non admittit, ac per hoc nec veniae. At vero hominis vice nullam condidit creaturam, innuens ex hoc ipso redimendum adhuc hominem, quippe quem supplantavit aliena malitia; ideo que prodesse ei potest caritas aliena."

3   See BERNARDUS CLARAEVALLENSIS, *Sermones in dominica I novembris* 1,4; 2,3; 3,1 (Bernardi opera 5,306.309.311–312; PL 183,345–349); ID., *Sermones in festo sancti Michaelis* 1,4; 2,2 (Bernardi opera 5,296–297.300–301; PL 183,449.451–452); ID., *Sermones in dedicatione ecclesiae* V,5–6 (Bernardi opera 5,392; PL 183,532–533); ID., *Sermones super Cantica Canticorum* 62,1; 77,4 (Bernardi opera 2,154.263–264; PL 183,1075.1157).

4   BERNARDUS CLARAEVALLENSIS, *Sermones super Cantica Canticorum* 78,1 (Bernardi opera 2,267; PL 183,1159): "Quid restat, nisi ut debitum iam solvamus? In explicatione sacramenti magni – illud loquor quod Doctor gentium interpretatus est in Christo et in Ecclesia, sanctum castum que connubium, ipsum est opus nostrae salutis –, in eo, inquam, tres sibi invicem cooperantur: Deus, angelus, homo. Et Deus quidem quidni operetur et curam gerat nuptiarum dilecti Filii sui? Ipse vero, ac tota voluntate. Et utique per se sufficeret ipse, et absque adminiculo horum; hi autem sine ipso possunt facere nihil. Ergo quod ex illis ascivit in opus ministerii huius, non sibi solatium, sed profectum quaesivit illis. Nam hominibus quidem

Any search for echoes of the argument in Bernard and other Cistercian authors would be in vain: their interests pointed in a different direction, as is the case, for example, with other brief references to our theme in Aelred of Rievaulx (c. 1100–1167) and John of Clairvaux († 1179).[5] Otto of Freising (c. 1112–1158), who joined the Cistercian order after completing his studies in Paris and went on to become bishop of Freising, engaged with Gregory's text in order to address the question concerning the number of men to be admitted into the place of the fallen angels.[6]

Simply because Anselm, Rupert, and Honorius had all connected our theme to the question as to whether man was created as a replacement for fallen angels or for his own sake, we would clearly be mistaken to assume that it had ever after been narrated only in this perspective. This has already been shown by our insights into the work of the Cistercians and is also apparent elsewhere. As a student of Hugh of St. Victor, Eckebert of Schönau ([before] 1132–1184) used the theme in a completely different way when he employed it in his polemic with the Cathars and their belief that human souls are identical to fallen demons, against which he uses the topos of Eph 1:10: everything in heaven and on the earth is in Christ, and is therefore contained in his predestination and election; the number of angels who fell in heaven will be restored, through Christ, by men who will be redeemed by him, whether that will be an identical number or a higher number. If, on the other hand, human souls are identical with fallen spirits, then it must hold that all fallen angels and all people will be saved. This would lead us to ask to whom the Lord was referring when he said: "Depart from me, you cursed, into the eternal fire prepared for the devil and his angels!" (Matt 25:41)[7]

---

merita locavit in opere [...] Angelorum autem cum ad salutem humani generis ministerio utitur, nonne facit ut ab hominibus angeli diligantur? Nam quia ab angelis homines diligantur, inde vel maxime adverti potest, quod antiqua suae civitatis damna ex hominibus resarcitum iri angeli non ignorant. Nec aliis profecto regi legibus regnum caritatis decebat, quam piis ipsorum, qui pariter regnaturi sunt, mutuis que amoribus, et puris affectionibus in invicem et in Deum."

5   AELREDUS RIEVALLENSIS, *De Iesu puero duodenni* I,7 (CCCM 1,255; PL 184,854): "Cunctis divino modo dispositis, altera die angelicis et archangelicis choris suavitatem sui vultus indulsit. Referens que antiquam civium supernorum ruinam post modicum reparandam, universam laetificavit civitatem Dei." See IOHANNES PRIOR CLARAEVALLENSIS, *Collectaneum exemplorum et visionum Claraevallense e codice Trecensi 946* 1,25 (CCCM 208,167).

6   OTTO FRISINGENSIS, *Chronica sive Historia de duabus civitatibus* 8,31–32, Hannoverae et Lipsiae: Impensis Bibliopolii Hahniani, 1912, 448–451 (MGH SSrG: Scriptores Rerum Germanicarum in usum scholarum ex Monumentis Germaniae Historicis separatim editi).

7   ECKBERTUS SCHONAUGIENSIS, *Sermones contra Catharos* XIII,2 (PL 195,97–98): "Ex an-

Alain of Lille (c. 1124–1202/03) raised similar questions.[8] He assumed that the number of saved people will be higher than the number of fallen angels and inferred from this that man was not created only as a replacement for the fallen angels but rather as the ornament of the heavenly Jerusalem that is to be adorned by a diversity of creatures (*non propter supplendam ruinam tantum, sed potius ad coelestem Hierusalem exornandam, et ex diversorum graduum civibus, quasi ex diversis parietibus, componendam, homo creatus est potius ad coelestem Hierusalem exornandam*), as it was fitting for both spiritual and physical nature to enjoy God in that heavenly bliss.[9] Aside from this echo of the then still recent discussions, Alain referred to the patristic thesis in his commentary on the sequence *Ad celebres Rex caelice* (11th century), but without criticizing it, altering it,[10]

tiquo hoc in communi fide est, et sacra scripta attestantur, quod ad hoc creavit Deus humanum genus, ut ex eo restauraret coelesti curiae numerum angelorum, qui ex ea ceciderunt in exordio mundi. Postquam autem per invidiam diaboli etiam humanum genus lapsum est in peccatum, et de paradiso expulsum est in primis parentibus; Filius Dei in his novissimis temporibus factus est homo, ut humanum genus a peccatis suis, et a potestate diaboli liberaret, quatenus adhuc in eo perficeret quod proposuerat, videlicet ut ex eo coelestem curiam restauraret, et impleret numerum angelorum suorum, qui fuerat imminutus per ruinam illorum, qui proiecti fuerant de coelo propter superbiam suam. Creditis hoc vos qui ex paradiso estis? Si non creditis, ecce inducam vobis verba apostoli Pauli, ex quibus intelligere potestis ita esse ut dixi. [...] Item omnia quae in coelis sunt, id est totum numerum angelorum, qui fuerat imminutus per ruinam lapsorum spirituum, proposuit instaurare per Christum, ita ut redimeretur humanum genus per ipsum, et loco angelorum collocaretur electorum hominum numerus, atque coelestis curia ita ad integritatem plenitudinis suae rediret, in quo primo condita fuerat. Nam si ille numerus ministrorum Dei, quem in principio ad laudem nominis sui creavit, per Christum redintegratus non fuerit, non omnia in coelis per Christum instaurantur; si vero per ipsum impletus fuerit ille numerus, ita ut tot homines salventur, quod angeli ceciderunt, aut plures, sicut asserunt quidam; et si nihil aliud sunt animae, quam illi spiritus qui ceciderunt, necessario concedendum est, quod et omnes angeli qui ceciderunt, et omnes homines salvandi sint. Qui erunt ergo angeli quibus Dominus in novissimo dicturus est, et qui erunt homines quibus dicturus est: Ite, maledicti, in ignem aeternum, qui praeparatus est diabolo et angelis eius? Nunquid non cognoscitis hic quoque vos esse mendaces?"

8   ALANUS DE INSULIS, *Contra haereticos* I,17 (PL 210,320): "Item, si mali angeli salvandi sunt, quomodo homo creatus est ad supplendam ruinam angelorum, si lapsus angelorum in ipsis est reparandus?"

9   ALANUS DE INSULIS, *Contra haereticos* I,14 (PL 210,318–319): "Etiamsi angelus non cecidisset, tamen homo creatus fuisset, quia plures salvabuntur homines, quam sint angeli qui ceciderunt; et ita, non propter supplendam ruinam tantum, sed potius ad coelestem Hierusalem exornandam, et ex diversorum graduum civibus, quasi ex diversis parietibus, componendam, homo creatus est. Decens enim fuit, ut tam corporea quam incorporea natura divinae bonitatis particeps fieret, et ea frueretur, et feliciter viveret."

10   ALANUS DE INSULIS, *Expositio prosae de Angelis*, in ALAIN DE LILLE, *Textes inédits*, avec une introduction sur sa vie et ses oeuvres par Marie-Thérèse d'Alverny, Paris: J. Vrin, 1965, 191–192 (sequence), 215–216 (commentary). For further commentary on the same sequence

or speculating about how human beings might become affiliated to the orders of the good and evil angels.[11]

It is worth noting that in some authors a new topos appears in connection with an interpretation of the words from Ps 109:6: *implebit ruinas.* Among these we find Odo of Asti (c. first half of the 12th century), Gerhoch of Reichersberg (1093–1169), Alain of Lille (c. 1124–1202/03), Bernard of Clairvaux (1090–1153), and Alexander of Hales (c. 1185–1245).[12]

We could name other twelfth-century representatives of the monastic tradition who spoke about the creation of man as a replacement for fallen angels, or that *homo decimus est creates,*[13] such as Hildegard of Bingen (1098–1179).[14] None of them, however, comment on the discussion around our theme that was taking place in the early part of that century, and they all approach it in much the same way as the authors of the early Middle Ages.

It is a different matter, however, with contemporaries of theirs who were involved in the beginnings of the scholastic movement and to whom we will now turn.

2. Hugh of St. Victor

With Rupert and Honorius we followed the theme established in Laon as it spread into Germany. With Hugh of St. Victor (1096–1141) we return

---

see Erika KIHLMAN, *Expositiones Sequentiarum: Medieval Sequence Commentaries and Prologues: Editions with Introductions,* Stockholm: Stockholm University, 2006, 89, 125, 166, 211, 255, 277.

11 ALANUS DE INSULIS, *Hierarchia Alani,* ibid., 226; ID., *Sermo in die sancti Michaelis,* ibid., 249–251.

12 See ODO ASTENSIS, *Expositio in Psalmos – Psalmus CIX,* v. 6 (PL 165,1295): "Implebit etiam ruinas, quia sancti illuc ascendent, unde angeli ceciderunt"; GERHOHUS REICHERSPERGENSIS, *Expositio in Psalmos – Psalmus CIX,* v. 6 (PL 194,696): "implebit ruinas angelorum de hominibus"; ALANUS DE INSULIS, *Distinctiones dictionum theologicalium – R* (PL 210,928): "Ruina, proprie. Dicitur lapsus angelorum, unde David: Iudicabit in nationibus, implebit ruinas; Christus enim genus humanum sublevando in coelum, implevit ruinas angelorum"; BERNARDUS CLARAEVALLENSIS, *In dedicatione ecclesiae* V,5–6 (Bernardi opera 5,392; PL 183,532–533); ALEXANDER HALENSIS, *Summa theologica* l. 3, pars 1, inquisitio unica, tr. 2, q. 1, m. 1, cap. 1–2, n. 65 (Summa Fratris Alexandri sive Summa universae theologiae IV,97); ID., *Summa theologica* l. 3, pars 1, inquisitio unica, tr. 3, q. 1, tit. 2, m. 2, cap. 3, art. 2, prob. 2, n. 113 (Summa Fratris Alexandri sive Summa universae theologiae IV,159).

13 For example, ALULFUS SANCTI MARTINI TORNACENSIS, *Expositio Novi Testamenti – ad Ephesios* 2 (PL 73,1349); BOTO PRUVENINGENSIS, *Omelie in Ezechielem* 8, in Joseph Anton ENDRES, *Honorius Augustodunensis,* 115.

14 HILDEGARDIS BINGENSIS, *Scivias* 3,2 (PL 197,585–587); ID., *Expositiones Euangeliorum* 49 (CCCM 226,315); ID., *Liber divinorum operum aimplicis hominis* (PL 197,886); ID., *Epistulae* XLVII (PL 197,242).

to France and to the theological school founded in 1108 by William of Champeaux, where we are able to observe how our theme now launches itself into the nascent arena of systematic theology. Of all Hugh's works, the only one so far shown to be of relevance to us is the treatise *De Sacramentis*, which represents one of the first Western examples of a theological *summa*. Hugh began writing *De Sacramentis* before 1133 and worked on it until his death prevented its completion. It was thus written immediately after the time when Rupert and Honorius had been addressing the subject.

The first book begins with the *opus conditionis*, the "work of creation," a consequence of which is the state in which man exists at the moment God comes to him with the "work of restoration." Because Hugh wanted his work to follow the *series narrationis* of Scripture, he first considers, after a prologue on theology, the creation of the material world before going on to the creation of man. Discussions on the creation of the angels and about God who is one in three persons appear later, as these themes are also implied in the narration of the first pages of the Bible.

Hugh's reflections on creation gave him occasion to ask why man was created at all (*quare creatus sit homo*). He answers that God himself, as the fullness of all that is good, had no need of creatures or their service, but willed man simply so that he could do him good. The sum of this good lies in what God did for man and what man himself was made for. With respect to what God did for man, we are told that God created the world for man so that he would find good in it, and this would assist him with his basic needs. Although chronologically speaking man was created last, causally he preceded everything since the whole world was created for him. Therefore, *causa omnium homo est*. With respect to what man himself was made for, we are told that God created man that he might find goodness and joy in his service of God. Therefore, the cause of the world is man (*causa mundi homo est*) as the world was made for man, and the cause of man is God (*causa hominis deus est*) as man was made for God. Man was made that he might serve God, and the world was made that it might serve man, who therefore stands at the centre of all reality (*positus est in medio homo*) as the one who is served and the one who serves, each of these being purely for his good.[15]

---

15 HUGO DE SANCTO VICTORE, *De sacramentis* I,2,1 (PL 176,205–206): "Prius siquidem opifex Deus mundum fecit; ac deinde hominem possessorem et dominum mundi, ut caeteris omnibus iure conditionis dominaretur homo, ipsi a quo factus fuerat soli voluntaria libertate subiectus. Unde constat creationem hominis, rerum omnium visibilium conditione posterio-rem quidem tempore, sed causa priorem fuisse: quia qui factus est post omnia, propter eum

Rational beings are therefore the cause of everything; men and angels themselves, however, have their cause only in their Creator.[16] Both were created because God in his eternal goodness wanted them to participate in his eternal blessedness, which he can share with them without being in any way diminished. The good that he himself was, and by which he was blessed, led him to share this blessedness out of goodness, not out of necessity.[17]

omnia facta sunt. Causa ergo conditionis humanae ante omnia est; et ipsam investigare oportet supra omnia et ante omnia quae tempore orta sunt, et ante tempora ordinata sunt. Si enim omnia Deus fecit propter hominem, causa omnium homo est; et causaliter homo prior omnibus est, ipsum vero propter quod homo factus est prius homine est; et multo ante omnia quibus homo causaliter prior est. Id autem propter quod factus est homo, quid aliud erit nisi ipse a quo factus est homo? Si ergo causa mundi homo est, quia propter hominem factus est mundus et causa hominis Deus est, quia propter Deum factus est homo; ergo Deus erat et mundus non erat, neque homo erat; factus est homo propter Deum et quod propter hominem mundus factus est. Nam et homo factus est ut Deo serviret propter quem factus est; et mundus factus est ut serviret homini propter quem factus est. [...] Deus perfectus erat et plenus bono consummato; neque opus habuit aliunde iuvari, quoniam nec minui potuit aeternus, nec immensus augeri. Nam et homo factus est ut Deo serviret propter quem factus est; et mundus factus est ut serviret homini propter quem factus est. [...] Ita positus est in medio homo, ut et ei serviretur et ipse serviret, et acciperet utrinque ipse, et totum sibi vindicaret; et reflueret totum ad bonum hominis, et quod accepit obsequium et quod impendit. Voluit enim Deus ut ab homine sibi serviretur; sic tamen ut ea servitute non Deus sed homo ipse serviens iuvaretur, et voluit ut mundus serviret homini, et exinde similiter iuvaretur homo, et totum hominis esset bonum, quia propter hominem totum hoc factum est. Ergo totum bonum hominis erat: videlicet et quod factum est propter ipsum, et propter quod factus est ipse. Sed aliud bonum deorsum erat et de subtus sumebatur ad necessitatem, aliud bonum sursum erat, et desuper sumebatur ad felicitatem. Bonum quippe illud quod in creatura positum erat, bonum erat necessitatis; quod vero in Creatore erat bonum, bonum erat felicitatis. Et utrumque ad hominem ferebatur quia utrumque homini debebatur; quia propter alterum factus est homo, ut illud possideret et frueretur; alterum propter hominem factum est ut illud acciperet et iuvaretur."

16 HUGO DE SANCTO VICTORE, *De sacramentis* I,2,1 (PL 176,206): "In tantum ergo rationalis creaturae conditio caeteris omnibus quae propter ipsam facta sunt excellentior esse probatur; quod omnium causa ipsa est. Causa vero eius alia nulla est, nisi ipse a quo ipsa est. [...] Et hoc fortassis diligentius consideratum aliquem movere possit; propterea causam conditionis rationalium quam in solo rerum auctore constituimus, non solum pro hominibus de quibus sermo propositus erat, verum etiam pro angelis; quoniam et ipsi sicut eiusdem naturae participes sunt, ita quoque ab eodem fonte originis causam trahunt: generali quadam consideratione investigare oportet; quoniam in ipsa principium consistit universorum quae facta sunt."

17 HUGO DE SANCTO VICTORE, *De sacramentis* I,2,4 (PL 176,208): "Hinc ergo primam causam sumpsit creaturae rationalis conditio, quod voluit Deus aeterna bonitate suae beatitudinis participes fieri quam vidit et communicari posse, et minui omnino non posse. Illud itaque bonum quod ipse erat et quo ipse beatus erat, bonitate sola non necessitate trahebatur ad communicandum. Quoniam et optimi erat prodesse velle, et potentissimi nocere non posse." See ID., *De arca Noe* I,1 (CCCM 176,4; PL 176,619): "Primus itaque homo ad hoc conditus fuit, ut si non peccasset per contemplationis presentiam vultui Creatoris semper assisteret, ut eum semper videndo semper amaret, semper amando semper ei adhereret, semper ei adherendo qui

Hugh's position reminds us of the school of Laon, but only because of their common patristic roots. The concept of *laus perfecta* does not appear in Hugh, and neither does the idea that man had to be created and saved for his own sake so that his unique voice might resound in all of creation as it celebrates God. Stress is laid more on the assertion that *causa omnium homo est*. Unlike Honorius, Hugh does not refute the idea that this is precisely why the creation of man could not depend on the arbitrary nature of the free actions of the angels.

Hugh does not ask whether man was created as a replacement for fallen angels. This question does not emerge until an exposition on angels, in which Hugh discusses his view of a proper interpretation of the patristic thesis: the assumption of those who assert that the creation of man as a replacement for fallen angels happened in such a way that man would not have been created if the angels had not fallen is false (*non enim ut quidam putant conditio hominis ita ad restaurationem angelorum provisa est, quasi homo non fuisset factus, nisi angelus cecidisset*). The assertion that man was created to restore and complete the number of fallen angels indicates that when, after he was created, man is led to the place from which the angels had fallen, the depleted population of the heavenly community is being restored (*cum homo postmodum creatus illuc unde illi ceciderunt ductus est, illius societatis numerus qui in cadentibus diminutus fuerat, per hominem reparatur*).[18] In other words, although man was not created as a replacement for fallen angels, he did in reality fulfil this role in the history of salvation.

<hr />

immortalis est etiam ipse vitam sine termino possideret. Hoc erat ergo unum et verum bonum hominis, plena videlicet et perfecta cognitio sui Conditoris, plena scilicet secundum illam plenitudinem quam creatus acceperat, non secundum illam quam post peractam obedientiam accepturus erat."

18 HUGO DE SANCTO VICTORE, *De sacramentis* I,5,30 (PL 176,260–261): "Non enim ut quidam putant conditio hominis ita ad restaurationem angelorum provisa est, quasi homo non fuisset factus, nisi angelus cecidisset; sed idcirco ad restaurandum et supplendum lapsorum angelorum numerum factus homo dicitur, quia cum homo postmodum creatus illuc unde illi ceciderunt ductus est, illius societatis numerus qui in cadentibus diminutus fuerat, per hominem reparatur. Novem enim ordines angelorum ab initio conditi sunt, et ex illis qui ceciderunt (quia in una simul omnes malitia consenserunt) quasi unum ex se perversae societatis ordinem effecerunt. Habet autem traditio ex singulis ordinibus aliquos cecidisse. Unde et Apostolus Paulus cum de malignorum spirituum tyrannide mentionem faceret, principatus et potestates tenebrarum nominavit. Ut videlicet ostenderet quod idem nunc quisque in malo ministerium ex perversitate exercet, quod ad bonum perficiendum ex conditione accepit. Nusquam tamen in Scriptura nequam spiritus seraphim appellatos invenio; quia licet caetera dona post ruinam adhuc in malo possideant, charitatem tamen in dilectione Dei nequaquam potuerunt habere."

When we compare Hugh's idea with other known formulations of the problem, we find certain features that it has in common with Rupert and Honorius, such as the references to the opinion of certain theologians that man would not have been created if the angels had not fallen (*quidam putant* – *solent plerique arbitrari* – *plerique arbitrantur* – *videtur* – *solet quaeri a quibusdam*), and also the rejection of this opinion. But if we take into account the line of argument by which Hugh presented his refutation, what becomes clear is an obvious link with the approach taken by the school of Laon:

HUGO DE SANCTO VICTORE, *De sacramentis christianae fidei*	Non enim ut quidam putant conditio hominis ita ad restaurationem angelorum provisa est, quasi homo non fuisset factus, nisi angelus cecidisset; sed idcirco ad restaurandum et supplendum lapsorum angelorum numerum factus homo dicitur, quia cum homo postmodum creatus illuc unde illi ceciderunt ductus est, illius societatis numerus qui in cadentibus diminutus fuerat, per hominem reparatur.
DIVINA ESSENTIA TESTE = SENTENTIAE ATREBATENSES	Qui homo propter restaurationem predictorum angelorum factus dicitur; non quin factus esset etsi illi non cecidissent, sed quia in gloriam quam illi perdiderunt homo suscipitur, quasi locum illorum subintrare videtur; et ideo propter eorum restaurationem factus dicitur.
DE SENTENTIA DIVINE = SENTENTIE DIVINE PAGINE	Unde, cum dicat auctoritas, quod tot ascensuri sunt quot ceciderunt, dicimus, quod non ideo factus est homo principaliter, ut restitueretur numerus angelorum; consecutus est quidem ille effectus, scilicet restauratio, sed etiamsi angelus non cecidisset, tamen homo fieret.
PRINCIPIUM ET CAUSA = SENTENTIAE ANSELMI	Hinc homo loco perditorum angelorum factus dicitur, non quin factus esset etiam, si illi non cecidissent, sed cum in gloriam, quam illi perdiderunt, homo suscipitur, quasi locum illorum subintrare videtur.

It therefore appears that it is to the school of Laon we must look for the source of inspiration for Hugh's formulation of, and answer to, the problem.[19] The subsequent argument refers to the seraphim in a way that is very close to Rupert.[20]

19 See Cédric GIRAUD, *Per verba magistri*, 454–464.
20 See RUPERTUS TUITIENSIS, *De glorificatione Trinitatis et processione Spiritus sancti* III,17 (PL 169,69); ID., *De sancta Trinitate et operibus eius* 2, *In Genesim* II,15 (CCCM 21,200; PL 167,259–260). See also GILBERTUS PORRETANUS, *Sententiae* XIII,41–42: Nicholas M.

3. *Summa sententiarum*

Special reference should be made to the work *Summa sententiarum,* the author of which is yet to be clearly and successfully identified. A number of modern-day scholars support Gastaldelli's theory that the work should be attributed to Otto of Lucca († 1146/1154), who studied in France – where he came to know the teaching of Anselm of Laon and his school and the teaching of Hugh of St. Victor – and who by the end of the 1130s had been made bishop of Lucca. He is said to have written *Summa sententiarum* before then, perhaps between 1138 and 1141.[21] Not everyone shares this opinion as there are some serious objections to this particular attribution. Luscombe, Colish, and Quinto are of the opinion – either openly or cautiously – that the author of *Summa sententiarum* was a student of Hugh of St. Victor and that it was written between 1138 and 1142.[22]

The exposition on creation in *Summa sententiarum* II,1 is a faithful echo of the school of Laon: God wished for some creatures to participate in his blessedness and since that is possible only by the means of an intellect, he created rational beings that they might know, and therefore love, and possess what they love, and therefore also enjoy what they love. God also decided that one part of these rational beings would consist of angels, and the second part, connected to a body, would consist of men.[23]

HÄRING, Die Sentenzie magistri Gisleberti episcopi Pictavensis, *Archives d'histoire doctrinale et littéraire du moyen âge* 45 (1978), 168; ID., Die Sentenzie magistri Gisleberti episcopi Pictavensis, *Archives d'histoire doctrinale et littéraire du moyen âge* 46 (1979), 100.

21 See Ferruccio GASTALDELLI, La "Summa sententiarum" di Ottone da Lucca: conclusione di un dibattito secolare, *Salesianum* 42/3 (1980), 537–546; ID., Introduzione, in WILHELMUS LUCENSIS, *Commentum in Tertiam Ierarchiam Dionisii que est De Divinis Nominibus,* Firenze: Olschki Ed., 1983, XXVII–XL and 537–541.

22 David E. LUSCOMBE, *The School of Peter Abelard: The Influence of Abelard's Thought in the Early Scholastic Period,* Cambridge: Cambridge University Press, 1969, 198–223; Marcia L. COLISH, *Peter Lombard,* vol. 1, Leiden – New York – Köln: Brill, 1993, 57–65; Ronald G. WITT, *The Two Latin Cultures and the Foundation of Renaissance Humanism in Medieval Italy,* Cambridge: Cambridge University Press, 2012, 264; Riccardo QUINTO, Trivium e teologia: l'organizzazione scolastica nella seconda metà del secolo dodicesimo e i maestri della sacra pagina, in Giulio D'ONOFRIO (ed.), *Storia della teologia nel medioevo,* vol. II, *La grande fioritura,* Casale Monferrato: Edizioni Piemme, 1996, 458–460.

23 [ANONYMOUS], *Summa sententiarum* II,1 (PL 176,79) = [ANONYMOUS], *Tractatus theologicus* XVII (PL 171,1106): "Cum enim summe bonus et perfecte beatus aeternaliter esset, voluit aliquos esse participes suae beatitudinis. Et quia non potest eius beatitudo participari nisi per intellectum, et quanto magis intelligitur tanto magis habetur; fecit rationalem creaturam ut intelligeret, intelligendo amaret, amando possideret, possidendo frueretur; et eam hoc modo distinxit, ut pars in sui puritate permaneret scilicet angeli; pars corpori iungeretur ut animae." On the relations to the school of Laon see Cédric GIRAUD, *Per verba magistri,* 465–477.

From here, the author moved on to an exposition on angels, and in
II,5 on the differentiation of their orders. In connection with this he felt
led to add that although, according to Eph 1:10, that which fell in the
angels will be repaired through men, this cannot be understood in terms
of man having been created only for the angels who fell; he would have
been created even if the angels had not fallen (*non tamen intelligendum est
quod solummodo propter illos qui ceciderunt factus sit homo; licet enim angelus
non cecidisset, homo non minus factus esset*).[24] This assertion connects with
Gregory's interpretation in which the fact that men will be admitted into
particular angelic orders according to the measure of their merits, and
that they are to compose a new tenth order in heaven, is qualified by
the assertion that they will be admitted into the heavens not according
to the number of angels who fell but according to the number of those
who remained: different gifts will result in differences in belonging to
the particular orders, but the unity of human nature means that men will
compose a separate tenth order.[25]

The author thus reinterprets the topos of Eph 1:10 and takes his place
in the increasingly animated discussion on how to understand Gregory's
homily. The source of his inspiration is not clear, however, as specific
indications are lacking.

---

24 [ANONYMUS], *Summa sententiarum* II,5 (PL 176,87): "Et quamvis de hominibus restauretur
quod lapsum est in angelis, propter quod ait apostolus: Proposuit Deus instaurare omnia in
Christo quae sunt in coelo et quae in terris, non tamen intelligendum est quod solummodo
propter illos qui ceciderunt factus sit homo. Licet enim angelus non cecidisset, homo non minus factus esset. Unde Gregorius dicit quod non sunt homines electi iuxta numerum eorum qui
ceciderunt; sed iuxta eorum numerum qui permanserunt. Gregorius: Quia superna civitas ex
angelis et hominibus constat, ad quam tantos humani generis credimus conscendere, quantos
illic contigit angelos remansisse, sicut scriptum est: Statuit terminos gentium iuxta numerum
angelorum Dei."

25 [ANONYMUS], *Summa sententiarum* II,5 (PL 176,87): "Quaeritur an omnes eiusdem ordinis
pares sunt et aequales. Quod quibusdam visum est. Sed illud non potest stare cum Scriptura
dicat Luciferum cunctis aliis excellentiorem; quem constat fuisse de ordine supremo, et tamen
in ordine illo caeteris fuit excellentior. Sicut enim omnes virgines unius ordinis sunt, et tamen
alius excellit alium in virginitate; sic et in angelis potest esse. Legimus quod decimus ordo
de hominibus impleri debeat. Mali enim angeli cum de singulis ordinibus caderent, fecerunt
unum ordinem; quia in malitia similes, licet improprie in eis dicatur ordo. Et ille decimus ordo,
ut Scriptura dicit, de hominibus restauratur. Sed cum Gregorius dicat assumendos esse homines in ordines angelorum; quidam in ordinem superiorum qui scilicet magis ardent charitate;
quidam in ordinem inferiorum qui scilicet minus perfecti sunt; non videtur quod decimus
ordo de hominibus fiat, sed novem tantum remaneant. Ad quod potest dici quod secundum
convenientiam donorum quam habent cum angelis dicuntur assumendi in ordines angelorum;
sed secundum naturam quam habent differentem ab illis, alium ordinem dicuntur facturi."

4. Alcher of Clairvaux

We will now return, briefly, to the monastic tradition. The treatise *De diligendo Deo,* the author of which may have been the Cistercian Alcher of Clairvaux (second half of the 12th century),[26] made a not insignificant contribution to the history of our theme. In it the author, who was seeking to ignite his readers' love for God, presented his thoughts on why man was actually created. His answer is provided through a mosaic of texts from St. Augustine (*Enchiridion* 3,9) and Hugh of St. Victor (*De sacramentis* I,2,1; I,2,4; and *Summa sententiarum* II,1), to which the author added his own words: *Ad quid autem creata est rationalis creatura? Ad laudandum Deum, ad serviendum ei, ad fruendum eo: in quibus ipsa proficit, non Deus.*[27]

---

26 An edition of Augustine's works compiled at the end of the seventeenth century by the Benedictine Congregation of St. Maur included a note in *De diligendo Deo* that pointed to the fact that although in some manuscripts it is attributed to Augustine, in reality it contains statements from Hugh of St. Victor, Bernard, and Anselm. The note also reveals the author of *Liber de spiritu et anima.* This other more famous work was, in PL 40,779–780, attributed to a Cistercian called Alcherus Claraevallensis, who led a correspondence on this subject at the beginning of the 1160s with the Cistercian, Isaac of Stella (1105/20–1178). In PL 40, *De diligendo Deo* was published still without any clear identification of the author. PL 194,1895, however, identified the author as Alcher. But we should stress that internal analysis of the work does not provide clear evidence that would confirm this attribution. It is based on three facts: that the author of *De diligendo Deo* worked with sources in a similar way to the author of *Liber de spiritu et anima;* that these sources enable the origins of the work to be dated somewhere in the second half of the twelfth century; and that the author gave the work the title of a famous work by Bernard of Clairvaux, thus aligning himself with Cistercian spirituality. See [AUGUSTINUS], *Sancti Aurelii Augustini Hipponensis Episcopi Operum* tomus sextus, continens moralia, post Lovaniensium theologorum recensionem castigatus ... Opera & Studio Monachorum Ordinis Sancti Benedicti è Congregatione Sancti Mauri, editio altera, Antwerpiae: Sumptibus Societatis, 1701, 553–554; Teresa REGAN, *A study of the Liber de Spiritu et Anima: Its Doctrine, Sources and Historical Significance: A thesis...*, University of Toronto, 1948; Palémon *GLORIEUX, Pour revaloriser Migne: tables rectificatives*, Lille: Facultés catholiques, 1952, 27.

27 [ALCHERUS CLARAEVALLENSIS?], *De diligendo Deo* 2 (PL 40,850): "Ut autem amor Dei in te amplius excitetur et crescat, considera diligenter, a quo, quare, vel ad quid creatus sit homo, quaeve Deus propter hominem creavit. Sciendum est ergo rerum creatarum, coelestium et terrestrium, visibilium et invisibilium causam non esse nisi bonitatem Creatoris, qui est Deus unus et verus: cuius est tanta bonitas, quod alios suae beatitudinis qua aeternaliter beatus est, velit esse participes, quam vidit communicari posse, minui omnino non posse. Illud igitur bonum, quod ipse erat et quo ipse erat beatus, sola bonitate, non necessitate aliis communicare voluit: quia summi boni erat prodesse velle, et omnipotentissimi nocere non posse. Et quia non valet eius beatitudinis particeps existere aliquis, nisi per intelligentiam, quae quanto magis intelligitur, tanto plenius habetur; fecit Deus rationalem creaturam, quae summum bonum intelligeret, intelligendo amaret, amando possideret, et possidendo frueretur: eamque hoc modo distinxit, ut pars in sui puritate permaneret, nec corpori uniretur, scilicet angelus; pars corpori iungeretur, scilicet anima. Distincta est igitur rationalis creatura in incorpoream

These reflections upon the reasons for the creation of man, or rational beings, conclude with the assertion that even angels were in a certain sense created for man. The service they render for him is described in words taken from Bernard of Clairvaux's *In festo S. Michaelis* 1,4, and with these words our theme returns as in them Bernard (or Alcher) states that the angels render this service for their own sake as they wish that from among us their damaged ranks will be restored.[28]

5. Peter Lombard

The author who exerted the most significant influence on the continuing history of our theme was Peter Lombard (1095/1100–1160), who tackled the question in *Sententiae in IV libris distinctae*, which was completed between 1155 and 1158.[29] The theme appears in two contexts: in connection with the question of the goal of creation and in connection with angelology.

Very near the beginning of his tractate, although without stating his sources, the "Master" from Paris quoted from *De diligendo Deo*, which provided him with a ready-made synthesis of the above-mentioned sources. Like *De diligendo Deo,* he expressed his belief in the fact that the one and only cause of all heavenly and earthly things is the goodness of the Creator, and that this sovereignly and eternally blessed God entirely

---

et corpoream. Incorporea, angelus; corporea vero, homo vocatur, ex anima rationali et carne subsistens. Conditio igitur rationalis creaturae primam causam habuit, Dei bonitatem. Creatus est igitur homo vel angelus propter bonitatem Dei. Nam quia bonus est Deus, sumus; et in quantum sumus, boni sumus. Ad quid autem creata est rationalis creatura? Ad laudandum Deum, ad serviendum ei, ad fruendum eo: in quibus ipsa proficit, non Deus. Deus enim perfectus et summa bonitate plenus, nec augeri potest nec minui. Quod ergo creatura rationalis facta est a Deo, referendum est ad Creatoris bonitatem, et ad creaturae utilitatem. Cum igitur quaeritur, quare vel ad quid facta sit rationalis creatura; respondendum est, Propter Dei bonitatem, et creaturae utilitatem: utile nempe est ei servire Deo et frui eo."

28 [ALCHERUS CLARAEVALLENSIS?], *De diligendo Deo* 3 (PL 40,851): "De excelso igitur coelorum habitaculo ad consolandos, ad visitandos et ad adiuvandos nos attrahit supereminens charitas angelos, propter Deum, propter nos, propter se ipsos. Propter Deum utique, cuius tanta erga nos pietatis viscera ipsi quoque, ut dignum est, imitantur: propter nos, quibus nimirum propter propriam similitudinem miserantur: propter se ipsos, quorum ordines instaurandos ex nobis toto desiderio praestolantur." BERNARDUS CLARAEVALLENSIS, *Sermones in festo sancti Michaelis* 1,4 (Bernardi opera 5,296–297; PL 183,449).

29 See Marcia L. COLISH, *Peter Lombard*, vol. 1, Leiden – New York – Köln: Brill, 1993, 15–32. See also Heinrich WEISWEILER, La "Summa Sententiarum" source de Pierre Lombard, *Recherches de théologie ancienne et médiévale* 6 (1934), 143–183.

freely wished that others should also participate in his blessedness.[30] Lombard then immediately asks himself why rational creatures were created. The answer is again taken from *De diligendo Deo* and reflects, faithfully, the teaching of the school of Laon: the participation in God's blessedness presupposes intelligence, so God created rational creatures that would come to know sovereign good, and through this knowing to love the good, and through loving to enjoy it.[31]

The same question is then asked once more: Why were man and the angels created? The author provides the answer by first quoting from Augustine's *De doctrina christiana* I,32[32] and then once more from *De diligendo Deo,*[33] but concluded this latter quotation before arriving at the words of St. Bernard's *In festo S. Michaelis* 1,4, which means our theme is missing here, although the author does arrive at it eventually. Immediately after addressing himself to the causes of the creation of rational creatures, angels and men, he asks in what sense it is said that man was made for the restoration of the angelic fall (*Quomodo dicitur homo factus propter reparationem angelici casus*). It is, he continued, because Scripture said so. His answer also states that it must not be assumed that man would not have been created if the angels had not sinned, but that among other principle causes stands this not insignificant cause. Everything else exists for man.[34]

The way in which Lombard dealt with our patristic thesis recalls the school of Laon:

30 PETRUS LOMBARDUS, *Sententiae in IV libris distinctae* l. II, d. 1, c. 3, n. 5 (Spicilegium Bonaventurianum 4,332).
31 PETRUS LOMBARDUS, *Sententiae in IV libris distinctae* l. II, d. 1, c. 4, n. 1 (Spicilegium Bonaventurianum 4,332).
32 PETRUS LOMBARDUS, *Sententiae in IV libris distinctae* l. II, d. 1, c. 4, n. 3 (Spicilegium Bonaventurianum 4,332); AUGUSTINUS, *De doctrina christiana* I,32,35 (CCSL 32,26; PL 34,32).
33 PETRUS LOMBARDUS, *Sententiae in IV libris distinctae* l. II, d. 1, c. 4, n. 4–7 (Spicilegium Bonaventurianum 4,332–333).
34 PETRUS LOMBARDUS, *Sententiae in IV libris distinctae* l. II, d. 1, c. 5 (Spicilegium Bonaventurianum 4,334): "De homine quoque in Scriptura interdum reperitur quod factus sit propter reparationem angelicae ruinae. Quod non ita est intelligendum, quasi non fuisset homo factus si non peccasset angelus; sed quia inter alias causas praecipuas, haec etiam nonnulla exstitit. Nostra igitur sunt superiora et aequalia; nostra etiam sunt inferiora, quia ad serviendum nobis facta."

PETRUS LOMBARDUS, *Sententiae in IV libris distinctae*	De homine quoque in Scriptura interdum reperitur quod factus sit propter reparationem angelicae ruinae. Quod non ita est intelligendum, quasi non fuisset homo factus si non peccasset angelus; sed quia inter alias causas praecipuas, haec etiam nonnulla exstitit.
De sententia divine = *Sententie divine pagine*	Unde, cum dicat auctoritas, quod tot ascensuri sunt quot ceciderunt, dicimus, quod non ideo factus est homo principaliter, ut restitueretur numerus angelorum; consecutus est quidem ille effectus, scilicet restauratio, sed etiamsi angelus non cecidisset, tamen homo fieret.

Secondly, our theme appears in the context of angelology. The author asked in what sense Scripture (Tradition) declares that the tenth order is to be completed from among men (*Quomodo dicat Scriptura, decimum ordinem compleri de hominibus*). He answers in the manner of *Summa sententiarum* II,5[35] and with an echo of the usual commentary on Eph 1:10, which he adopted as his own.[36]

The Parisian "Master" also asked, alongside *Summa sententiarum* and other authors of his time, how the tenth angelic order can be restored from among men when there are not, and according to Scripture never were, more than nine. Gregory's teaching that men are admitted into particular angelic orders according to their merits means that men will

---

35 PETRUS LOMBARDUS, *Sententiae in IV libris distinctae* l. II, d. 9, c. 6, n. 1–3 – c. 7, n. 1–2 (Spicilegium Bonaventurianum 4,375–376): "Notandum etiam quod decimus ordo legitur de hominibus restaurandus. Sed cum non sint nisi novem ordines, nec plures fuissent etiam si illi perstitissent qui ceciderunt, moventur lectores quomodo Scriptura dicat decimum ordinem compleri ex hominibus. Gregorius namque dicit homines assumendos in ordine angelorum: Quorum alii assumuntur in ordine superiorum, qui scilicet magis ardent caritate; alii in ordine inferiorum, qui scilicet minus perfecti sunt. Ex quo apparet non esse de hominibus formandum decimum ordinem, tamquam novem sint angelorum et decimus hominum, sed homines pro qualitate meritorum statuendos in ordinibus angelorum. Quod ergo legitur decimus ordo complendus de hominibus, ex tali sensu dictum fore accipi potest: Quia de hominibus restaurabitur quod in angelis lapsum est; de quibus tot corruerunt unde posset fieri decimus ordo. Propter quod apostolus dicit restaurari omnia in Christo, quae in caelis et quae in terris sunt; quia per Christum redemptum est humanum genus, de quo fit reparatio ruinae angelicae; tamen non minus salvaretur homo, etsi angelus non cecidisset. Non enim iuxta numerum eorum qui ceciderunt, sed eorum qui permanserunt, homines ad beatitudinem admittuntur. Unde Gregorius [...]. Quidam dicunt secundum numerum lapsorum angelorum homines reparandos. A quibusdam tamen putatur quod homines reparentur iuxta numerum angelorum qui ceciderunt, ut illa caelestis civitas nec suorum civium numero privetur, nec maiori copia regnet. Quod Augustinus in Enchiridion sentire videtur [...]. Ecce aperte dicit non minus de hominibus salvari quam corruit de angelis, sed plus non asserit."

36 See PETRUS LOMBARDUS, *Collectanea in epistolas Pauli – In epistolam ad Ephesios* 1 (PL 192,172).

not compose a distinct tenth order. If this is what was being said, then perhaps (*fore*) we should take such a statement to mean there were so many fallen angels to be replaced by men that a tenth order could have been created. But at the very end of his exposition, Lombard departs from *Summa sententiarum* when he adds not that man would have been *created* even if the angels had not fallen, but that he would have been *saved*. His conclusion therefore corresponds more closely to statements from the school of Laon.

Summa sententiarum	Proposuit Deus instaurare omnia in Christo quae sunt in coelo et quae in terris, non tamen intelligendum est quod solummodo propter illos qui ceciderunt factus sit homo. Licet enim angelus non cecidisset, homo non minus factus esset.
PETRUS LOM-BARDUS, *Sententiae in IV libris distinctae*	Propter quod apostolus dicit restaurari omnia in Christo, quae in caelis et quae in terris sunt; quia per Christum re-demptum est humanum genus, de quo fit reparatio ruinae angelicae; tamen non minus salvaretur homo, etsi angelus non cecidisset.
Liber pancrisis	... Quem ordinem si diligenter attendis, videbis hominem debuisse salvari, etsi nullus angelus cecidisset.

Twice, therefore, Peter Lombard briefly addresses the debate of the time. He did not work with our theme in any creative way, however, and it appears to have stood more on the fringes of his interest and only to have been registered for the sake of thoroughness. He did not even use the thesis to resolve the question as to why man was created. This an-swer was provided for him by Alcher, or rather Hugh of St. Victor and *Summa sententiarum*. The controversy was, in other words, basically of no interest to him.

6. The influence of Lombard's *Sententiae*

Up until the fifteenth and sixteenth centuries Lombard's *Sententiae* was compulsory reading for students in theological faculties. More than 1,400 commentaries were written so we do not of course have time to go into all of them here.[37] What is certain, however, is that this was one way

---

37 See G. R. EVANS, *Mediaeval Commentaries on the Sentences of Peter Lombard*, vol. 1, Leiden – Boston – Köln: Brill, 2002; Philipp W. ROSEMANN (ed.), *Mediaeval Commentaries on the Sentences of Peter Lombard*, vol. 2, Leiden – Boston – Köln: Brill, 2010.

in which our theme was kept alive – in addition, of course, to a direct reading of Augustine, Gregory, and other significant authors in whose works the theme occurs.

It should come as no surprise that the theme appears in various guises – not all of them betraying a clear link with Lombard – among theologians who had connections with Paris immediately after Lombard's time: Peter the Chanter (c. 1130–1197),[38] Magister Bandinus (12th century),[39] Simon of Tournai (1170/1180–c. 1203),[40] and Peter of Poitiers (c. 1130–c. 1216/1230). This later Peter incorporated into his exposition infrequent references to the topos of the tithe,[41] and three questions that evolve from our theme but which we have not yet registered: whether John the Baptist will assume the place of Lucifer; whether Christ will receive the place of one of the fallen angels; and whether man will be resurrected in the perfection the angels enjoyed before the fall, or in the perfection they were to have obtained had they, the angels, not fallen.[42] Peter of Blois (c. 1130/1135–1212) also studied in Paris; our theme is used in one of his homilies, but simply as an exhortation to humility.[43]

Evidence of the rapid expansion of Peter Lombard's influence lies in the fact that the text devoted to our theme was quoted (without stating its source) by Martin of Laon (c. 1130–1203), whose biographical connection with the Parisian "Master" remains unclear.[44] He also connected the relevant text in the *Sententiae* to the topos of Eph 1:10 and to a text written by Isidore of Seville.[45]

---

38 PETRUS CANTOR, *Summa quae dicitur Verbum adbreviatum (textus prior)* 137 (CCCM, 196A,699; PL 205,365): "... supplebit enim et restituet Ecclesia cavernam et ruinam angelorum."

39 BANDINUS, *Sententiarum libri quatuor* l. II, d. 9 (PL 192,1038).

40 SIMON TORNACENSIS, *Institutiones in sacram paginam* d. IV, in Richard HEINZMANN, *Die "Institutiones in sacram paginam" des Simon von Tournai: Einleitung und Quästionenverzeichnis*, München-Paderborn-Wien: Verlag Ferdinand Schöningh, 1967, 47: "Quaeritur cum novem fuerint et sint ordines angelorum, cur decimus dicitur reparandus. Redditur: non quia reparandus sit ex hominibus decimus ordo discretus ab aliis, sed singuli novem ex tot hominibus supplendi sunt ex quot decimus ordo posset fieri." See ID., *Sententiae*, in ALAIN DE LILLE, *Textes inédits*, 307–312.

41 PETRUS PICTAVIENSIS, *Sententiae* l. II, c. 5 (PL 211,953): "Quaeritur postea qualiter intelligendum sit quod dicitur decimus ordo angelorum cecidisse; propter quod etiam adhuc dicuntur homines decimas dare, ut in illo decimo ordine angelorum lapsorum ponantur."

42 PETRUS PICTAVIENSIS, *Sententiae* l. II, c. 5 (PL 211,954).

43 PETRUS BLESENSIS, *Sermones* 39 (PL 207,677–678).

44 MARTINUS LEGIONENSIS, *Sermones* 7 (PL 208,569–570). See Antonio VIÑAYO GONZÁLEZ, San Martín de León, el primer español que cita a Pedro Lombardo, *Scriptorium victoriense* 1 (1954), 51–62.

45 MARTINUS LEGIONENSIS, *Sermones* 25 (PL 208,928–929); ID., *Expositio libri Apocalypsis* V,11–12 (PL 209,332–333).

Most interesting of all in this respect is the way in which the greatest authors addressed our theme in their commentaries on the *Sententiae* or other works of systematic theology. From these significant authors we will select Albert the Great, Bonaventure of Bagnoregio, and Thomas Aquinas. The remainder we will leave to one side.[46]

7. Albert the Great

In his commentary on the *Sententiae,* from between 1244 and 1249, Albert (c. 1200–1280) touched on our subject only in passing: in the context of creation not at all;[47] in the context of angelology only briefly and cautiously.[48] In *Summa theologiae* (1270–1274), he offered a more detailed exposition on the angelological question, which is again to some extent a commentary on the *Sententiae.*

In this context, Albert asked whether the tenth order of angels – the order that fell – will indeed be repaired from among men.[49] By reference to the topos of Eph 1:10, his answer in the affirmative is developed into the assertion that although it is through humankind, redeemed by Christ, that the angelic ruins are restored, man would have been saved even if the angels had not fallen. Human salvation is not caused by the angels' fall (*homo ex ruina angelorum non habet*): man is saved in order to earn his salvation by his service to God, and only as a consequence of this does the one who is admitted into salvation restore the angelic ruins (*ex hominibus restauratur ruina angelorum ex consequenti*).[50]

---

46 For example: ALEXANDER HALENSIS, *Summa theologica* l. 3, pars 1, inquisitio unica, tr. 2, q. 1, m. 1, cap. 1–2, n. 65 (Summa Fratris Alexandri sive Summa universae theologiae IV,97); l. 3, pars 1, inquisitio unica, tr. 3, q. 1, tit. 2, m. 2, cap. 3, art. 2, prob. 2, n. 113 (Summa Fratris Alexandri sive Summa universae theologiae IV,159); PETRUS IOHANNES OLIVI, *Quaestiones in secundum librum Sententiarum* q. 48 (ed. B. Jansen, tomus I, Quaracchi: Ex Typographia Collegii S. Bonaventurae, 1922, 754–763); IOHANNES DUNS SCOTUS, *Lectura in Librum Secundum Sententiarum* d. 20, q. 2 (Ioannis Duns Scoti Opera omnia 19,192–197).

47 ALBERTUS MAGNUS, *Super II Sententiarum* d. 1 (B. Alberti Magni Opera omnia 27,31–39).

48 ALBERTUS MAGNUS, *Super II Sententiarum* d. 9, I, art. 8 (B. Alberti Magni Opera omnia 27,207–208).

49 ALBERTUS MAGNUS, *Summa theologiae sive scientia de mirabili scientia Dei* II, tract. 10, q. 42, m. 3 (B. Alberti Magni Opera omnia 32,502–504).

50 ALBERTUS MAGNUS, *Summa theologiae sive scientia de mirabili scientia Dei* II, tract. 10, q. 42, m. 3 (B. Alberti Magni Opera omnia 32,503): "... per Christum redemptum est genus humanum, de quo fit reparatio angelicae ruinae: tamen non minus salvaretur homo, si angelus non cecidisset. Causa dicti est, quia homo ex ruina angelorum non habet, quod salvetur: sed quia ad hoc salvandus est, quod serviendo Deo mereatur salutem, ex consequenti accidit, quod

Albert also addresses the question as to how many men will be admitted into the place of the fallen angels, and outlines the three main answers that had been proffered: according to Gregory there will be as many men admitted into heaven as there are angels who abided with God; according to Augustine there will not be admitted into heaven fewer people than there were fallen angels; and according to a third thesis, which draws on the assertions of Anselm, there will be admitted into heaven as many virgins as there were good and evil angels, and as many non-virgins as there are virgins and good and evil angels together. None of the advocates of these propositions can, however, authoritatively prove that theirs is true, and the answer is known only to the one who established the precise number of those elected for eternal bliss.

It is clear that Albert works with our theme somewhat guardedly and on the whole only when it is presented to him on the authority of Lombard, but he does at least attempt to tease out the meaning of the statement that man would have been saved even if the angels had not fallen. In his other works, our subject can be found only in a commentary on Luke 2:14 (15:8) and Rev 11:13.[51]

8. Bonaventure of Bagnoregio

In his commentary on the *Sententiae,* from between 1248 and 1255, Bonaventure (c. 1217–1274) touches on our subject in the contexts of creation and angelology.

With respect to the former context, after addressing the matter of the main goal of creation, Bonaventure posed a question concerning the relationship between individual creatures, and that is whether spiritual nature is superior to the being composed of both a spiritual and a physical

---

assumptus ad salutem, ruinam restaurat angelorum. [...] ex hominibus restauratur ruina angelorum ex consequenti."

51 ALBERTUS MAGNUS, *Super Lucam* I,26 (B. Alberti Magni Opera omnia 22,46): "Ruina etiam angelorum ex hoc reparatur, sicut significatur, Luc. XV,8 de drachma quae perdita erat, et est inventa. Sic etiam dicitur, Apocal. XXI,17: Mensura hominis quae est angeli, scilicet in beatitudine. Et ideo homines assumuntur in sortem angelorum, ut decimus chorus ex hominibus reparetur, qui cecidit ex angelis. Non quod decem chori sint futuri, sicut dicunt Sancti, sed quod de quolibet ordine (supple, cuniunctim) tot ceciderunt quot sunt in choro, et ille numerus ex hominibus reparatur." ALBERTUS MAGNUS, *In Apocalypsim B. Joannis* visio III,XI,13 (B. Alberti Magni Opera omnia 38,644): "Per civitatem intelligitur gaudium paradisi, de quo corruerunt Angeli, et facti sunt daemones: et cum essent novem ordines Angelorum, tot ceciderunt de ipsis quod posset fieri ordo decimus."

nature. He answers that with respect to the dignity of their nature angels are superior to man, but with respect to their goal they are equal, since men and angels are both headed directly for the same end: eternal bliss. Therefore man is not for the angel, and neither is the angel for man (*nec homo propter angelum, nec angelus propter hominem*). Love, however, begets mutuality: angels by their steadfastness help man in his weakness, and man through his resurrection repairs the angelic ruins (*homo resurgens reparat ruinam angelicam*). In this sense, therefore, the angel is somehow for man; and likewise man for the angel (*quodam modo angelus propter hominem, et quodam modo homo propter angelum*); in this they are equal.[52]

In the second context, Bonaventure first clarified the exposition *de ordinum reparatione* by asking whether those who are to be saved will be admitted into particular angelic orders. The answer is again in the affirmative: just as some angels fell from particular orders, these orders will be repaired from among men; even though men and angels are of different natures they can together form one order according to the particular grace to which they are elevated and by which the damage to the angelic ranks is repaired.[53]

Bonaventure also asked himself whether there are nine, or more than nine angelic orders. The problem is set in the context of Gregory's interpretation of Luke 15:8–10, according to which man is likened to the tenth drachma – the tenth order – which is added to the nine angelic orders. Bonaventure mentioned three existing ideas:

According to the first of these, people will be admitted into angelic orders so there will be nine orders in the heavenly Jerusalem. It is, however, necessary to take into account that man would have been created and would have attained blessedness even if the angels had not sinned (*si angelus nunquam peccasset, homo factus esset et ad beatitudinem perveniret*). If this had been the case, admittance into the angelic orders would simply be a matter of human beatification; in reality, however, the angels did sin so it is therefore a matter not only of human beatification but also of the repair of the angelic ruins (*tunc illa assumtio esset hominum beatificatio solum, nunc autem est hominum beatificatio et ruinae angelorum per quandam*

---

52 BONAVENTURA DE BAGNOREGIO, *Commentaria in quatuor libros sententiarum* l. II, d. 1, p. 2, art. 3, q. 1, (Opera omnia S. Bonaventurae 2,45–46).

53 BONAVENTURA DE BAGNOREGIO, *Commentaria in quatuor libros sententiarum* l. II, d. 9, q. 5 (Opera omnia S. Bonaventurae 2,250): "Quia vero homines possunt ad eminentiam gratiae et gloriae, in qua sunt angeli, elevari, potest ex hominibus et angelis idem ordo constitui, quia, quamvis non conveniant in natura, assimilantur tamen et aequantur in hac gratia; et per hunc modum reparatur angelorum ruina."

aequivalentiam reparatio). Bonaventure believes such an interpretation to contain a certain amount of validity.[54]

A second thesis suggests that men themselves will compose one whole order, the tenth, as only virgins will be admitted into the nine angelic orders, and only virgins will restore the ranks of angels (*solas virgines ad ordines angelorum dicunt assumi, et ex eis solis ruinam angelicam restauri*). Against this, however, Bonaventure suggests not only that the tenth drachma signifies both virgins (*virgines*) and others (*corrupti*) but that many of the latter take precedence over the virgins (*multi carne corrupti multis virginibus praeferuntur*), as is the case, for example, with Mary Magdalene and the apostle Peter. Bonaventure therefore feels that this interpretation lacks credibility.[55]

The third thesis asserts that in addition to the nine orders of angels there will be added a tenth order from among those who, in this life, did not attain sufficient merit to enable them to join the ranks of angels; through the merit of Christ, however, they are made into a tenth order. Bonaventure considers this interpretation the most likely, as on the one hand it respects the fact that many people are imperfect, and on the other it maintains the perfect number of ten heavenly orders.[56]

Bonaventure therefore works with our theme when Tradition presents it to him, and attempts to find arguments by which he may satisfactorily address the questions that the theme evokes for him. He does not, however, develop his own argument concerning the idea of man as a "replacement angel," and this guardedness is especially apparent in his detailed interpretation of the parables of the lost sheep and the lost drachma from Luke chapter 15. Although the interpretation is soaked in traditional exegesis, our theme is entirely absent.[57]

---

54 BONAVENTURA DE BAGNOREGIO, *Commentaria in quatuor libros sententiarum* l. II, d. 9, q. 7 (Opera omnia S. Bonaventurae 2,253–254).

55 BONAVENTURA DE BAGNOREGIO, *Commentaria in quatuor libros sententiarum* l. II, d. 9, q. 7 (Opera omnia S. Bonaventurae 2,254).

56 BONAVENTURA DE BAGNOREGIO, *Commentaria in quatuor libros sententiarum* l. II, d. 9, q. 7 (Opera omnia S. Bonaventurae 2,253–254): "Probabile esse videtur, quod novem angelorum ordinibus additur ordo decimus hominum imperfectorum, sed meritis Christi salvatorum. [...] supra novem ordines angelorum addetur ordo decimus ex his, qui in vita ista non pervenerunt ad tantam meritorum excellentiam, ut exaltentur ad ordines angelorum; sed meritis Christi salvati, decimum tenent gradum..."

57 BONAVENTURA DE BAGNOREGIO, *Commentarius in Evangelium S. Lucae* c. XV, n. 6–20 (Opera omnia S. Bonaventurae 7,383–389).

9. Thomas Aquinas

In his commentary on the *Sententiae* (redaction from 1253–1257 [1254/55–1256]), Thomas (1215–1274) makes frequent mention of our theme.

One such reference in the context of the causes of creation addresses the question as to whether everything was made for man. Thomas asserts that God brought into existence two orders: the principle order, in which beings are directed towards him, God, and a second order, in which one being assists the other in attaining the likeness of God. There are beings to whom is given absolute participation in God's goodness, from which arises their usefulness to the other, and this is the sense in which angels and all other creatures are made for man (*angeli et omnes creaturae propter hominem a Deo factae sunt*) and man is made for the repair of the angelic ruins. This usefulness is only consequential, but is nonetheless foreknown and ordained by God.[58]

All of the other places where Thomas touches on the patristic thesis are in the context of angelology. First, he raises the question as to whether men will be admitted into angelic orders. Here he mentions three existing theses. According to the first, there will be a tenth order made up from among human beings and this order will be subordinated to angelic orders. Thomas rejects this thesis as it contradicts the statements of the saints and the fact that the Virgin Mary is superior to the angels. In the second thesis, some people will be admitted into angelic orders and others will make up a tenth order, by which the parable of the lost drachma from Luke 15 will be fulfilled. This interpretation has many variants, however. According to some, only virgins will be admitted into angelic orders; the remainder will form the tenth. This is not true, however, as many non-virgins, for example Mary Magdalene and Peter, will surpass the angels. Others say that perfect people will be admitted into angelic orders, while the imperfect, those of lesser merit, will form the tenth order; it is, however, unlikely that to the single celestial hierarchy that is divided into three triads, and is as such a sign of the Trinity, will be added a tenth order from among men. This leaves us with the third thesis, which Thomas truly liked the most as it corresponds most closely to the

---

58 THOMAS AQUINAS, *Scriptum super Sententiis* l. II, d. 1, q. 2, a. 3 (*Opera omnia*. <http://www.corpusthomisticum.org> [2013-07-01]): "… quaedam sunt quae habent participationem divinae bonitatis absolutam, ex qua provenit aliqua utilitas alicui rei: et talia essent etiam si illud cui provenit ex eis utilitas non foret: et per hunc modum dicitur, quod angeli et omnes creaturae propter hominem a Deo factae sunt; et sic etiam homo factus est propter reparationem ruinae angelicae: quia haec utilitas consecuta est et a Deo praevisa et ordinata."

statements of the saints. This thesis suggests that all elect human beings
will be admitted into angelic orders, each according to their own merits:
some into the higher orders and others to the lower orders; and the Virgin
Mary will be above all. But whether this means that as many people will
be admitted as there were angels who fell, or as many as remained, or
as many as there were altogether – or more or fewer – this is something
that is known only to the one who knows the number of the elect who
are to be admitted into heavenly bliss. (It appears that Thomas took the
first two positions from Bonaventure; his conclusion suggests an echo
of Albert.)[59]

We will find a further reference in the context of the question as to
whether the fallen angels could have been evil since the beginning of creation. Thomas set this argument out as follows: according to Augustine,
angels and men were created simultaneously; if, however, man was created in order to repair the angelic ruins, then angels must already have
been evil at the beginning of God's creation.[60] Thomas's assertion was
that even assuming man was created at the same time as the angels, it
does not necessarily follow that the evil angels already existed at the time
man was created since the restoration of the angelic ruins is not the main
goal of the creation of man, but rather provides some kind of consequent
utility, which God, nonetheless, foreknew.[61]

The third reference is made in the context of explaining why it was an
angel who was charged with the annunciation. One reason is that he was
announcing the king of angels and men, whose birth brought salvation
to men and restoration to the angelic ruins.[62]

Besides the texts mentioned above, Thomas also touched on our
theme in others of his works.

---

59 THOMAS AQUINAS, *Scriptum super Sententiis* l. II, d. 9, q. 1, a. 8.

60 THOMAS AQUINAS, *Scriptum super Sententiis*, l. II, d. 3, q. 2, a. 1, arg. 3: "secundum Augustinum, angelus et homo, ad minus secundum animam, simul creati sunt. Sed homo factus est
propter reparationem ruinae angelicae; non autem hoc esset, angelo adhuc non ruente. Ergo
videtur quod angelus in principio creationis suae malus et ruens fuit."

61 THOMAS AQUINAS, *Scriptum super Sententiis*, l. II, d. 3, q. 2, a. 1, ad 3: "... etiam supposito
quod homo simul cum angelo creatus sit, non oportet quod angelo existente malo, creatus sit
homo: quia non est principalis finis creationis hominis, reparatio ruinae angelicae, sed quaedam utilitas consequens, ut supra dictum est. Et hanc utilitatem Deus praevidebat, in cuius
praescientia eventus omnium rerum erant."

62 THOMAS AQUINAS, *Scriptum super Sententiis*, l. III, d. 3, q. 3, a. 2, qc. 1 co.: "quia ille
annuntiabatur qui est rex hominum et angelorum; et eius nativitas sicut in salutem hominum
fuit, ita et in reparationem ruinae angelicae; et ideo decuit ut tam homines quam angeli huic
mysterio ministerium exhiberent."

In *Summa theologiae*, the first part of which was written between 1265 and 1268, he did so in the context of exploring how it was that angels became evil. Here, Thomas contended that if, as some were claiming, the devil, the highest of all evil angels, fell from the highest order, then in all likelihood other angels fell from each of the other orders, in which case to restore the angelic ruins man will be admitted into all orders.[63] In the same work, Thomas also asked whether men will in fact be admitted into the angelic orders. His answer was that angelic orders differ according to the status of their nature and according to the gifts of grace. Regarding natures, men can never be admitted into angelic orders as the distinction between the natures will always exist. Regarding the gifts of grace, however, men can earn sufficient grace to become equal to angels according to their particular level. This is what is meant by being admitted into angelic orders. Thomas rejected the thesis that not all of those who attain salvation will be admitted into angelic orders – only virgins and the perfect – on the grounds that there will not ultimately be two cities, of men and angels, since they will all share the same blessedness from cleaving to the one God.[64] A direct allusion to the fact that this is how the angelic fall would be repaired is missing here.

In *Quaestiones disputatae de malo* (1265–1266 [1267]), we find the same question as in the commentary on the *Sententiae,* that is, whether the devil sinned, or could have sinned, in the first instant of his creation. We already know one of the arguments used here: man was created as a replacement for fallen angels and if he was created together with the

63 THOMAS AQUINAS, *Summa theologiae* I, q. 63, a. 9, ad 3: "Secundum vero illos qui ponunt maiorem diabolum de supremo fuisse ordine, probabile est quod de quolibet ordine aliqui ceciderunt; sicut et in quemlibet ordinem homines assumuntur in supplementum ruinae angelicae."
64 THOMAS AQUINAS, *Summa theologiae* I, q. 108, a. 8: "Respondeo dicendum quod, sicut supra dictum est, ordines angelorum distinguuntur et secundum conditionem naturae, et secundum dona gratiae. Si ergo considerentur angelorum ordines solum quantum ad gradum naturae, sic homines nullo modo assumi possunt ad ordines angelorum: quia semper remanebit naturarum distinctio. Quam quidam considerantes, posuerunt quod nullo modo homines transferri possunt ad aequalitatem angelorum. Quod est erroneum: repugnat enim promissioni Christi, dicentis, Lucae XX, quod filii resurrectionis erunt aequales angelis in caelis. Illud enim quod est ex parte naturae, se habet ut materiale in ratione ordinis; completivum vero est quod est ex dono gratiae, quae dependet ex liberalitate Dei, non ex ordine naturae. Et ideo per donum gratiae homines mereri possunt tantam gloriam, ut angelis aequentur secundum singulos angelorum gradus. Quod est homines ad ordines angelorum assumi. Quidam tamen dicunt quod ad ordines angelorum non assumuntur omnes qui salvantur, sed soli virgines vel perfecti; alii vero suum ordinem constituent, quasi condivisum toti societati angelorum. – Sed hoc est contra Augustinum, qui dicit XII de Civ. Dei, quod non erunt duae societates hominum et angelorum, sed una, quia omnium beatitudo est adhaerere uni Deo."

angels, then the devil sinned in the first moment of his creation. Thomas responds that man was not created simply to repair the angelic ruins, but to enjoy God and the perfection of the universe; he would have been made in this way even if the angelic fall had not happened.[65]

Finally, we should mention the topos of Eph1:10.[66]

We conclude that Thomas has no doubts as to the validity of the theme we are following, and that he perceives as truth that which is contained in the statements of the saints, and therefore in the Tradition of the church. But he feels an understandable need to explain the theme with great correctness and is more active in using it than are Albert and Bonaventure.

---

65   THOMAS AQUINAS, *Quaestiones disputatae de malo* q. 16, a. 4, arg. 16 + ad 16: "… homo non est simpliciter factus propter reparationem ruinae angelicae, sed propter fruitionem Dei et perfectionem universi, etiam si nunquam fuisset ruina angelica."

66   THOMAS AQUINAS, *Super Epistolam B. Pauli ad Ephesios lectura* cap. 1, l. 3: "Omnia, inquam, quae in caelis, id est Angelos: non quod pro Angelis mortuus sit Christus, sed quia redimendo hominem, reintegratur ruina angelorum. Ps. CIX, 6: implevit ruinas, et cetera. Ubi cavendus est error Origenis, ne per hoc credamus angelos damnatos redimendos esse per Christum, ut ipse finxit. Et quae in terris, inquantum caelestia terrenis pacificat. Col. I, 20: pacificans per sanguinem crucis eius, sive quae in terris, sive quae in caelis sunt; quod est intelligendum quantum ad sufficientiam, etsi omnia non restaurentur quantum ad efficaciam."

Conclusion

1. In the foregoing pages we have attempted to present a history of the thesis that man was created as a replacement for fallen angels, and which implies that his redemption was also primarily for the benefit of the angels.

We have seen how and by what manner of argument the thesis originated with St. Augustine, who may have gained inspiration on certain points from some of his predecessors, especially perhaps from Origen, but who generally speaking was undoubtedly original. We have seen that a further author to embrace this train of thought was St. Gregory the Great, and we have identified his points of departure from the bishop of Hippo. Although these divergences are fundamental, they were not generally recognized as such and the words of the bishop of Rome have simply been interpreted along the lines of St. Augustine. The apparent accord between these two great authorities was then carried through by the writers of the early Middle Ages, who referred to our theme by rote in a number of standard contexts without genuinely thinking it through for themselves (with the exception, perhaps, of Johannes Scotus Eriugena).

Early scholasticism in the eleventh and twelfth centuries, however, embraced our theme with great interest and enthusiasm. St. Anselm of Canterbury reflected upon why the sin of angels needs to be restored by human nature, and incorporated these reflections into his treatise *Cur Deus homo*: if men are to be admitted into the place of the fallen angels, and are to be holy even though they had sinned, it was necessary for them to be redeemed through the incarnation of the Word of God. This logic suggests that the question *cur homo* was being answered in terms of man having been created as a replacement for fallen angels (Augustine) or for completing the angels who had persevered (Gregory). However, in the reflections as to whether more people will be justified and admitted into heaven than there were angels who fell, we saw in Anselm a glimpse of the assertion that it is also possible that men were not created for this reason alone: that human nature was made for itself (*pro se ipsa ibi facta est*).

Theologians at the school of Laon noticed that Anselm was asking whether man was created only for this purpose or also for his own sake (*an etiam propter se*). They themselves arrived at the latter conclusion from different sources. They rejected Augustine's idea that man was created in order to beget offspring that would replace the fallen angels, and asserted rather that God created man so that through knowing, loving, and praising he should participate in God's blessedness. Man was needed for the praise of God to be complete and perfect (*laus perfecta*). He was therefore, first and foremost, made for his own sake, that is, for the praise that only he can offer to God. This praise is necessary because in it resounds the voice of the whole of the physical creation. If, therefore, the purpose of creation is to be fulfilled, man must praise God, which also, to a certain degree, makes the work of redemption necessary, and for this the angels in turn give praise to God. The number of angels was diminished by the fall and by this also their glory. But redeemed man makes up for these fallen angels in praise, although he would have been created and redeemed even if the angels had not fallen.

The question was approached in a highly original way by Rupert of Deutz, who linked the patristic thesis with reflections upon God's plan of salvation, which has its entire focus in the predestination of the incarnate and glorified Word. God's predestination should not be imagined in terms of there being a kind of sequence to God's intentions – that while prior to the fall of the angels he had no intention of creating man, he later resolved to do so prompted by the idea that he needed to replenish the depleted number of his family members. It cannot be said in any way, therefore, that man was created for angels: angels and all other creatures, including men, were created for man – for the man Jesus Christ, the incarnate Word of God. The cause of the creation of all things, and thus also of angels and men, was the Son of Man, who by the Father's will was, through the incarnation, to share in communion with all creatures, and through suffering to attain among them unutterable glory.

Rupert's theology was embraced by Honorius of Autun, but with certain shifts in emphasis. First, Honorius did not truly consider the question of the causes of the creation of man alongside the question of the primary causes of the incarnation; the two subjects were thought through independently. God the Father willed and anticipated the whole of creation in the eternal Son. Therefore to assert that man's creation is

conditional upon the arbitrary actions of angels and that man was created only so that through him the angelic fall might be repaired is absurd.
Every kind of being was made for its own sake and in the order of creation to each belongs its own incommutable place. Man also was created
propter semetipsum. It is also possible, however, to say that everything is
made for man and that his creation is, in fact, the prerequisite for the
creation of all other beings. The goal of his creation is, then, deification.
This discovery follows from the answer that Honorius gave to the question *cur Deus homo*: the primary cause of the incarnation of the Son of
God was not sin, but that man would be brought to the goal for which
he was created, that is, deification.

In holding to their supra-lapsarian understanding of the primary
causes of the incarnation, Rupert and Honorius were essentially alone;
they represented the minority opinion. Most theologians either held that
the cause of the incarnation was human sin, or left the answer somewhat
undefined. This in turn influenced the way in which people approached
the subjects of the causes of man's creation and his being a "replacement
angel." Only St. Anselm of Canterbury, the school of Laon, and Rupert
and Honorius made a link between the questions *cur Deus homo* and *cur
homo* in the context of our theme. With these authors, however, the disputation brought to our attention by Chenu virtually exhausted itself,
there being only a few distant echoes in the years that followed. It cannot definitely be assumed, either, that the narration of our theme always
focused on the question as to whether man was created as a replacement
angel or for his own sake. The following history outlines the variety of
positions taken by thinkers who applied themselves to our theme.

Among authors from the monastic tradition, the motif of the "replacement angel" appears in a variety of spiritual contexts not dissimilar
to those we have seen in the theologians of the early Middle Ages. It is
integrated into an understanding of monastic life and human existence
collectively denoted by the term *bios angelikos*.

The second approach is presented by representatives of speculative
theology. The first of these is the younger contemporary of Rupert and
Honorius, Hugh of St. Victor, who integrated our theme into the very
beginnings of the systematization of theology. He did not connect it with
the question as to why the incarnation took place, or even with the question as to why God created the world and man, to which he answered:
causa omnium homo est. The cause of the world is man because the world
was created for man, and the cause of man is God, because man was created for God. Angels and men were created because God in his eternal

goodness wished them to participate in his eternal bliss. The question as to whether man was created as a replacement for fallen angels arose only with the discourse on angels. Hugh's view was that although man was not created as a replacement for angels, he nonetheless fulfilled this role in the reality of the history of salvation. A similar assertion was made in *Summa sententiarum*: even though that which fell in the angels will be restored through men, this cannot be understood in terms of man having been created only because of those angels who fell; he would have been created even if the angels had not fallen.

A little later, in *Sententiae in IV Libris distinctae,* Peter Lombard recalled our theme in two contexts: in relation to the question concerning the goal of creation, and in connection with angelology. With regard to the former he posed the question: *Quomodo dicitur homo factus propter reparationem angelici casus*; with the latter: *Quomodo dicat Scriptura, decimum ordinem compleri de hominibus.* The answers Lombard himself provided to these questions – without really extending the argument beyond that of his sources – are of less consequence than the fact that due to the significant influence his work had on successive centuries, his questions were taken on by other writers. Among these were some of the greatest theologians of the late Middle Ages. Peter Lombard, Albert the Great, and Bonaventure of Bagnoregio, in an echo of the now extinct disputation, all agreed that man would have been created and saved even if the angels had not sinned.

St. Thomas Aquinas, in his commentary on Lombard's *Sententiae,* noted that there are certain beings that enjoy absolute participation in God's goodness, from which stems their usefulness to others: thus, angels and all other creatures are made for man, and man is made for the restoration of the angelic ruins. This usefulness is only consequential, but is foreknown and foreordained by God (*et sic etiam homo factus est propter reparationem ruinae angelicae: quia haec utilitas consecuta est et a Deo praevisa et ordinata*): the restoration of the angelic ruins is not the main goal of the creation of man but a kind of concomitant benefit that stems from his creation; God, however, foresaw it (*non est principalis finis creationis hominis, reparatio ruinae angelicae, sed quaedam utilitas consequens*). In *Quaestiones disputatae de malo,* Thomas then stated that man was not created simply to restore the angelic ruins but to enjoy God and the perfection of the universe, and he would have been created like this even if the angels had not fallen (*homo non est simpliciter factus propter reparationem ruinae angelicae, sed propter fruitionem Dei et perfectionem universi, etiam si nunquam fuisset ruina angelica*).

With these statements we conclude our survey of the thesis that man was created as a replacement for fallen angels and that his redemption therefore took place primarily for the benefit of the angels. It would be a simple matter to demonstrate that our theme continued its journey through the successive centuries, whether on a more spiritual[1] and spec-ulative[2] level, or by way of reminiscence,[3] or of course in poetry, as we see in John Milton's (1608–1674) *Paradise Lost* (1667), in which God, in wishing to limit the pride of the fallen angels, creates, with the help of his Son and his Spirit, a new world, and also man, who by his own merits is to ascend among the celestials.[4]

Evidence of this kind appears until the present day, and in most cases the authors simply take their lead from a text from some earlier author-ity. In English-speaking countries, however, there still exist thinkers of various Christian confessions who speak with some certainty about man having been created as a replacement for fallen angels.[5] For the most part this assertion is no longer taken seriously, however, so very few see the need to take issue with it: "Are we merely the replacement for the angels he lost, the first date he can find on the rebound?"[6] Only very occasionally do theologians actually work with it, for example Sergei N. Bulgakov (1871–1944), who after criticizing the patristic thesis states that

1   For example Pius KÜNZLE, *Heinrich Seuses Horologium Sapientiae*, Freiburg: Universitätsverlag Freiburg, 1977, 461–462 (l. I, m. XI).

2   For example FRANCISCUS SUAREZ, *Opera omnia*, tomus I, Parisiis: apud Ludovicum Vivès, 1856, 282, 285 (Tractatus de divina substantia ejusque attributis l. I, c. XII); ID., *Opera omnia*, tomus II, Parisiis: apud Ludovicum Vivès, 1856, 45 (Tractatus de Angelis l. I, c. XI).

3   For example DANTE ALIGHIERI, *Convivio* II,V,12, in ID., *Il Convivio: Testo*, ed. Franca Brambilla Ageno, Florenzia: Casa editrice Le lettere, 1995, 89: "Dico che di tutti questi ordini si perderono alquanti tosto che furono creati, forse in numero de la decima parte; a la quale restaurare fu l'umana natura poi creata." *Divi Dionysii Carthusiani In Sententiarum librum II commentarii locupletissimi*. Venetiis: sub signo Angeli Raphaelis, 1584, 99 (Augustine), 168 (Hugh), 184 (Bonaventure), 234 (Gregory), 257 (Thomas of Strasbourg), 280 (Bonaventure), 401–402 (Augustine).

4   John MILTON, *Paradise Lost* (1667) VII,139–191, in *The Poetical Works of John Milton*, edited after the Original Texts by the Rev. H. C. Beeching M.A., Oxford: Clarendon Press, 1900, 321–323.

5   William A. SCHACKLEFORD, *Replacing the Fallen Angels*, [s.l.]: Xulon Press 2007; Dollard DORAIS, *The Reverse of the Fall*, Lake Mary (Florida): Creation House, 2005; Robert D. LUGINBILL, *The Satanic Rebellion: Background to the Tribulation*, Part 3: *The Purpose, Creation and Fall of Man*. <http://ichthys.com/Fall-sr3.htm> [2013-07-27]; *Anthropology 1.1.2: Man created to replace Satan and his angels*. <http://biblesurvey.net/?p=381> [2013-07-27].

6   Brent CURTIS – John ELDREDGE, *The Sacred Romance: Drawing Closer to the Heart of God*, Nashville, TN: Thomas Nelson, 1997, 77.

if the fallen angels were replaced by anybody it was by good angels, who became the protectors of men.[7]

2. Even so, however, our theme is still surprisingly current: the question as to whether and in what sense man was created for his own sake is once more being debated, and the lessons we can draw from the history we have presented can still be of some use. It is to this fact that we will now, finally, turn our attention.

In 1985, the Swiss philosopher and theologian Romano Amerio (1905–1997) published *Iota Unum*. He devoted a lengthy section of his book to criticism of what he saw as the "anthropocentric theology" of the pastoral constitution of the Second Vatican Council, *Gaudium et spes*.[8] He particularly perceived this kind of anthropocentrism in the assertion that believers and non-believers agree that all things on earth should relate to man as their centre and crown (article 12: *omnia quae in terra sunt ad hominem, tamquam ad centrum suum et culmen, ordinanda sunt*), and especially in the assertion that man is the only creature on earth that God willed for itself (article 24: *qui in terris sola creatura est quam Deus propter seipsam voluerit*).[9]

Amerio held that the Council was accommodating inappropriately to the anthropocentrism of the modern world, which emphasized man's autonomy and ignored the fact that the whole world has its purpose in God. Against the authority of the conciliar text the author therefore posited the authority of the Word of God: *universa propter semet ipsum operatus est Dominus* (Proverbs 16:4 Vulg.); and the authority of St. Thomas Aquinas: *Sic igitur [Deus] vult et se esse, et alia: sed se ut finem, alia vero ut ad finem* (*STh* I, q. 19, a. 2). God created everything that is – and therefore also man – for himself and for his glory, not for its intrinsic or original value. Man is not a goal in himself but is here, *ad finem*, for God. Amerio's conclusion was that by its statement the Council was departing from revealed truth and from the Tradition of the Catholic Church.

7   Sergej N. BULGAKOV, *L'Échelle de Jacob: des anges*, Lausanne: Éditions l'Age d'Homme, 1987, 50–51.

8   Romano AMERIO, *Iota Unum: Studio delle variazioni della Chiesa Cattolica nel secolo XX*, Milano-Napoli: R. Ricciardi, 1985, 401–408 (§§ 205–208). The cited critique of the Council spread widely, as is attested by, for example, Paolo PASQUALUCCI, La cristologia antropocentrica del Concilio Ecumenico Vaticano II, *Divinitas* 2 (2011), 163–187.

9   SACROSANCTUM CONCILIUM OECUMENICUM VATICANUM II, Constitutio pastoralis de Ecclesia in mundo hiuius temporis Gaudium et spes, *AAS* 50 (1966), 1034, 1035, 1045.

But a closer reading of the conciliar statements and a study of their genesis leads to a different conclusion.[10] According to the constitution, believers and non-believers agree that it is necessary to assign to man the central place (article 12), but this does not imply that they will all understand this statement in the same way. On the contrary, the constitution immediately suggests that each will understand it according to how they answer the question "What is man?" Christians will have in mind, for example, a being that in its physicality draws together all of the elements of the material world, which "reach their crown through him, and 'through him raise their voice in free praise of the Creator' (see Dan 3:57–90)" (article 14).[11] God assigned to human beings a place of central importance in the whole of the creation, subordinated everything to them, and arranged that creatures fulfil their purpose only in relation to the free actions of man, that is, in the measure to which he himself freely relates to God as his goal.

Christian anthropocentrism is therefore characterised by the fact that it is theocentric; as is, contrary to Amerio's belief, the statement according to which *homo in terris sola creatura est quam Deus propter seipsam voluerit* (article 24). From the genesis of the text it is clear that it is inspired directly from St. Thomas Aquinas. In the schema of the "Pastoral Constitution on the Church in the Modern World" (May 1965), where it featured in article 16, a reference to *Contra Gentiles* III,112 was added, which does not, however, feature in any other version. In the passage

---

10 See *Acta synodalia Sacrosancti Concilii Oecumenici Vaticani II*, volumen IV, pars I, Città del Vaticano: Typis Polyglottis Vaticanis, 1976, 443, 446; *Acta synodalia Sacrosancti Concilii Oecumenici Vaticani II*, volumen IV, pars I, Città del Vaticano: Typis Polyglottis Vaticanis, 1978, 434, 435, 447.

11 From the genesis of the text it follows that article 12 and article 14 of the pastoral constitution *Gaudium et spes* should be read together. The schema of the "Pastoral Constitution on the Church in the Modern World" (May 1965) contained the following words in article 11: "Secundum credentium et non credentium fere concordem sententiam, tota socialis vitae ordinatio ad hominem respicere debet, si intimiori eius cordis desiderio respondere velit," and in article 12: "Corporali sua conditione homo universas mundanas creaturas in se colligit et culmen vitae terrestris constituit. In eo elementa mundi materialis et cuncta quae super faciem terrae vita moventur, fastigium suum attingunt, et ad liberam sui Creatoris laudem vocem attolunt, in totius mundi symphonia, ore hominis proferenda (cf. Dan 3:57–90)." In October 1965 article 12 contained the sentence, "Secundum credentium et non credentium fere concordem sententiam, omnia quae in terra sunt ad hominem, tamquam ad centrum suum et culmen, ordinanda sunt." As is clear, it came from the joining together of two originally independent statements. The continuation of the second sentence was moved to article 14: "Corpore et anima unus, homo per ipsam suam corporalem condicionem elementa mundi materialis in se colligit, ita ut, per ipsum, fastigium suum attingant et ad liberam Creatoris laudem vocem attollant (cf. Dan 3:57–90)." These formulations made their way into the final version of *Gaudium et spes*.

referred to, Thomas speaks about God's providence concerning rational and free beings in a special way: *gubernantur propter seipsas, aliae vero in ordine ad eas.* It is here in this statement that we find an echo of the reflections that Thomas developed in relation to the motif of man as a replacement angel.

Thomas emphasized that like all other creatures, human beings are integrated into a wider complex of mutual relationships (*ordo partium universi*) that are ordered in such a way that the perfection of the whole of reality was reflected in them and attained through them (*perfectio universi, bonum ordinis universi*).[12] The truth about this whole is mainly that its individual parts exist for their own sake, for their own perfection, and for their own deeds (*unaquaeque creatura est propter suum proprium actum et perfectionem*); in their uniqueness they are a partial expression of God's goodness, as for God to express his perfection in the world a diversity of beings is necessary, each of which, whatever their nature, is irreplaceable. We can therefore say, for example, that the world is a better place for containing angels and rocks than it would be if it contained only angels.[13] In another sense, however, it holds that the less perfect beings exist for the more perfect being – for man. It further holds that every being, including man, is here for the perfection of the universe. This, however, is not only arranged according to the mutual relationships between individual beings, but also, and principally, according to their relationship to their goal, which is God. Each individual part of the whole – and the whole itself – is therefore directed towards God, not so that he might perfect it but in order to reflect his glory in it. And it is here that a unique place is

---

12 In terms of sources and interpretation, the discussion in a number of authors on the relationship between Thomas's understanding of the "common good" (*bonum commune*) and personalism is still beneficial for what is being hinted at here. See: Jacques MARITAIN, *Humanisme intégral*, Paris: Aubier, 1936; François HERTEL, *Pour un ordre personnaliste*, Montréal: Éditions de l'Arbre, 1942; Charles de KONINCK, *De la primauté du bien commun contre les personnalistes*, Québec et Montréal: Presses de l'université Laval et Fides, 1943; Ignace ESCHMANN, In Defense of Jacques Maritain, *The Modern Schoolman* 4 (1945), 183–208; Charles de KONINCK, In Defence of Saint Thomas: A Reply to Father Eschmann's Attack on the Primacy of the Common Good, *Laval théologique et philosophique* 2 (1945), 9–109; Jacques MARITAIN, *La personne et le bien commun*, Paris: Desclée de Brouwer, 1947.

13 THOMAS AQUINAS, *Scriptum super Sententiis*, l. I, d. 44, q. 1, a. 2, ad 6: "Ad sextum dicendum, quod quamvis angelus absolute sit melior quam lapis, tamen utraque natura est melior quam altera tantum: et ideo melius est universum in quo sunt angeli et aliae res, quam ubi essent angeli tantum: quia perfectio universi attenditur essentialiter secundum diversitatem naturarum, quibus implentur diversi gradus bonitatis, et non secundum multiplicationem individuorum in una natura."

assigned to rational beings since they are able to attain to God through their acts of knowing and loving.[14]

Since rational creatures are unique objects of God's care and providence, God gave them power over their actions, which implies not only that they are ontologically incommutable (in the sense of the maxim quoted above: *unaquaeque creatura est propter suum proprium actum et perfectionem*), but also that they do not exist as a function of another creature. Rather, they exist for themselves (*propter se*), and thus everything else exists for them.[15] Rational nature is thus the only nature that God requires in the universe for itself; everything else is willed only for the sake of rational nature (*sola igitur intellectualis natura est propter se quaesita in universo, alia autem omnia propter ipsam*).[16] This does not mean to say, however, that beings of a rational nature would not relate to God and to the perfection of the universe, but that they do not exist for the benefit of anything else.[17] They are free, and God treats them as such

---

14 THOMAS AQUINAS, *Summa theologiae* I, q. 65, ad 2 co. 1: "... considerandum est quod ex omnibus creaturis constituitur totum universum sicut totum ex partibus. Si autem alicuius totius et partium eius velimus finem assignare, inveniemus primo quidem, quod singulae partes sunt propter suos actus; sicut oculus ad videndum. Secundo vero, quod pars ignobilior est propter nobiliorem; sicut sensus propter intellectum, et pulmo propter cor. Tertio vero, omnes partes sunt propter perfectionem totius, sicut et materia propter formam, partes enim sunt quasi materia totius. Ulterius autem, totus homo est propter aliquem finem extrinsecum, puta ut fruatur Deo. Sic igitur et in partibus universi, unaquaeque creatura est propter suum proprium actum et perfectionem. Secundo autem, creaturae ignobiliores sunt propter nobiliores sicut creaturae quae sunt infra hominem, sunt propter hominem. Ulterius autem, singulae creaturae sunt propter perfectionem totius universi. Ulterius autem, totum universum, cum singulis suis partibus, ordinatur in Deum sicut in finem, inquantum in eis per quandam imitationem divina bonitas repraesentatur ad gloriam Dei, quamvis creaturae rationales speciali quodam modo supra hoc habeant finem Deum, quem attingere possunt sua operatione, cognoscendo et amando. Et sic patet quod divina bonitas est finis omnium corporalium."

15 THOMAS AQUINAS, *Contra Gentiles*, l. 3, cap. 112, n. 1: "Primum igitur, ipsa conditio intellectualis naturae, secundum quam est domina sui actus, providentiae curam requirit qua sibi propter se provideatur: aliorum vero conditio, quae non habent dominium sui actus, hoc indicat, quod eis non propter ipsa cura impendatur, sed velut ad alia ordinatis. Quod enim ab altero tantum agitur, rationem instrumenti habet: quod vero per se agit, habet rationem principalis agentis. Instrumentum autem non quaeritur propter seipsum, sed ut eo principale agens utatur. Unde oportet quod omnis operationis diligentia quae circa instrumenta adhibetur, ad principale agens referatur sicut ad finem: quod autem circa principale agens vel ab ipso vel ab alio adhibetur, inquantum est principale agens, propter ipsum est. Disponuntur igitur a Deo intellectuales creaturae quasi propter se procuratae, creaturae vero aliae quasi ad rationales creaturas ordinatae."

16 THOMAS AQUINAS, *Contra Gentiles*, l. 3, cap. 112, n. 3. See ibid., n. 4: "Naturae ergo intellectuales sunt propter se a divina providentia procuratae, alia vero omnia propter ipsas."

17 THOMAS AQUINAS, *Contra Gentiles*, l. 3, cap. 112, n. 10: "Per hoc autem quod dicimus substantias intellectuales propter se a divina providentia ordinari, non intelligimus quod ipsa

expressly for their own sake.[18] And they are to relate to him in a similar way: even though God is the ultimate end of the entire universe, only beings of a rational nature can attain to him the way he is, by knowing and loving Him (*constat autem ex praemissis finem ultimum universi Deum esse, quem sola intellectualis natura consequitur in seipso, eum scilicet cognoscendo et amando*).[19] What Thomas is describing here can be expressed as follows: people are not a medium through which God might fulfil some kind of purpose. Even though God created them as part of the whole – its mutual immanent finalities and its constitutive transcendental finality – their participation in these relationships is *personal*. God relates to them in such a way that he establishes their distinctiveness, which he then utterly respects; he relates to men with selfless love that wills them and that accompanies them by his care *propter seipsas*. In the same way they are to relate to the Father, the Son, and the Holy Spirit, as in such consists the very essence of love.[20] God is to be the end for man, and the goal, the one to be unselfishly known, loved, and praised. As we have seen, this is how the question as to why rational creatures were created was answered by those writing in the first part of the twelfth century, and subsequently by those from other Christian traditions such as St. Ignatius of Loyola (1491–1556) and John Calvin (1509–1564).[21]

ulterius non referantur in Deum et ad perfectionem universi. Sic igitur propter se procurari dicuntur et alia propter ipsa, quia bona quae per divinam providentiam sortiuntur, non eis sunt data propter alterius utilitatem; quae vero aliis dantur, in eorum usum ex divina ordinatione cedunt."

18 THOMAS AQUINAS, *Contra Gentiles*, l. 3, cap. 112, n. 2: "In quolibet autem regimine, liberis providetur propter seipsos: servis autem ut sint in usum liberorum. Sic igitur per divinam providentiam intellectualibus creaturis providetur propter se, ceteris autem creaturis propter ipsas."

19 THOMAS AQUINAS, *Contra Gentiles*, l. 3, cap. 112, n. 3. See ID., *Summa theologiae* I–II, q. 1, a. 8 co.: "Si ergo loquamur de ultimo fine hominis quantum ad ipsam rem quae est finis, sic in ultimo fine hominis omnia alia conveniunt, quia Deus est ultimus finis hominis et omnium aliarum rerum. Si autem loquamur de ultimo fine hominis quantum ad consecutionem finis, sic in hoc fine hominis non communicant creaturae irrationales. Nam homo et aliae rationales creaturae consequuntur ultimum finem cognoscendo et amando Deum, quod non competit aliis creaturis, quae adipiscuntur ultimum finem inquantum participant aliquam similitudinem Dei, secundum quod sunt, vel vivunt, vel etiam cognoscunt."

20 ANSELMUS CANTUARIENSIS, *Cur Deus homo* II,1 (S. Anselmi Cantuariensis Opera omnia II, 97): "Ad hoc itaque factam esse rationalem naturam certum est, ut summum bonum super omnia amaret et eligeret, non propter aliud, sed propter ipsum. Si enim propter alium, non ipsum sed aliud amat."

21 IGNATIUS DE LOYOLA, *Exercitia Spiritualia: Textuum antiquissimorum nova editio*, Roma: Institutum Historicum Societatis Jesu, 1969, 164–167 (n. 23) (Monumenta Historica SJ 100): "El hombre es criado para alabar, hacer reverencia y servir a Dios nuestro Señor y, mediante

We must conclude that the conciliar statements that Amerio and others criticized are in fact entirely traditional. They are not intended in the sense of modern-day immanent anthropocentrism but in the sense of a theologically understood anthropic principle that is integrated into a wider context of Christocentrism and theocentrism (1 Cor 3:22–23: "All are yours; and you are Christ's; and Christ is God's.") Furthermore, this is not some kind of impersonal automatism but an economic expression of the immanent finality of the Trinity: just as out of selfless love the Father and the Son desire in the Holy Spirit a divine person, their eternal "You," *propter seipsam*, so does the whole Trinity selflessly desire, *propter seipsam*, a human person united with Jesus Christ.

By this we are arriving at what can be intuited from the words of Rupert of Deutz. Men were not created for angels, for the numerical completeness of God's house and some kind of mechanism of salvation, as God's predestination wholly and only concerns Jesus Christ. From the beginning, the Father pursues a single goal: the revelation of the glory of his resurrected and ascended Son. Likewise the Son pursues a single goal: the revelation of the glory of his heavenly Father. Therefore, all creatures exist so that through them and before them the Father and the Son can, in the Holy Spirit, and in complete freedom and under no obligation, express love to each other – supremely in the Easter drama – and so in this way men and angels are included into this selfless loving exchange. This is precisely why the human creature, willed by God for its own sake, can fully find himself only through a sincere gift of himself (*Gaudium et spes,* article 24).

The ultimate expression of such selfless love that allows others to be what they are, and that rejoices in their glory, is the church, especially in its eschatological expression in the perfect kingdom of God, the heavenly city of God. In this community, the love between the Father and the Son in the Holy Spirit, expressed through and before men and other creatures, achieves its completion. This is the intuition expressed by Jacques-Bénigne Bossuet (1627–1704) when he penned the words in which our theme appears once more, in reinterpreted form, and which

---

esto, salvar su ánima; y las otras cosas sobre la haz de la tierra son criadas para el hombre, y para que le ayuden en la prosecución del fin para que es criado..." Jean CALVIN, *Catechismus seu christianae religionis institutio ecclesiae genevensis.* 1538 (CR 33, 323): "... nos in hunc finem creatos omnes esse constat, ut maiestatem agnoscamus creatoris nostri, agnitam suspiciamus, omnique et timore, et amore, et reverentia colamus." AUGUSTINUS, *Confessionum libri tredecim* I,1 (CCSL 27,1): "Tu excitas, ut laudare te delectet, quia fecisti nos ad te et inquietum est cor nostrum, donec requiescat in te."

also implies the ideas that inspired the statements of the Second Vatican Council noted above. With these words we will conclude our study:

"VII. In the unity of the church appears the Trinity in unity: the Father, as a principle to which we reunite; the Son as the place in which we reunite; the Holy Spirit as a knot through which we reunite; and all is one. Amen to God, so be it.

VIII. In the unity of the church, all creatures are reunited. All creatures visible and invisible are something to the church. The angels are ministers of her salvation: and through the church their ranks are filled up of their legions decimated by the desertion of Satan and his accomplices; but in this recruitment it is not so much we who are incorporated with the angels as the angels who come to be united with us; because of Jesus, our common chief, and more ours than theirs.

IX. Even the rebellious and corrupted creatures such as Satan and his angels, through their own moral wandering and mischief which God uses despite them, are applied to the service, the purposes, and the sanctification of the church; God willing that all contributes to the unity – even schism, rupture, and revolt. Praise be to God for the effectiveness of his power and may each heart tremble at his judgement!

X. The inanimate creatures speak to the church about the wonders of God; and not being able to praise him themselves they praise him through the church as the universal temple where we give sacrifice of a fitting tribute for all creation, which is delivered by the church from its servitude to sin by being used for holy purposes.

XI. Regarding men, they are all something intimately connected with the church, all of whom are incorporated into it, or called to the banquet where everything becomes one."[22]

---

22 Jacques-Bénigne BOSSUET, Lettre 4 à une demoiselle de Metz (1662), in *Oeuvres complètes de Bossuet*, tome 26, Paris: Librairie de Louis Vivès, 1864, 305–306 (translated from the French). See Gérard RÉMY, Une lettre sur l'Eglise de Bossuet, in Anne-Élisabeth SPICA, *Bossuet à Metz (1652–1659): Les années de formation et leurs prolongements: Actes du Colloque international de Metz (21–22 mai 2004)*, Berne: Peter Lang, 2005, 97–113, esp. 112.

Resume

The monograph *Cur homo? A history of the thesis concerning man as a replacement for fallen angels* has set itself the goal to examine, outline, elucidate, and supplement the existing body of knowledge concerning a theme from patristic and medieval theology recalled in 1953 by Marie--Dominique Chenu, and that is the assertion that man was created as a replacement for fallen angels (Yves Congar: *créature de remplacement*; Louis Bouyer: *ange de remplacement*). The study first shows that the idea of man having being created to take the place of fallen angels was introduced by St. Augustine and developed by other church fathers. It then identifies the typical contexts in which the subject was raised by authors of the early Middle Ages, but goes on to focus on the discussion that developed during the twelfth century (Anselm of Canterbury, the school of Laon, Rupert of Deutz, Honorius of Autun), which represents the high point of the theme under investigation, culminating in the assertion that man is an "original" being, created for its own sake, for whom God created the world – a world which together with, and through, man is destined for the heavenly Jerusalem. The question as to whether man would have been created if the angels had not sinned (*cur homo*) bears a clear similarity to a further controversy, the origins of which also go back to the twelfth century, and that is whether the Son of God would have become incarnate if man had not sinned (*cur Deus homo*). Next, the book sheds light on how the subject begins to gradually fade away through the twelfth and thirteenth centuries, both within monastic tradition, which nonetheless held onto Augustine's motif, and within scholastic theology, which asserted that man was created for his own sake. The conclusion summarizes the findings and points to the surprisingly contemporary relevance of the foregoing reflections, particularly in relation to the critique that the Swiss philosopher and theologian Romano Amerio († 1997) offers concerning a statement in the pastoral constitution of the Second Vatican Council (*Gaudium et spes* 24), according to which man is "the only creature on earth that God willed for itself."

Bibliography

1. Abbreviations

AAS	*Acta Apostolicae Sedis*
CC-LLS	Corpus Christianorum Latin Lexicographical Series
CCCM	Corpus Christianorum, Continuatio Mediaevalis
CCSL	Corpus Christianorum, Series Latina
CSEL	Corpus Scriptorum Ecclesiasticorum Latinorum
FC	Fontes Christiani
L	Odon LOTTIN, *Psychologie et morale aux XIIe et XIIIe siècles*, tome 5, *Problèmes d'histoire littéraire. L'école d'Anselme. L'école de Guillaume de Champeaux*, Louvain: Abbaye de Mont César, 1959
PL	*Patrologiae cursus completus omnium patrum, doctorum scriptorumque ecclesiasticorum*, Series Latina, J.-P. Migne ed., Paris 1844–1855
SC	Sources chrétiennes

2. Electronic sources

Alberti Magni e-corpus. <http://albertusmagnus.uwaterloo.ca/newFiles/index.html>
Alcuin: Infothek der Scholastik. <http://www-app.uni-regensburg.de/Fakultaeten/PKGG/Philosophie/Gesch_Phil/alcuin/index.php>
Corpus thomisticum. <http://www.corpusthomisticum.org>

Dante Alighieri. <http://www.interbooks.eu/poesia/duecento/dantealighieri.html>

Digitale Monumenta Historiae Germanica. <http://www.dmgh.de>

Documenta Catholica Omnia. <http://www.documentacatholicaomnia.eu>

Europeana. <http://www.europeana.eu/>

Gallica: Bibliothèque numérique. <http://gallica.bnf.fr>

Google Books. <http://books.google.com>

International Medieval Bibliography. <http://apps.brepolis.net/bmb/search.cfm>

Internet Archive. <http://archive.org/>

Library of Latin Texts – Series A. <http://apps.brepolis.net/BrepolisPortal/default. aspx>

Mittelalterliche Handschriften in österreichischen Bibliotheken. <http://manuscripta. at/>.

Patrologia Latina Database. <http://pld.chadwyck.co.uk>

Post-Reformation Digital Library. <http://www.prdl.org>

Repertorium „Geschichtsquellen des deutschen Mittelalters". <http://www.geschichts-quellen.de>

Sant'Agostino. <http://www.augustinus.it>

San Bonaventura online. <http://dionysiana.wordpress.com/2010/12/24/san-bona-ventura-online>

The Digital Library of Catholic Reformation. <http://solomon.tcpt.alexanderstreet. com>

The Digital Library of Classic Protestant Texts. <http://solomon.tcpt.alexanderstreet. com>

Verzeichnis der im deutschen Sprachbereich erschienenen Drucke des 16. Jahrhunderts (VD 16) – *Verzeichnis der im deutschen Sprachraum erschienenen Drucke des 17. Jahrhunderts* (VD 17). <http://www.bsb-muenchen.de/>

Verzeichnis der im deutschen Sprachraum erschienenen Drucke des 18. Jahrhunderts (VD 18). <http://vd18-proto.bibliothek.uni-halle.de/>

3. Primary sources

ÆLFRIC, *The Sermones Catholici, or Homilies of Ælfric: In the original Anglo-Saxon, with an English version*, ed. Benjamin Thorpe, vol. 1–2. London: Richard and John E. Taylor, 1844, 1846

AELREDUS RIEVALLENSIS, *De Iesu puero duodenni* (CCCM 1), Turnhout: Brepols, 1971, 249–278

AELREDUS RIEVALLENSIS, *Tractatus de Jesu puero duodenni* (PL 184,849–869)

ALANUS DE INSULIS, *Contra haereticos* (PL 210,305–429)

ALANUS DE INSULIS, *Distinctiones dictionum theologicalium* (PL 210,685–1011)

ALANUS DE INSULIS, *Expositio prosae de Angelis*, in ALAIN DE LILLE, *Textes inédits*, avec une introduction sur sa vie et ses oeuvres par Marie-Thérèse d'Alverny, Paris: J. Vrin, 1965, 194–217

ALANUS DE INSULIS, *Hierarchia Alani*, in ALAIN DE LILLE, *Textes inédits*, avec une introduction sur sa vie et ses oeuvres par Marie-Thérèse d'Alverny, Paris: J. Vrin, 1965, 223–235

ALANUS DE INSULIS, *Sermo in die sancti Michaelis*, in ALAIN DE LILLE, *Textes inédits*, avec une introduction sur sa vie et ses oeuvres par Marie-Thérèse d'Alverny, Paris: J. Vrin, 1965, 249–251

ALBERTUS MAGNUS, *In Apocalypsim B. Joannis*, ed. A. Borgnet, Parisiis: apud Ludovicum Vivès 1890, 465–792 (B. Alberti Magni Opera omnia 38)

ALBERTUS MAGNUS, *Summa theologiae sive scientia de mirabili scientia Dei*, ed. A. Borgnet, Parisiis: apud Ludovicum Vivès, 1894 (B. Alberti Magni Opera omnia 31)

ALBERTUS MAGNUS, *Summa theologiae sive scientia de mirabili scientia Dei*, ed. A. Borgnet, Parisiis: apud Ludovicum Vivès, 1895 (B. Alberti Magni Opera omnia 32)

ALBERTUS MAGNUS, *Summa theologiae sive scientia de mirabili scientia Dei*, ed. A. Borgnet, Parisiis: apud Ludovicum Vivès, 1895 (B. Alberti Magni Opera omnia 33)

ALBERTUS MAGNUS, *Super Lucam*, ed. A. Borgnet, Parisiis: apud Ludovicum Vivès, 1894 (B. Alberti Magni Opera omnia 22)

ALBERTUS MAGNUS, *Super Lucam*, ed. A. Borgnet, Parisiis: apud Ludovicum Vivès, 1895 (B. Alberti Magni Opera omnia 23)

ALBERTUS MAGNUS, *Super Matthaeum*, ed. A. Borgnet, Parisiis: apud Ludovicum Vivès, 1893 (B. Alberti Magni Opera omnia 20)

ALBERTUS MAGNUS, *Super Matthaeum – Super Marcum*, ed. A. Borgnet, Parisiis: apud Ludovicum Vivès, 1894 (B. Alberti Magni Opera omnia 21)

ALBERTUS MAGNUS, *Super I Sententiarum*, ed. A. Borgnet, Parisiis: apud Ludovicum Vivès, 1893 (B. Alberti Magni Opera omnia 25)

ALBERTUS MAGNUS, *Super I Sententiarum*, ed. A. Borgnet, Parisiis: apud Ludovicum Vivès, 1893 (B. Alberti Magni Opera omnia 26)

ALBERTUS MAGNUS, *Super II Sententiarum*, ed. A. Borgnet, Parisiis: apud Ludovicum Vivès, 1894 (B. Alberti Magni Opera omnia 27)

ALBERTUS MAGNUS, *Super III Sententiarum*, ed. A. Borgnet, Parisiis: apud Ludovicum Vivès, 1894 (B. Alberti Magni Opera omnia 28)

ALBERTUS MAGNUS, *Super IV Sententiarum*, ed. A. Borgnet, Parisiis: apud Ludovicum Vivès, 1894 (B. Alberti Magni Opera omnia 29)

ALBERTUS MAGNUS, *Super IV Sententiarum*, ed. A. Borgnet, Parisiis: apud Ludovicum Vivès, 1894 (B. Alberti Magni Opera omnia 30)

[ALCHERUS CLARAEVALLENSIS?], *De diligendo Deo* (PL 40,847–863)

ALCUINUS, *Commentaria in Apocalypsin* (PL 100,1085–1156)

ALEXANDER HALENSIS, *Summa theologica* (*Summa Fratris Alexandri sive Summa universae theologiae*), tomus I–IV, Quaracchi: Ex Typographia Collegii S. Bonaventurae, 1924–1948

ALULFUS SANCTI MARTINI TORNACENSIS, *Expositio Novi Testamenti* (PL 73,1137–1424)

AMBROSIUS, *De fide ad Gratianum Augustum*, ed. Otto Faller, Vindobonae: Holder-Pichler-Tempsky, 1962, 3–307 (CSEL 78)

AMBROSIUS, *De fide ad Gratianum Augustum* (PL 16,527–698)

AMBROSIUS, *Expositio Evangelii secundum Lucam*, eds. M. Adriaen – P. A. Ballerini, Turnhout: Brepols, 1957, 1–400 (CCSL 14)

AMBROSIUS, *Expositio Evangelii secundum Lucam* (PL 15,1527–1850)

AMBROSIUS, *Expositio Psalmi CXVIII*, ed. M. Petschenig, Vindobonae: Tempsky; Lipsiae: Freytag, 1913 (CSEL 62)

AMBROSIUS, *Expositio in psalmum David CXVII* (PL 15,1197–1526)

AMBROSIUS AUTPERTUS, *Expositio in Apocalypsin*, ed. R. Weber, Turnhout: Brepols, 1975 (CCCM 27)

[ANONYMUS], *Epistola Hugonis a Sancto Victore* (Paris, Bibliothèque nationale de France, latin 14366, fol. 8v–23r, *Gallica: Bibliothèque numérique*. <http://gallica.bnf.fr>)

[ANONYMUS], *Summa sententiarum* (PL 176,41–174)

[ANONYMUS], *Tractatus theologicus* (PL 171,1067–1150)

ANSELME DE CANTORBERY, *Pourquoi Dieu s'est fait homme*, Paris: Cerf, 1963 (SC 91)

ANSELMUS CANTUARIENSIS, *Cur Deus homo*, in *S. Anselmi Cantuariensis Opera omnia*, tomus II, ed. F. S. Schmitt, Romae: [s.n.], 1940, 37–133

ANSELMUS CANTUARIENSIS, *De casu diaboli*, in *S. Anselmi Cantuariensis Opera omnia*, tomus I, ed. F. S. Schmitt, Edinburgi: apud Thomam Nelson et filios, 1946, 227–276

ANSELMUS CANTUARIENSIS, *Orationes*, in *S. Anselmi Cantuariensis Opera omnia*, tomus III, ed. F. S. Schmitt, Edinburgi: apud Thomam Nelson et filios, 1946, 5–75

[ANSELMUS LAUDUNENSIS?], *Enarrationes in Apocalypsin* (PL 162,1499–1586)

ATHANASE D'ALEXANDRIE, *Vie d'Antoine*, Paris: Cerf, 1994 (SC 400)

ATHANASIUS, *Vita Antonii* (PG 26,833–976)

ATTO VERCELLENSIS, *Expositio epistolarum S. Pauli – ad Colossenses* (PL 134, 607–644)

AUCTOR INCERTUS, *Expositio super missam* (PL 138,1163–1186)

AUDRADUS MODICUS, *Carmina*, in Ludovicus TRAUBE (ed.), *Poetae latini aevi Carolini*, tomus III, Berolini: apud Weidmannos 1896, 73–121, 740–745 (MGH Poetae 3)

AUGUSTINUS, *Collatio cum Maximino episcopo Arianorum* (PL 42,709–742)

AUGUSTINUS, *Confessionum libri tredecim*, ed. L. Verheijen, Turnhout: Brepols, 1981 (CCSL 27)

AUGUSTINUS, *De catechizandis rudibus*, ed. J.-B. Bauer, Turnhout: Brepols, 1969, 121–178 (CCSL 46)

AUGUSTINUS, *De catechizandis rudibus* (PL 40,309–348)

AUGUSTINUS, *De civitate Dei*, eds. B. Dombart, A. Kalb, Turnhout: Brepols, 1955 (CCSL 47)

AUGUSTINUS, *De civitate Dei*, eds. B. Dombart, A. Kalb, Turnhout: Brepols, 1955 (CCSL 48)

AUGUSTINUS, *De civitate Dei* (PL 41,13–803)

AUGUSTINUS, *De correptione et gratia* (PL 44,915–959)

AUGUSTINUS, *De doctrina christiana*, ed. J. Martin, Turnhout: Brepols, 1962, 1–167 (CCSL 32)

AUGUSTINUS, *De doctrina christiana* (PL 34,15–121)

AUGUSTINUS, *De Genesi ad litteram libri duodecim*, ed. J. Zycha, Pragae-Vindobonae: Tempsky; Lipisiae: Freytag, 1894, 3–435 (CSEL 28/1)

AUGUSTINUS, *De Genesi ad litteram* (PL 34,245–486)

AUGUSTINUS, *De Genesi contra Manicheos* (PL 34,173–220)

AUGUSTINUS, *Enarrationes in Psalmos I-L*, eds. E. Dekkers, J. Fraipont, Turnhout: Brepols, 1956 (CCSL 38)

AUGUSTINUS, *Enarrationes in Psalmos LI-C*, eds. E. Dekkers, J. Fraipont, Turnhout: Brepols, 1956 (CCSL 39)

AUGUSTINUS, *Enarrationes in Psalmos CI-CL*, eds. E. Dekkers, J. Fraipont, Turnhout: Brepols, 1956 (CCSL 40)

AUGUSTINUS, *Enarrationes in Psalmos* (PL 36,67–1026; 37,1033–1967)

AUGUSTINUS, *Enchiridion de fide et spe et caritate*, ed. M. Evans, Turnhout: Brepols, 1969, 49–114 (CCSL 46)

AUGUSTINUS, *Enchiridion* (PL 40,231–290)

[AUGUSTINUS], *Oeuvres de saint Augustin 9, Exposés généraux de la foi*, texte, traduction, et notes par Jean Rivière, Paris: Desclée de Brouwer, 1947

AUGUSTINUS, *Retractationum libri duo*, ed. A. Mutzenbecher, Turnhout: Brepols, 1984 (CCSL 57)

AUGUSTINUS, *Retractationes* (PL 32,581–656)

[AUGUSTINUS], *Sancti Aurelii Augustini Hipponensis Episcopi Operum* tomus sextus, continens moralia, post Lovaniensium theologorum recensionem castigatus ... Opera & Studio Monachorum Ordinis Sancti Benedicti è Congregatione Sancti Mauri, editio altera, Antwerpiae: Sumptibus Societatis, 1701

AUGUSTINUS, *Sermones post Maurinos reperti*, éd. G. Morin, Romae: Typis polyglottis Vaticanis, 1930 (Miscellanea Agostiniana 1)

BANDINUS, *Sententiarum libri quatuor* (PL 192,969–1112)

BEDA VENERABILIS, *In Lucae evangelium expositio*, ed. D. Hurst, Turnhout: Brepols, 1960, 5–425 (CCSL 120)

BEDA VENERABILIS, *In Evangelium S. Lucae* (PL 92,301–633)

BEDA VENERABILIS, *Homeliarum evangelii libri II*, ed. D. Hurst, Turnhout: Brepols, 1955, 1–378 (CCSL 122)

BEDA VENERABILIS, *Homiliae* (PL 94,9–268)

BEDA VENERABILIS, *In Marci evangelium expositio*, ed. D. Hurst, Turnhout: Brepols, 1960, 431–648 (CCSL 120)

BEDA VENERABILIS, *In Evangelium S. Marci* (PL 92,131–302)

BEDA VENERABILIS, *Homiliae subditae* (PL 94,267–513)

BERNARDUS CLARAEVALLENSIS, *Sermones in adventu Domini* (PL 183,35–56)

BERNARDUS CLARAEVALLENSIS, *Sermones in adventu Domini*, in Jean Leclercq – Henri Rochais (eds.), *Bernardi opera*, tomus 4, Romae: Ed. cistercienses, 1966, 161–196

BERNARDUS CLARAEVALLENSIS, *Sermones in dedicatione ecclesiae* (PL 183,517–536)

BERNARDUS CLARAEVALLENSIS, *Sermones in dedicatione ecclesiae*, in Jean Leclercq – Henri Rochais (eds.), *Bernardi opera*, tomus 5, Romae: Ed. cistercienses, 1968, 370–398

BERNARDUS CLARAEVALLENSIS, *Sermones in Cantica Canticorum* (PL 183, 785–1197)

BERNARDUS CLARAEVALLENSIS, *Sermones super Cantica Canticorum*, in Jean Leclercq – Charles H. Talbot – Henri Rochais (eds.), *Bernardi opera*, tomus 1–2, Romae: Ed. cistercienses, 1957–1958

BERNARDUS CLARAEVALLENSIS, *Sermones in dominica I novembris* (PL 183,343–360)

BERNARDUS CLARAEVALLENSIS, *Sermones in dominica I novembris*, in Jean Leclercq – Henri Rochais (eds.), *Bernardi opera*, tomus 5, Romae: Ed. cistercienses, 1968, 304–326

BERNARDUS CLARAEVALLENSIS, *Sermones in festo sancti Michaelis* (PL 183,447–454)

BERNARDUS CLARAEVALLENSIS, *Sermones in festo sancti Michaelis*, in Jean Leclercq – Henri Rochais (eds.), *Bernardi opera*, tomus 5, Romae: Ed. cistercienses, 1968, 294–303

Biblia cum glossa ordinaria, pars I–IV, Straßburg: Adolf Rusch, 1480/1481

BOETHIUS, *De consolatione philosophiae; Opuscula theologica*, ed. Claudio Moreschini, editio altera, Monachii et Lipsiae: In aedibus K. G. Saur, 2005

BONAVENTURA DE BAGNOREGIO, *Commentaria in quatuor libros Sententia-rum magistri Petri Lombardi*, Ad Claras Aquas (Quaracchi): Collegium S. Bo-naventurae, 1882 (Opera omnia S. Bonaventurae 1/1)

BONAVENTURA DE BAGNOREGIO, *Commentaria in quatuor libros Sententia-rum magistri Petri Lombardi*, Ad Claras Aquas (Quaracchi): Collegium S. Bo-naventurae, 1882 (Opera omnia S. Bonaventurae 1/2)

BONAVENTURA DE BAGNOREGIO, *Commentaria in quatuor libros Sententia-rum magistri Petri Lombardi*, Ad Claras Aquas (Quaracchi): Collegium S. Bo-naventurae, 1885 (Opera omnia S. Bonaventurae 2)

BONAVENTURA DE BAGNOREGIO, *Commentaria in quatuor libros Sententia-rum magistri Petri Lombardi*, Ad Claras Aquas (Quaracchi): Collegium S. Bo-naventurae, 1887 (Opera omnia S. Bonaventurae 3)

BONAVENTURA DE BAGNOREGIO, *Commentaria in quatuor libros Sententia-rum magistri Petri Lombardi*, Ad Claras Aquas (Quaracchi): Collegium S. Bo-naventurae, 1887 (Opera omnia S. Bonaventurae 4)

BONAVENTURA DE BAGNOREGIO, *Commentarii in Sacram Scripturam*, Ad Claras Aquas (Quaracchi): Collegium S. Bonaventurae, 1893 (Opera omnia S. Bonaventurae 6)

BONAVENTURA DE BAGNOREGIO, *Commentarius in Evangelium S. Lucae*, Ad Claras Aquas (Quaracchi): Ex typographia Colegii S. Bonaventurae, 1895 (Opera omnia S. Bonaventurae 7)

Jacques-Bénigne BOSSUET, *Oeuvres complètes de Bossuet*, tome 26, Paris: Librairie de Louis Vivès, 1864

BRUNO ASTENSIS, *Expositio in Pentateuchum* (PL 164,147–550)

BRUNO ASTENSIS, *Expositio in Apocalypsim* (PL 165,603–736)

[BRUNO CARTHUSIANORUM?], *Expositio in Psalmos* LXXXVIII (PL 152, 637–1419)

[BRUNO CARTHUSIANORUM?], *Expositio in epistolas Pauli – Epistola ad Ephe-sios* (PL 153,315–350)

BURCHARDUS WORMACIENSIS, *Libri decretorum* (PL 140,537–1057)

CASSIODORI DISCIPULUS, *Commentaria in epistulas sancti Pauli – Ad Ephesios* (PL 68,607–626)

Clavis Patrum Latinorum, ed. E. Dekkers, Turnhout: Brepols, 1995

Corpus iuris canonici, tomus 1–2, Graz: Akademische Druck- u. Verlagsanstalt, 1959

CYRILUS ALEXANDRINUS, *Commentarius in Lucam* (PG 72,475–950)

DANTE ALIGHIERI, *Il Convivio: Testo*, ed. Franca Brambilla Ageno, Florenzia: Casa editrice Le lettere, 1995

Divi Dionysii Carthusiani In Sententiarum librum II commentarii locupletissimi. Vene-tiis: sub signo Angeli Raphaelis, 1584

Eadmeri Cantuariensis monachi Scriptum de beatitudine perennis vitae sumptum de verbis beati Anselmi, in *Anselmo d'Aosta nel ricordo dei discepoli: parabole, detti, miracoli*, eds. Inos Biffi – Aldo Granata – Costante Marabelli – Davide Riserbato, Milano: Jaca Book, 2008, 486–532

ECKBERTUS SCHONAUGIENSIS, *Sermones contra Catharos* (PL 195,11–98)

Emonis Chronicon 1204–1234, ed. L. Weiland, in Georgius Heinricus PERTZ (ed.), *Monumenta Germaniae Historica: Scriptorum* tomus XXIII, Hannoverae: Impensis Bibliopolii Aulici Hahniani, 1874, 454–572 (MGH SS 23)

EUCHERIUS LUGDUNENSIS, *Instructionum ad Salonium libri II*, ed. C. Mandolfo, Turnhout: Brepols, 2004, 77–216 (CCSL 66)

EUCHERIUS LUGDUNENSIS, *Instructiones* (PL 50,773–822)

EVAGRIUS, *Vita Antonii* (PL 73,125–170 ed. B. Montfaucon; PG 26,833–976 ed. H. Rosweyde)

EVAGRIUS, *Vita Antonii*, in Pascal Henricus Elisabeth BERTRAND, *Die Evagrius-übersetzung der Vita Antonii: Rezeption-Überlieferung-Edition: Unter besonderer Berücksichtigung der Vitas Patrum-Tradition* (Proefschrift University of Utrecht), [s. l.]: [s.n.], 2006, 155–310 <http://igitur-archive.library.uu.nl/dissertations/2006-0221-200251>

FLORUS LUGDUNENSIS, *De expositione missae* (PL 119,15–72)

FRANCISCUS SUAREZ, *Opera omnia*, tomus I, Parisiis: apud Ludovicum Vivès, 1856

FRANCISCUS SUAREZ, *Opera omnia*, tomus II, Parisiis: apud Ludovicum Vivès, 1856

FULGENTIUS RUSPENSIS, *Liber de Trinitate ad Felicem*, ed. J. Fraipont, Turnhout: Brepols, 1968, 633–644 (CCSL 91A)

GERHOHUS REICHERSPERGENSIS, *Expositio in Psalmos (continuatio)* (PL 194,9–1002)

GILBERTUS PORRETANUS, *Commentaria in librum De duabus naturis et una persona Christi* (PL 64,1353–1412)

GILBERTUS PORRETANUS, *Sententiae*: Nicholas M. HÄRING, Die Sententiae magistri Gisleberti episcopi Pictavensis, *Archives d'histoire doctrinale et littéraire du moyen âge* 45 (1978), 83–180; Nicholas M. HÄRING, Die Sententiae magistri Gisleberti episcopi Pictavensis, *Archives d'histoire doctrinale et littéraire du moyen âge* 46 (1979), 45–105

[GILBERTUS PORRETANUS], *Sententiae divinitatis*: Bernhard GEYER, *Die Sententiae divinitatis: Ein Sentenzenbuch der gilbertschen Schule aus den Handschriften zum ersten Male herausgegeben und historisch untersucht*, Münster: Aschendorffische Buchhandlung, 1909, 1*–171*

GRÉGOIRE LE GRAND, *Commentaire sur le Premier livre des Rois*, tome 1, Paris: Cerf, 1989 (SC 351)

GRÉGOIRE LE GRAND, *Commentaire sur le Premier livre des Rois*, tome 2, Paris: Cerf, 1993 (SC 391)

GRÉGOIRE LE GRAND, *Commentaire sur le Premier livre des Rois*, tome 3, Paris: Cerf, 1998 (SC 432)

GRÉGOIRE LE GRAND, *Commentaire sur le Premier livre des Rois*, tome 4, Paris: Cerf, 2000 (SC 449)

GRÉGOIRE LE GRAND, *Commentaire sur le Premier livre des Rois*, tome 5, Paris: Cerf, 2003 (SC 469)

GRÉGOIRE LE GRAND, *Commentaire sur le Premier livre des Rois*, tome 6, Paris: Cerf, 2004 (SC 482)

GRÉGOIRE LE GRAND, *Homélies sur l'Évangile*, tome I, Paris: Cerf, 2005 (SC 485)

GRÉGOIRE LE GRAND, *Homélies sur l'Évangile*, tome II, Paris: Cerf, 2008 (SC 522)

GREGOR DER GROSSE, *Homiliae in evangelia = Evangelienhomilien*, Bd. 2, Freiburg im Breisgau: Herder, 1998 (FC 28/2)

GREGORIUS MAGNUS, *Moralia in Iob*, ed. M. Adriaen, Turnhout: Brepols, 1979–1985 (CCSL 143; 143A; 143B)

GREGORIUS MAGNUS, *Moralia in Iob* (PL 75,509–1162; 76,9–780)

GREGORIUS MAGNUS, *Homiliae in evangelia*, ed. R. Étaix, Turnhout: Brepols, 1999 (CCSL 141)

GREGORIUS MAGNUS, *Homiliae in evangelia* (PL 76,1075–1312)

GREGORIUS MAGNUS, *Expositio in Canticum canticorum*, ed. P.-P. Verbraken, Turnhout: Brepols, 1963, 3–46 (CCSL 144)

GREGORIUS MAGNUS, *Expositio super Canticum canticorum* (PL 79,471–548)

GUIBERTUS S. MARIAE DE NOVIGENTO, *Tropologiae in prophetas Osee et Amos ac Lamentationes Jeremiae* (PL 156,337–488)

GUILLELMUS DE CONCHIS, *Glossae super Platonem*, ed. E. A. Jeauneau, Turnhout: Brepols, 2006, 5–324 (CCCM 203)

GUILLELMUS DE CONCHIS, *Sententiae*, in Odon LOTTIN, *Psychologie et morale aux XIIe et XIIIe siècles*, tome 5, *Problèmes d'histoire littéraire. L'école d'Anselme. L'école de Guillaume de Champeaux*, Louvain: Abbaye de Mont César, 1959, 191–227; Georges LEFÈVRE, *Les Variations de Guillaume de Champeaux et la question des universaux: Étude suivie de documents originaux*, Lille: au siège de l'Université, 1898, 21–79

HAYMO HALBERSTATENSIS, *Expositio in D. Pauli epistolas – In epistolam ad Ephesios* (PL 117,699–734)

HAYMO HALBERSTATENSIS, *Expositio in Apocalypsin* (PL 117,937–1220)

HAYMO HALBERSTATENSIS, *Homiliae* (PL 118,11–815)

HAYMO HALBERSTATENSIS, *De varietate librorum* (PL 118,875–958)

HERMANNUS TORNACENSIS, *De incarnatione Christi* (PL 180,9–38)

HERVAEUS BURGIDOLENSIS, *Commentaria in epistolas Pauli – In epistolam ad Ephesios* (PL 181,1201–1280)

HILAIRE DE POITIERS, *Sur Matthieu*, tome 1, Paris: Cerf, 2007 (SC 254)

HILAIRE DE POITIERS, *Sur Matthieu*, tome 2, Paris: Cerf, 1979 (SC 258)

HILARIUS PICTAVIENSIS, *Commentarius in Mattheum* (PL 9,917–1078)

HILARIUS PICTAVIENSIS, *Tractatus super Psalmos*, ed. A. Zingerle, Mediolani: Hoepli, 1891 (CSEL 22)

HILARIUS PICTAVIENSIS, *Tractatus super Psalmos* (PL 9,231–890)

HILDEBERTUS CENOMANENSIS, *Sermones* (PL 171,339–964)

HILDEGARDIS BINGENSIS, *Expositiones Euangeliorum*, ed. B. M. Kienzle – C. A. Muessig, Turnhout: Brepols, 2007, 187–333 (CCCM 226)

HILDEGARDIS BINGENSIS, *Epistulae* XLVII (PL 197,145–382)

HILDEGARDIS BINGENSIS, *Scivias* (PL 197,383–738)

HILDEGARDIS BINGENSIS, *Liber divinorum operum simplicis hominis* (PL 197,739–1040)

HONORIUS AUGUSTODUNENSIS, *De cognitione verae vitae* (PL 40,1005–1032)

HONORIUS AUGUSTODUNENSIS, *Hexaemeron* [*De Neocosmo*] (PL 172, 253–266)

HONORIUS AUGUSTODUNENSIS, *Expositio in Cantica canticorum* (PL 172, 347–496)

HONORIUS AUGUSTODUNENSIS, *Speculum Ecclesiae* (PL 172,807–1108)

HONORIUS AUGUSTODUNENSIS, *Elucidarium* (PL 172,1109–1176)

HONORIUS AUGUSTODUNENSIS, *Liber XII quaestionum* (PL 172,1177–1185)

HONORIUS AUGUSTODUNENSIS, *Liber VIII quaestionum* (PL 172,1185–1192)

HONORIUS AUGUSTODUNENSIS, *Inevitabile* (PL 172,1192–1222)

HONORIUS AUGUSTODUNENSIS, *Inevitabile*, in Walter A. HANNAM, *The Inevitabile of Honorius Augustodunensis: A Study in the Textures of Early Twelfth--Century Augustianisms: a dissertation*, Boston College: The Graduate School of Arts and Sciences: Department of Theology, 2013, 197–510 <http://gradworks. umi.com/35/60/3560655.html> [2013-08-01]

HONORIUS AUGUSTODUNENSIS, *Inevitabile*, in Johann KELLE, Unter-suchungen über des Honorius Inevitabile sive de praedestinatione et libero arbitrio dialogus, *Sitzungsberichte der Akademie der Wissenschaften in Wien. Philosophisch-historische Klasse* 150/3 (1905), 9–33

HONORIUS AUGUSTODUNENSIS, *De anima et de Deo*, in Marie-Odile GAR-RIGUES, Honorius Augustodunensis: De anima et de Deo, quaedam ex Au-gustino excerpta, sub dialogo exarata, *Recherches augustiniennes et patristiques* 12 (1977), 212–278

HONORIUS AUGUSTODUNENSIS, *Quod monachis liceat predicare*, in Joseph Anton ENDRES, *Honorius Augustodunensis: Beitrag zur Geschichte des geistigen Lebens im 12. Jahrhundert*, Kempten-München: Verlag der Josef Kösel'schen Buchhandlung, 1906, 147–150

HUGO DE SANCTO VICTORE, *De sacramentis* (PL 176,173–618)

HUGO DE SANCTO VICTORE, *De arca Noe*, ed. P. Sicard, Turnhout: Brepols, 2001, 3–117

HUGO DE SANCTO VICTORE, *De arca Noe morali* (PL 176,617–680)

HUMBERTUS SILVAE CANDIDAE, *Adversus Graecas calumnias* (PL 143, 929–983)

IGNATIUS DE LOYOLA, *Exercitia Spiritualia: Textuum antiquissimorum nova editio*, Roma: Institutum Historicum Societatis Jesu, 1969 (Monumenta Historica SJ 100)

IOHANNES CASSIANUS, *Collationes XXIII*, ed. M. Petschenig, Vindobonae: apud C. Geroldi filium, 1886 (CSEL 13)

IOHANNES DUNS SCOTUS, *Lectura in Librum Secundum Sententiarum*, in *Ioannis Duns Scoti Opera omnia*, tomus 19, ed. Commissio Scotistica, Città del Vaticano, Typis Vaticanis, 1993

IOHANNES PRIOR CLARAEVALLENSIS, *Collectaneum exemplorum et visionum Claraevallense e codice Trecensi 946*, ed. O. Legendre, Turnhout: Brepols, 2005 (CCCM 208)

IOHANNNES SCOTUS ERIUGENA, *Periphyseon (De divisione naturae)*, ed. E. A. Jeauneau, Turnhout: Brepols, 1996–2003 (CCCM 161; 162; 163; 164; 165)

ISIDORUS HISPANENSIS, *Etymologiarum sive originum libri XX*, tomus I, ed. W. M. Lindsay, Oxonii: E Typographeo Clarendoniano, 1911, [s. p.]

ISIDORUS HISPANENSIS, *Etymologiae* (PL 82, 73–728)

ISIDORUS HISPALENSIS, *Sententiae*, ed. p. Canzier, Turnhout: Brepols, 1998 (CCSL 111)

ISIDORUS HISPALENSIS, *Sententiae* (PL 83,537–738)

ISIDORUS HISPALENSIS, *Allegoriae sacrae Scripturae* (PL 83,97–130)

ISIDORUS HISPANENSIS (incertus), *Expositio in missa* (PL 83,1145–1154)

IVO CARNOTENSIS, *Decretum* (PL 161,48–1022)

JEAN CALVIN, *Catechismus seu christianae religionis institutio ecclesiae genevensis. 1538*, in *Ioannis Calvini opera quae supersunt omnia*, ed. G. Baum – E. Cunitz – E. Reuss, tomus V (= *Corpus reformatorum*, tomus XXXIII), Brunsvigae: apud C. A. Schwetschke et filium, 1865, 317–362

JOANNES CASSIANUS, *Collationes XXIII* (PL 49,477–1328)

JOANNES DUNS SCOTUS, *Quaestiones in primum librum Sententiarum*, Parisiis: apud Ludovicum Vivès, 1813 (Joannis Duns Scoti Opera omnia 9)

JOANNES DUNS SCOTUS, *Quaestiones in primum librum Sententiarum*, Parisiis: apud Ludovicum Vivès, 1813 (Joannis Duns Scoti Opera omnia 10)

JOANNES DUNS SCOTUS, *Quaestiones in secundum librum Sententiarum*, Parisiis: apud Ludovicum Vivès, 1810 (Joannis Duns Scoti Opera omnia 11)

JOANNES DUNS SCOTUS, *Quaestiones in secundum librum Sententiarum*, Parisiis: apud Ludovicum Vivès, 1893 (Joannis Duns Scoti Opera omnia 12)

JOANNES DUNS SCOTUS, *Quaestiones in tertium librum Sententiarum*, Parisiis: apud Ludovicum Vivès, 1894 (Joannis Duns Scoti Opera omnia 13)

JOANNES DUNS SCOTUS, *Quaestiones in tertium librum Sententiarum*, Parisiis: apud Ludovicum Vivès, 1894 (Joannis Duns Scoti Opera omnia 14)

JOANNES DUNS SCOTUS, *Quaestiones in tertium librum Sententiarum*, Parisiis: apud Ludovicum Vivès, 1894 (Joannis Duns Scoti Opera omnia 15)

JOANNES DUNS SCOTUS, *Quaestiones in quartum librum Sententiarum*, Parisiis: apud Ludovicum Vivès, 1894 (Joannis Duns Scoti Opera omnia 16)

JOANNES DUNS SCOTUS, *Quaestiones in quartum librum Sententiarum*, Parisiis: apud Ludovicum Vivès, 1894 (Joannis Duns Scoti Opera omnia 17)

JOANNES DUNS SCOTUS, *Quaestiones in quartum librum Sententiarum*, Parisiis: apud Ludovicum Vivès, 1894 (Joannis Duns Scoti Opera omnia 18)

JOANNES DUNS SCOTUS, *Quaestiones in quartum librum Sententiarum*, Parisiis: apud Ludovicum Vivès, 1894 (Joannis Duns Scoti Opera omnia 19)

JOANNES DUNS SCOTUS, *Quaestiones in quartum librum Sententiarum*, Parisiis: apud Ludovicum Vivès, 1894 (Joannis Duns Scoti Opera omnia 20)

JOANNES DUNS SCOTUS, *Quaestiones in quartum librum Sententiarum*, Parisiis: apud Ludovicum Vivès, 1894 (Joannis Duns Scoti Opera omnia 21)

JOANNES SCOTUS ERIUGENA, *De divisione naturae* (PL 122,441–1021)

Erika KIHLMAN, *Expositiones Sequentiarum: Medieval Sequence Commentaries and Prologues: Editions with Introductions*, Stockholm: Stockholm University, 2006

Pius KÜNZLE, *Heinrich Seuses Horologium Sapientiae*, Freiburg: Universitätsverlag Freiburg, 1977

LANFRANCUS CANTUARIENSIS, *Commentarius in omnes epistolas Pauli – Epistola B. Pauli apostoli ad Ephesios* (PL 150,287–306)

LAON

– *Liber pancrisis*: Odon LOTTIN, *Psychologie et morale aux XIIe et XIIIe siècles*, tome 5, *Problèmes d'histoire littéraire. L'école d'Anselme. L'école de Guillaume de Champeaux*, Louvain: Abbaye de Mont César, 1959, 19–142

– *Deus non habet*: John C. WEI, The Sentence Collection: Devs Non Habet Initivm Vel Terminvm and Its Reworking, Devs Itaqve Svmme atqve Ineffabiliter Bonvs, *Mediaeval Studies* 73 (2011), 1–118: 39–115

– *Deus de cujus*: Heinrich WEISWEILER, Le recueil de sentences Deus de cujus principio et fine tacetur et son remaniement, *Recherches de théologie ancienne et médiévale* 5 (1933), 245–274: 252–274

- *Principium et causa = Sententiae Anselmi*: Franz BLIEMETZRIEDER (ed.), *Anselms von Laon systematische Sentenzen*, Münster: Verlag der Aschendorffschen Verlagsbuchhandlung, 1919, 47–153
- *De sententia divine = Sententie divine pagine*: Franz BLIEMETZRIEDER (ed.), *Anselms von Laon systematische Sentenzen*, Münster: Verlag der Aschendorffschen Verlagsbuchhandlung, 1919, 3–46
- *Divina essentia teste = Sententiae Atrebatenses*: Odon LOTTIN, *Psychologie et morale aux XIIe et XIIIe siècles*, tome 5, *Problèmes d'histoire littéraire. L'école d'Anselme. L'école de Guillaume de Champeaux*, Louvain: Abbaye de Mont César, 1959, 403–440
- *Quid de sancta = Sententiae Berolinenses*: Friedrich STEGMÜLLER, Sententiae Berolinenses: Eine neugefundene Sentenzensammlung aus der Schule des Anselm von Laon, *Recherches de théologie ancienne et médiévale* 11 (1939), 39–61
- *Potest queri*: Heinrich WEISWEILER, *Das Schrifttum der Schule Anselms von Laon und Wilhelms von Champeaux in Deutschen Bibliotheken: ein Beitrag zur Geschichte der Verbreitung der ältesten scholastischen Schule in Deutschen Landen*, Münster i. W.: Verlag der Aschendorffschen Verlagsbuchhandlung, 1936, 258–269
- *Deus est sine = De conditione angelica et humana*: Yves LEFÈVRE, Le De conditione angelica et humana et les Sententiae Anselmi, *Archives d'histoire doctrinale et littéraire du moyen âge* 26 (1959), 249–275: 256–275
- *Augustinus. Semel immolatus est Christus*: Heinrich WEISWEILER, *Das Schrifttum der Schule Anselms von Laon und Wilhelms von Champeaux in Deutschen Bibliotheken: ein Beitrag zur Geschichte der Verbreitung der ältesten scholastischen Schule in Deutschen Landen*, Münster i. W.: Verlag der Aschendorffschen Verlagsbuchhandlung, 1936, 281–291
- *Deus hominem fecit perfectum*: Heinrich WEISWEILER, *Das Schrifttum der Schule Anselms von Laon und Wilhelms von Champeaux in Deutschen Bibliotheken: ein Beitrag zur Geschichte der Verbreitung der ältesten scholastischen Schule in Deutschen Landen*, Münster i. W.: Verlag der Aschendorffschen Verlagsbuchhandlung, 1936, 292–311
- *Dubitatur a quibusdam*: Heinrich WEISWEILER, *Das Schrifttum der Schule Anselms von Laon und Wilhelms von Champeaux in Deutschen Bibliotheken: ein Beitrag zur Geschichte der Verbreitung der ältesten scholastischen Schule in Deutschen Landen*, Münster i. W.: Verlag der Aschendorffschen Verlagsbuchhandlung, 1936, 314–358
- *Decretum Dei fuit*: Heinrich WEISWEILER, *Das Schrifttum der Schule Anselms von Laon und Wilhelms von Champeaux in Deutschen Bibliotheken: ein Beitrag zur*

Geschichte der Verbreitung der ältesten scholastischen Schule in Deutschen Landen, Münster i. W.: Verlag der Aschendorffschen Verlagsbuchhandlung, 1936, 358–379

- *Origo et principium*: Odon LOTTIN, *Psychologie et morale aux XIIe et XIIIe siècles, tome 5, Problèmes d'histoire littéraire. L'école d'Anselme. L'école de Guillaume de Champeaux*, Louvain: Abbaye de Mont César, 1959, 330–332
- *Antequam quicquam fieret*: Odon LOTTIN, *Psychologie et morale aux XIIe et XIIIe siècles, tome 5, Problèmes d'histoire littéraire. L'école d'Anselme. L'école de Guillaume de Champeaux*, Louvain: Abbaye de Mont César, 1959, 333–338
- *Filius a Patre gigni*: Odon LOTTIN, *Psychologie et morale aux XIIe et XIIIe siècles, tome 5, Problèmes d'histoire littéraire. L'école d'Anselme. L'école de Guillaume de Champeaux*, Louvain: Abbaye de Mont César, 1959, 338–342
- *Voluntas Dei relata*: Odon LOTTIN, *Psychologie et morale aux XIIe et XIIIe siècles, tome 5, Problèmes d'histoire littéraire. L'école d'Anselme. L'école de Guillaume de Champeaux*, Louvain: Abbaye de Mont César, 1959, 342–31
- *De novissimis*: Odon LOTTIN, *Psychologie et morale aux XIIe et XIIIe siècles, tome 5, Problèmes d'histoire littéraire. L'école d'Anselme. L'école de Guillaume de Champeaux*, Louvain: Abbaye de Mont César, 1959, 393–400
- *In primis hominibus*: Bernd MATECKI, *Der Traktat In primis hominibus: eine theologie- und kirchengeschichtliche Untersuchung zu einem Ehetext der Schule von Laon aus dem 12. Jahrhundert*, Frankfurt am Main: Lang, 2001, 1*–54*
- Cédric GIRAUD, Théologie et Pédagogie au XIIe siècle: les sentences d'Anselme de Laon et de son école dans le manuscrit Paris, BNF, n.a.l. 181, *Archives d'histoire doctrinale et littéraire du Moyen Âge* 1 (2012), 193–287: 224–280
- *Ut autem hoc evidenter*: John C. WEI, A Twelfth-Century Treatise on Charity: The Tract "Vt autem hoc euidenter" of the Sentence Collection Deus itaque summe atque ineffabiliter bonus, *Mediaeval Studies* 74 (2012), 1–50: 31–50
- *Sententie Magistri A.*: Heinrich J. F. REINHARDT, *Die Ehelehre der Schule des Anselms von Laon. Eine theologie- und kirchenrechtsgeschichtliche Untersuchung zu den Ehetexten der frühen pariser Schule des 12. Jahrhunderts. Anhang: Edition des Ehetraktates der Sententie Magistri A.* Münster: Aschendorff, 1974, 135–263
- RADULPHUS LAUDUNENSIS, *Sententiae*: Odon LOTTIN, *Psychologie et morale aux XIIe et XIIIe siècles, tome 5, Problèmes d'histoire littéraire. L'école d'Anselme. L'école de Guillaume de Champeaux*, Louvain: Abbaye de Mont César, 1959, 184–188
- cf. GISLEBERTUS PORRETANUS
- cf. GUILLELMUS DE CONCHIS

Libelli de lite Imperatorum et Pontificum saeculi XI. et XII. conscripti, tomus III, Hannoverae: Impensis Bibliopolii Hahniani, 1897
MARTINUS LEGIONENSIS, *Sermones* (PL 208,27–1349)

MARTINUS BRACARENSIS, *De correctione rusticorum*, in Claude W. BARLOW, *Martini episcopi Bracarensis opera omnia*, New Haven, CT: Yale University Press, 1950, 183–203

MARTINUS LEGIONENSIS, *Expositio libri Apocalypsis* (PL 209,299–420)

METHODIUS, *Convivium decem virginum* (PG 18,27–220)

John MILTON, *Paradise lost* (1667), in *The Poetical Works of John Milton*, edited after the Original Texts by the Rev. H. C. Beeching M.A., Oxford: Clarendon Press, 1900, 175–448

ODO ASTENSIS, *Expositio in Psalmos – Psalmus CIX*(PL 165,1141–1298)

ODO CLUNIACENSIS, *Moralia in Iob* (PL 133,105–512)

ORIGÈNE, *Homélies sur Ézéchiel*, Paris: Cerf, 1989 (SC 352)

ORIGÈNE, *Homélies sur le Lévitique*, tome 1, Paris: Cerf, 1981 (SC 286)

ORIGÈNE, *Homélies sur le Lévitique*, tome 2, Paris: Cerf, 1981 (SC 287)

ORIGENES, *In Numeros homilia* (PG 12,583–806)

ORIGENES, *In Genesim homilia* (PG 12,145–262)

ORIGENES, *Commentarius in Matthaeum* (PG 13,829–1800)

OSBERNUS CANTUARIENSIS, *Vita S. Dunstani* (PL 137,407–473)

OTTO FRISINGENSIS, *Chronica sive Historia de duabus civitatibus*, Hannoverae et Lipsiae: Impensis Bibliopolii Hahniani, 1912 (MGH SSrG: Scriptores Rerum Germanicarum in usum scholarum ex Monumentis Germaniae Historicis separatim editi)

PETRUS ABAELARDUS, *Theologia christiana*, ed. E. M. Buytaert, Turnhout: Brepols, 1969, 71–372 (CCCM 12)

PETRUS ABAELARDUS, *Sententiae magistri Petri Abaelardi*, ed. D. Luscombe, Turnhout: Brepols, 2006, 5–152 (CCCM 14)

PETRUS ABAELARDUS, *Sic et non: A Critical Edition*, ed. Blanche B. Boyer – Richard McKeon, Chicago: The University of Chicago Press, 1976

PETRUS BLESENSIS, *Sermones* (PL 207,559–776)

PETRUS CANTOR, *Summa quae dicitur Verbum adbreviatum (textus prior)*, ed. M. Boutry, Turnhout: Brepols, 2012 (CCCM, 196A)

PETRUS CANTOR, *Verbum abbreviatum* (PL 205,21–370)

PETRUS IOHANNES OLIVI, *Quaestiones in secundum librum Sententiarum*, ed. B. Jansen, tomus I–III, Quaracchi: Ex Typographia Collegii S. Bonaventurae, 1922–1926

PETRUS LOMBARDUS, *Sententiae in IV libris distinctae*, Roma: Quaracchi, 1971 (Spicilegium Bonaventurianum 4)

PETRUS LOMBARDUS, *Collectanea in epistolas Pauli – In epistolam ad Ephesios* (PL 192,169–221)

PETRUS PICTAVIENSIS, *Sententiae* (PL 211,789–1280)

PIRMINIUS, *Scarapsus de singulis libris canonicis* (PL 89,1029–1050)

PLATO, *Timaeus a Calcidio translatus commentariosque instructus*, ed. Jan Hendrik Waszink, London: The Warburg Institute – Leiden: Brill, 1962, 7–52 (Corpus Platonicum Medii Aevi: Plato Latinus 4)

PSEUDO-ATHANASIUS, *Quaestiones ad Antiochium ducem* (PG 28,597–710)

RABANUS MAURUS, *Enarrationes in epistolas B. Pauli* XVII – *Expositio in Epistolam ad Ephsesios* (PL 112,381–478)

RABANUS MAURUS, *Homiliae* (PL 110,9–468)

RABANUS MAURUS, *Liber de sacris ordinibus* (PL 112,1165–1190)

RATHERIUS VERONENSIS, *Sermones Monacenses*, in *Thesaurus Ratherii Veronensis necnon Leodiensis*, ed. F. Dolbeau, Turnhout: Brepols, 2005, XXX–XLII (CC-LLS, Series A-B, Formae et lemmata)

REMIGIUS ALTISSIODORENSIS, *Expositio missae*, in Jean-Paul BOUNHOT, Les sources de l'*Expositio missae* de Rémi d'Auxerre, *Révue des études augustiniennes* 1 (1980), 140–151

ROBERTUS PULLUS, *Sententiae* (PL 186,639–1010)

RUPERTUS TUITIENSIS, *Commentaria in evangelium sancti Iohannis*, ed. R. Haacke, Turnhout: Brepols, 1969 (CCCM 9)

RUPERTUS TUITIENSIS, *Commentaria in evangelium sancti Iohannis* (PL 169,201–826)

RUPERTUS TUITIENSIS, *Commentarium in Apocalypsim Iohannis apostoli* (PL 169,825–1214)

RUPERTUS TUITIENSIS, *De divinis officiis* (PL 170,9–332)

RUPERTUS TUITIENSIS, *De gloria et honore Filii hominis super Matheum*, ed. R. Haacke, Turnhout: Brepols, 1979, 3–421 (CCCM 29)

RUPERTUS TUITIENSIS, *De gloria et honore Filii hominis super Matthaeum* (PL 168,1307–1634)

RUPERTUS TUITIENSIS, *De glorificatione Trinitatis et processione Spiritus sancti* (PL 169,9–202)

RUPERTUS TUITIENSIS, *De sancta Trinitate et operibus eius*, ed. R. Haacke, Turnhout: Brepols, 1971–1972 (CCCM 21; 22; 23; 24)

RUPERTUS TUITIENSIS, *De sancta Trinitate et operibus eius* (PL 167,199–1828)

RUPERTUS TUITIENSIS, *De victoria Verbi Dei*, ed. Rhaban Haacke, Weimar: Hermann Böhlaus Nachfolger, 1970 (MGH Quellen zur Geistesgeschichte des Mittelalters 5)

SACROSANCTUM CONCILIUM OECUMENICUM VATICANUM II, Constitutio pastoralis de Ecclesia in mundo hiuius temporis Gaudium et spes, *AAS* 50 (1966), 1025–1120

SEDULIUS SCOTUS, *Collectanea in omnes B. Pauli epistolas* – *In epistolam ad Ephesios* (PL 103,195–212)

SEDULIUS SCOTUS, *Kommentar zum Evangelium nach Matthäus (1,1–11,1)*,

ed. B. Löfstedt, Freiburg im Breisgau: Verlag Herder, 1989 (Vetus Latina, Aus
der Geschichte der lateinischen Bibel 14)
Sermones S. Ambrosio hactenus ascripti (PL 17,603–734)
SIMON TORNACENSIS, *Institutiones in sacram paginam*, in Richard HEINZ-
MANN, *Die „Institutiones in sacram paginam" des Simon von Tournai: Einleitung
und Quästionenverzeichnis*, München-Paderborn-Wien: Verlag Ferdinand Schö-
ningh, 1967, 25–93
SIMON TORNACENSIS, *Sententiae*, in ALAIN DE LILLE, *Textes inédits*, avec
une introduction sur sa vie et ses oeuvres par Marie-Thérèse d'Alverny, Paris:
J. Vrin, 1965, 307–312
SMARAGDUS S. MICHAELIS, *Collectiones in epistolas et evangelia* (PL 102,
15–552)
TAIO CAESARAUGUSTANUS, *Sententiae* (PL 80,727–990)
THOMAS DE AQUINO, *Opera omnia.* <http://www.corpusthomisticum.org>
Vitae Adae et Evae: Wilhelm MEYER, Vitae Adae et Evae, *Abhandlungen der köni-
glich bayerischen Akademie der Wissenschaften, Philosophische-philologische Klasse*
14.3 (1878), 185–250; J. H. MOZLEY, The Vita Adae, *Journal of Theological
Studies* 30 (1928–1929), 121–149; J. P. PETTORELLI, La vie latine d'Adam et
Eve, *Archivum Latinitatis Medii Aevi* 56 (1998), 18–67: 41–62, 72–77; Johannes
TROMP, *The Life of Adam and Eve in Greek: A Critical Edition*, Leiden-Boston:
Brill, 2005, 122–181
WALAFRIDUS STRABO, *Evangelium secundum Lucam* (PL 114,243–356)
WALAFRIDUS STRABO, *Apocalypsim B. Joannis* (PL 114,709–752)
WERNERUS S. BLASII, *Libri deflorationum* (PL 157,721–1255)
ZACHARIAS CHRYSOPOLITANUS, *De concordia evangelistarum* (PL 186,
11–620)

4. Secondary literature

Acta synodalia Sacrosancti Concilii Oecumenici Vaticani II, volumen IV, pars I, Città
del Vaticano: Typis Polyglottis Vaticanis, 1976
Acta synodalia Sacrosancti Concilii Oecumenici Vaticani II, volumen IV, pars I, Città
del Vaticano: Typis Polyglottis Vaticanis, 1978
Berthold ALTANER, *Kleine patristische Schriften*, Berlin: Akademie-Verlag, 1967
Romano AMERIO, *Iota Unum: Studio delle variazioni della Chiesa Cattolica nel secolo
XX*, Milano-Napoli: R. Ricciardi, 1985
Gary A. ANDERSON, The Exaltation of Adam and the Fall of Satan, in Gary A.
ANDERSON – Michael E. STONE – Johannes TROMP, *Literature on Adam
and Eve*, Leiden: Brill, 2000, 83–110

Alexander ANDRÉE, Anselm of Laon unveiled: The Glossae Super Iohannem and the Origins of the Glossa Ordinaria on the Bible, *Mediaeval Studies* 73 (2011) 217–260

Alexander ANDRÉE, *Gilbertus Universalis: Glossa ordinaria in Lamentationes Ieremie Prophete: Prothemata et Liber I: A Critical Edition with an Introduction and a Translation*, Stockholm: Almqvist & Wiksell International, 2005

Anthropology 1.1.2: Man created to replace Satan and his angels. <http://biblesurvey. net/?p=381> [2013-07-27]

Maria Lodovica ARDUINI, Di alcune analogie testuali tra il Liber Tertius del De apologeticis suis di Ruperto di Deutz e il Quid vasa honoris et quid vasa contumeliae di Onorio di Ratisbona (Augustodunensis), *Aevum* 64/2 (1990), 203–226

Maria Lodovica ARDUINI, Rupert von Deutz, in *Theologische Realenzyklopädie*, Bd. 29, Berlin-New York: Walter de Gruyter, 1998, 474–483

Maria Lodovica ARDUINI, Anselmo di Laon, Ruperto, sant'Agostino, *Aevum* 2 (2006), 377–387

R. AUBERT, Honorius Augustodunensis, *Dictionnaire d'histoire et de géographie ecclésiastiques*, Paris: Letouzey et Ané, 1993, tome 24, 1056–1058

Georges BAREILLE, Ange II. Angélologie d'après les Péres, in *Dictionnaire de théologie catholique*, ed. A. Vacant, tome I, Paris: Letouzey et Ané, 1909, 1192–1222

Franz BÄUMKER, *Das Inevitabile des Honorius Augustodunensis und dessen Lehre über das Zusammenwirken von Wille und Gnade*, Münster: Aschendorffschen Verlagsbuchhandlung, 1914

Pier Franco BEATRICE, Le tuniche di pelle: Antiche letture di Gen 3, 21, in Ugo BIANCHI (ed.), *La tradizione dell'Enkrateia: motivazioni ontologiche e protologiche*, Roma: Edizioni dell'Ateneo, 1985, 433–482

Wolfgang BEINERT, *Die Kirche-Gottes Heil in der Welt: die Lehre von der Kirche nach den Schriften des Rupert von Deutz, Honorius Augustodunensis und Gerhoch von Reichersberg: ein Beitrag zur Ekklesiologie des 12. Jahrhunderts*, Münster: Aschendorffsche Verlagsbuchhandlung, 1973

Pascal Henricus Elisabeth BERTRAND, *Die Evagriusübersetzung der Vita Antonii: Rezeption-Überlieferung-Edition: Unter besonderer Berücksichtigung der Vitas Patrum-Tradition* (Proefschrift University of Utrecht), [s.l.]: [s.n.], 2006 <http:// igitur-archive.library.uu.nl/dissertations/2006-0221-200251>

J. M. BISSEN, La tradition sur la prédestination absolue de Jésus-Christ du VIIe au XIVe siècles, *La France Franciscain* 22 (1939), 9–34

Franz BLIEMETZRIEDER, L'oeuvre d'Anselme de Laon et la littérature théologique contemporaine, *Recherches de théologie ancienne et médiévale* 5 (1933), 275–291

J. F. BONNEFOY, La question hypothétique: Utrum si Adam non peccasset... au XIIIe siècle, *Revista Española de Teología* 14 (1954), 327–368

Jean-Paul BOUHOT, Fragments attribués à Vigile de Thapse dans l'Expositio missae de Florus de Lyon, *Révue des études augustiniennes* 3–4 (1975), 301–316

Jean-Paul BOUHOT, Les sources de l'*Expositio missae* de Rémi d'Auxerre, *Révue des études augustiniennes* 1 (1980), 118–162

Louis BOUYER, *Le Sens de la vie monastique*, Paris: Les Éditions du Cerf, 2008

Damian BRACKEN, The Fall and the law in early Ireland, in Próinséas NÍ CHATHÁIN – Michael RICHTER (ed.), *Ireland and Europe in the early Middle Ages: texts and transmissions*, Dublin: Four Courts Press, 2002, 147–169

Sergej N. BULGAKOV, *L'Échelle de Jacob: des anges*, Lausanne: Éditions l'Age d'Homme, 1987

Robert BULTOT, *Christianisme et valeurs humaines: La doctrine du mépris du monde, en Occident, de S. Ambroise à Innocent III*, tome IV, *Le XI siècle*, vol. 1, *Pierre Damien*, Louvain-Paris: Éd. Nauwelaerts, 1963; vol. 2, *Jean de Fécamp, Hermann Contract, Roger de Caen, Anselme de Canterbury*, Louvain-Paris: Éd. Nauwelaerts, 1964

Claude CAROZZI, Hierarchie angelique et tripartition fonctionnelle chez Grégoire le Grand, in Claude CAROZZI – Huguette TAVIANI-CAROZZI (ed.), *Hiérarchies et services au Moyen-Age*, Aix-en-Provence: Publications de l'université de Provence, 2001, 31–51

Attilio CARPIN, *La redenzione in Origene, s. Anselmo e s. Tommaso*, Bologna: Edizioni Studio Domenicano, 2000

Marie-Dominique CHENU, Cur homo? Le sous-sol d'une controverse au XIIe siècle, *Mélanges de sciences religieuses* 10 (1953), 197–204

Marie-Dominique CHENU, *La théologie au douzième siècle*, Paris: J. Vrin, 1957

Y. CHRISTE – R. BONVIN, Les neufs choeurs angéliques; une création tardive de l'iconographie chrétienne, *Les Cahiers de Saint-Michel de Cuxa* 15 (1984), 67–99

Wanda CIZEWSKI, Interpreting the Hexaemeron: Honorius Augustodunensis De Neocosmo, *Florilegium* 7 (1985), 84–108

Jeremy COHEN, "Synagoga conversa": Honorius Augustodunensis, the Song of Songs, and Christianity's "Eschatological Jew", *Speculum* 2 (2004), 309–340

Marcia L. COLISH, *Peter Lombard*, vol. 1, Leiden – New York – Köln: Brill, 1993

Yves CONGAR, *L'Église: De saint Augustin à l'époque moderne*, Paris: Les Éditions du Cerf, 1997

Yves CONGAR, L'Église chez S. Anselme, in *Spicilegium Beccense*, tome I, *Congrès international du IXe centenaire de l'arrivée d'Anselme au Bec*, Paris: J. Vrin, 1959, 371–399

Yves-Marie-Joseph CONGAR, Église et Cité de Dieu chez quelques auteurs cisterciens à l'époque des croisades en particulier dans le De Peregrinante civitate Dei d'Henri d'Albano, in *Mélanges offerts à Étienne Gilson de l'Académie française*, Paris: Librairie philosophique J. Vrin, 1959, 173–202

Lellia CRACCO RUGGINI – Giorgio CRACCO, Gregorio Magno e i "Libri dei Re", in Philip ROUSSEAU – Emmanuel PAPOUTSAKIS (ed.), *Transformations of Late Antiquity: Essays for Peter Brown*, Farnham; Burlington, VT: Ashgate Publishing Limited, 2009, 223–258

Brent CURTIS – John ELDREDGE, *The Sacred Romance: Drawing Closer to the Heart of God*, Nashville, TN: Thomas Nelson, 1997

Richard C. DALES, A Medieval View of Human Dignity, *Journal of the History of Ideas* 4 (1977), 557–572

Marinus DE JONGE, *Pseudepigrapha of the Old Testament as Part of Christian Literature: The Case of the Testaments of the Twelve Patriarchs and the Greek Life of Adam and Eve*, Leiden: Brill, 2003

Werner DETTLOFF, Die Geistigkeit des hl. Franziskus in der Christologie des Johannes Duns Scotus, *Wissenschaft und Weisheit* 22 (1959), 17–28

Alger N. DOANE, *The Saxon Genesis: An Editon of the West Saxon Genesis B and the Old Saxon Vatican Genesis*, Madison, WI: University of Wisconsin Press, 1991

Dollard DORAIS, *The Reverse of the Fall*, Lake Mary, FL: Creation House, 2005

Frederick Homes DUDDEN, *The Life and Times of St. Ambrose*, vol. 2, Oxford: Clarendon Press, 1935

Martine DULAEY, L'apprentissage de l'exégèse biblique par Augustin. Première partie: Dans les années 386–389, *Revue des Études Augustiniennes* 48 (2002), 267–295

Martine DULAEY, L'apprentissage de l'exégèse biblique par Augustin (2). Années 390–392, *Revue des Études Augustiniennes* 49 (2003), 43–84

Martine DULAEY, L'apprentissage de l'exégèse biblique par Augustin (3). Années 393–394, *Revue des Études Augustiniennes* 51 (2005), 21–65

Judith Rachel DUNTHORNE, *Anselm of Canterbury and the Development of Theological Thought, c. 1070–1141* (Durham theses – submitted for examination for PhD), Durham: Durham University, 2012, 45–56 <http://etheses.dur.ac.uk/6360/> [2013-05-21].

Ludwig EISENHOFER, Augustinus in den Evangelien-Homilien Gregors des Großen: Ein Beitrag zur Erforschung der literarischen Quellen Gregors des Großen, in Heinrich M. GIETL – Georg PFEILSCHIFTER (Hrsg.), *Festgabe Alois Knöpfler zur Vollendung des 70. Lebensjahres gewidmet*, Freiburg im Breisgau: Herder, 1917, 56–66

Markus ENDERS, "Nichts liebt Gott mehr in dieser Welt als die Freiheit seiner Kirche": Anselm von Canterburys Verständnis der Kirche, kirchlicher Lebensformen und des Verhältnisses der kirchlichen zur weltlichen Gewalt, in Christoph STUMPF – Holger ZABOROWSKI (eds.), *Church as Politeia: The Political Self-Understanding of Christianity*, Berlin-New York: Walter de Gruyter, 2004, 29–68

Joseph Anton ENDRES, *Honorius Augustodunensis: Beitrag zur Geschichte des geistigen Lebens im 12. Jahrhundert*, Kempten-München: Verlag der Josef Kösel'schen Buchhandlung, 1906

Ignace ESCHMANN, In Defense of Jacques Maritain, *The Modern Schoolman* 4 (1945), 183–208

Valerie I. J. FLINT, Honorius Augustodunensis of Regensburg, in Patrick J. GEARY (ed.), *Authors of the Middle Ages: Historical and Religious Writers of the Latin West*, vol. II, Aldershot: Variorum, 1995, 89–183

Valerie I. J. FLINT, The career of Honorius Augustodunensis: some fresh evidence, *Revue bénédictine* 84 (1972), 63–86

Valerie I. J. FLINT, The chronology of the works of Honorius Augustodunensis, *Revue bénédictine* 82 (1972), 215–242

Valerie I. J. FLINT, The place and purpose of the works of Honorius Augustodunensis, *Revue bénédictine* 87 (1977), 97–127

Georg GÄBEL, *Die Kulttheologie des Hebräerbriefes: eine exegetisch-religionsgeschichtliche Studie*, Tübingen: Mohr Siebeck, 2006

Marie-Odile GARRIGUES, Honorius Augustodunensis: De anima et de Deo, quaedam ex Augustino excerpta, sub dialogo exarata, *Recherches augustiniennes et patristiques* 12 (1977) 212–278

Marie-Odile GARRIGUES, *Honorius Augustodunensis: Essai de bibliographie générale*, Montréal: [s.n.], 1972

Marie-Odile GARRIGUES, L'œuvre d'Honorius Augustodunensis: Inventaire critique, *Abhandlungen der Braunschweigischen Wissenschaftlichen Gesellschaft* 38 (1986), 7–136; 39 (1987), 123–228; 40 (1988), 129–190

Marie-Odile GARRIGUES, Utrum Honorius ubique sit totus? *Abhandlungen der Braunschweigischen Wissenschaftlichen Gesellschaft* 35 (1983), 31–64

Ferruccio GASTALDELLI, Introduzione, in WILHELMUS LUCENSIS, *Commentum in Tertiam Ierarchiam Dionisii que est De Divinis Nominibus*, Firenze: Olschki Ed., 1983, XXVII–XL a 537–541

Ferruccio GASTALDELLI, La "Summa sententiarum" di Ottone da Lucca: conclusione di un dibattito secolare, *Salesianum* 42/3 (1980), 537–546

Robert GILLET, Introduction, in GRÉGOIRE LE GRAND, *Morales sur Job*, tome I, Paris: Cerf, 1974 (SC 32 bis), 7–113

Cédric GIRAUD, *Per verba magistri: Anselme de Laon et son école au XIIe siècle*, Turnhout: Brepols, 2010

Cédric GIRAUD – Constant MEWS, Le Liber pancrisis, un florilège des Pères et des maîtres modernes du XIIe siècle, *Archivum latinitatis medii aevii (Bulletin Du Cange)* 64 (2006) 145–191

Palémon GLORIEUX, *Pour revaloriser Migne: tables rectificatives*, Lille: Facultés catholiques, 1952

Rudolf GOY, *Die Überlieferung der Werke Hugos von Sankt Viktor: Ein Beitrag zur Kommunikationsgeschichte des Mittelalters*, Stuttgart: Anton Hiersemann, 1976

Jean GRIBOMONT, Introduction, in RUPERT DE DEUTZ, *Les oeuvres du Saint--Esprit*, tome I, Paris: Cerf, 1967 (SC 131), 7–55

Karl HALM – Georg von LAUBMANN – Wilhelm MEYER, *Catalogus codicum latinorum Bibliothecae Regiae Monacensis*, Bd. 2,4, *Codices num. 21406 – 27268 complectens*, secundum Andreae Schmelleri indices composuerunt Carolus Halm et Gulielmus Meyer, Monachii, 1881

Walter A. HANNAM, *The Inevitabile of Honorius Augustodunensis: A Study in the Textures of Early Twelfth-Century Augustianisms: a dissertation*, Boston College: The Graduate School of Arts and Sciences: Department of Theology, 2013, 2–40 <http://gradworks.umi.com/35/60/3560655.html> [2013-08-01]

Nicholas M. HÄRING, The Sententiae Magistri A (Vat. Ms lat. 4361) and the School of Laon, *Medieval Studies* 17 (1955), 1–45

Barthélemy HAURÉAU, *Hugues de Saint-Victor: nouvel examen de l'édition de ses oeuvres avec deux opuscules inédits*, Paris: Pagnerre, 1859

György HEIDL, Did the young Augustine read Origen's homily on Paradise?, in Wolfgang BIENERT – Uwe KÜHNEWEG (ed.), *Origeniana septima*, Leuven: Peeters, 1999, 597–604

György HEIDL, *Origen's Influence on the Young Augustine: A Chapter of the History of Origenism*, Piscataway: Georgias Press, 2003

Yitzhak HEN, Martin of Braga's De correctione rusticorum and its uses in frankish Gaul, in Esther COHEN – Mayke B. DE JONG (eds.), *Medieval Transformations: Texts, Power, and Gifts in Context*, Leiden-Boston-Köln: Brill, 2001, 35–49

François HERTEL, *Pour un ordre personnaliste*, Montréal: Éditions de l'Arbre, 1942

Ludwig HÖDL – Rolf PEPPERMÜLLER – Heinrich J. F. REINHARDT, Anselm von Laon und seine Schule, in *Theologische Realenzyklopädie*, Bd. 3, Berlin--New York: Walter de Gruyter, 1978, 1–5

Daniel HORAN, How Original Was Scotus on the Incarnation? Reconsidering the History of the Absolute Predestination of Christ in Light of Robert Grosseteste, *The Heythrop Journal* 52 (2011), 374–391

David F. JOHNSON, The Fall of Lucifer in Genesis A and two Anglo-Latin Royal Charters, *Journal of English and Germanic Philology* 4 (1998), 500–521

Bruno JUDIC, Avant-propos au Livre II, in GRÉGOIRE LE GRAND, *Homélies sur l'Évangile*, tome II, Paris: Cerf, 2008 (SC 522), 7–17

Bruno JUDIC, Hiérarchie angélique et hiérarchie ecclésiale chez Grégoire le Grand, in François BOUGARD – Dominique IOGNA-PRAT – Régine LE JAN, *Hiérarchie et stratification sociale dans l'Occident médiéval (400–1100)*, Turnhout: Brepols, 2008, 39–54

Bruno JUDIC, Introduction, in GRÉGOIRE LE GRAND, *Homélies sur l'Évangile*, tome I, Paris: Cerf, 2005 (SC 485), 13–90

Johann KELLE, Untersuchungen über des Honorius Inevitabile sive de praedestinatione et libero arbitrio dialogus, *Sitzungsberichte der Akademie der Wissenschaften in Wien. Philosophisch-historische Klasse* 150/3 (1905), 1–34

Johann KELLE, Untersuchungen über den nicht nachweisbaren Honorius Augustodunensis ecclesiae presbyter et scholasticus und die ihm zugeschriebenen Werke, *Sitzungsberichte der Akademie der Wissenschaften in Wien. Philosophisch-historische Klasse* 152/2 (1906),1–27

Mark Stephen KINZER, *"All Things under his Feet": Psalm 8 in the New Testament and in other Jewisch Literature of Late Antiquity* (PhD dissertation), Ann Arbor, MI: University of Michigan, 1995

Rade KISIC, *Patria Caelestis: Die eschatologische Dimension der Theologie Gregors des Grossen*, Tübingen: Mohr Siebeck, 2011

Charles de KONINCK, *De la primauté du bien commun contre les personnalistes*, Québec et Montréal: Presses de l'université Laval et Fides, 1943

Charles de KONINCK, In Defence of Saint Thomas: A Reply to Father Eschmann's Attack on the Primacy of the Common Good, *Laval théologique et philosophique* 2 (1945), 9–109

Leopold KURZ, *Gregors des Großen Lehre von den Engeln*, Rottenburg: Bader'sche Verlagsbuhandlung, 1938

Anne-Marie LA BONNARDIÈRE, Jérôme "informateur" d'Augustin au sujet d'Origène, *Revue des Études Augustiniennes* 20 (1974), 42–54

Émilien LAMIRANDE, *L'Église céleste selon saint Augustin*, Paris: Études Augustiniennes, 1963

Émilien LAMIRANDE, Le thème de la Jérusalem céleste chez saint Ambroise, *Revue d'Études Augustiniennes* 3–4 (1983), 209–232

Artur Michael LANDGRAF, *Introduction à l'histoire de la littérature théologique de la scolastique naissante*, Paris: Librairie philosophique J. Vrin, 1973

Atria A. LARSON, The Influence of the School of Laon on Gratian: The Usage of the Glossa Ordinaria and Anselmian Sententiae in de Penitentia (Decretum C. 33 q. 3), *Mediaeval Studies* 72 (2010), 197–244

Yves LEFÈVRE, *L'Elucidarium et les Lucidaires: Contribution, par l'histoire d'un texte, à l'histoire des croyances religieuses en France au moyen âge*, Paris: E. de Boccard, 1954

Miguel LLUCH-BAIXAULI, *Boezio: La ragione teologica*, Milano: Jaca Book, 1997

Bernhard LOHSE, *Evangelium in der Geschichte: Studien zur Theologie der Kirchenväter und zu ihrer Rezeption in der Reformation*, Göttingen: Vandenhoeck & Ruprecht, 1998

174

Bernhard LOHSE, Zu Augustins Engellehre, *Zeitschrift für Kirchengeschichte* 70 (1959), 278–279

Claudia LOSEKAM, *Die Sünde der Engel: die Engelfalltradition in frühjüdischen und gnostischen Texten*, Tübingen: Franck Verlag, 2010

Robert LUFF, *Wissensvermittlung im europäischen Mittelalter: »Imago mundi«-Werke und ihre Prologe*, Tübingen: Niemeyer 1999

Robert D. LUGINBILL, *The Satanic Rebellion: Background to the Tribulation*, Part 3: *The Purpose, Creation and Fall of Man*. <http://ichthys.com/Fall-sr3.htm> [2013-07-27]

David E. LUSCOMBE, *The School of Peter Abelard: The Influence of Abelard's Thought in the Early Scholastic Period*, Cambridge: Cambridge University Press, 1969

Mariano MAGRASSI, *Teologia e storia nel pensiero di Ruperto di Deutz*, Roma: Apud Pontificiam Universitatem Urbanianam de Propaganda Fide, 1959

Albinia de la MARE, *Catalogue of the collection of medieval manuscripts bequeathed to the Bodleian Library, Oxford, by James P. R. Lyell*, Oxford: At the Clarendon Press, 1971

Mario MARITANO, Argomenti "filosofici" di Origene contro la metemsomatosi, in Lorenzo PERRONE (ed.), *Origeniana octava: Origen and the Alexandrian Tradition*, Leuven: Peeters, 2002–2003, 497–529

Mario MARITANO, L'argomentazione scritturistica di Origene contro la metem-somatosi, in Gilles DORIVAL – Alain LE BOLLUEC (ed.), *Origeniana sexta: Origène et la Bible*, Leuven: Peeters, 1995, 251–276

Jacques MARITAIN, *Humanisme intégral*, Paris: Aubier, 1936

Jacques MARITAIN, *La personne et le bien commun*, Paris: Desclée de Brouwer, 1947

C. W. MARX, *The Devil's Rights and the Redemption in the Literature of Medieval England*, Cambridge: D. S. Brewer, 1995

Bernd MATECKI, *Der Traktat In primis hominibus: eine theologie- und kirchen-geschichtliche Untersuchung zu einem Ehetext der Schule von Laon aus dem 12. Jahr-hundert*, Frankfurt am Main: Lang, 2001

Robert E. McNALLY, Isidoriana, *Theological Studies* 3 (1959), 432–442

Hermann MENHARDT, Der Nachlass des Honorius Augustodunensis, *Zeitschrift für deutsches Altertum* 89 (1958–1959), 23–69

Constant J. MEWS, Bruno of Rheims and Roscelin of Compiègne on the Psalms, in M. W. HERREN – C. J. MCDONOUGH – R. G. ARTHUR (eds.), *Public-ations of The Journal of Medieval Latin*, t. II: *Latin Culture in the Eleventh Century*, Turnhout: Brepols, 2002, 129–152

Walter MOHR, Audradus von Sens, Prophet und Kirchenpolitiker (um 850), *Archivum latinitatis medii aevi (Bulletin du Cange)* 29 (1959), 239–267

Martin MORARD, Le Commentaire des Psaumes et les écrits attribués à saint

Bruno le Chartreux: codicologie et problèmes d'authenticité, in Alain GI-RARD – Daniel LE BLÉVEC – Nathalie NABERT (eds.), *Bruno et sa posté-rité spirituelle: Actes du colloque international des 8 et 9 octobre 2001 à l'Institut catholique de Paris*, Salzburg: Insitut für Anglistik und Amerikanistik, 2003, 21–39

Bruno NARDI, *Dante e la cultura medievale*, Bari – Roma: Edizioni Laterza 1985

Antonio ORAZZO, Il mistero della Sposa nei Sermones sul Cantico dei Cantici di san Bernardo, in Enrico CATTANEO – Antonio TERRACCIANO (a cura di), *Credo Ecclesiam: Studi in onore di Antonio Barruffo S. I.*, Napoli: M. D'Auria Editore, 239–263

Shaun O'SULLIVAN, Anti-Jewish polemic and early Islam, in David RICHARD (ed.), *The Bible in Arab Christianity*, Leiden: Koninklijke Brill NV, 2007

Ludwig OTT, *Untersuchungen zur theologischen Briefliteratur der Frühscholastik, unter besonderer Berücksichtigung des Viktorinerkreises*, Münster i. W.: Aschendorff, 1937

Paolo PASQUALUCCI, La cristologia antropocentrica del Concilio Ecumenico Vaticano II, *Divinitas* 2 (2011), 163–187

Karl PELZ, *Die Engellehre des heiligen Augustinus: ein Beitrag zur Dogmengeschichte: Augustinus über die Natur der Engel*, Münster in Westfalen: Aschendorffsche Buchdruckerei, 1912

Joan M. PETERSEN, Did Gregory the Great know Greek?, in *Studies in Church History* 13 (1976), 121–134

Joan M. PETERSEN, Greek influences upon Gregory the Great's exegesis of Luke 15, 1–10 in *Homelia in evang.* II, 34, in Jacques FONTAINE (ed.), *Actes du colloque international CNRS Grégoire le Grand*, Paris: Éditions du CNRS, 1986, 521–529

Joan M. PETERSEN, Homo omnino latinus? The Theological and Cultural Background of Pope Gregory the Great, in *Speculum* 62 (1987), 529–551

Jeanne-Marie PONT, Homo angelorum decimus ordo, *Cahiers de civilisation mé-diévale* 31–121 (1988), 43–48

Riccardo QUINTO, Trivium e teologia: l'organizzazione scolastica nella seconda metà del secolo dodicesimo e i maestri della sacra pagina, in Giulio D'ONO-FRIO (ed.), *Storia della teologia nel medioevo*, vol. II, *La grande fioritura*, Casale Monferrato: Edizioni Piemme, 1996, 435–468

Vincenzo RECCHIA, La memoria di Agostino nella esegesi biblica di Gregorio Magno, *Augustinianum* 25 (1985), 405–434

Heinrich J. F. REINHARDT, *Die Ehelehre der Schule des Anselms von Laon. Eine theologie- und kirchenrechtsgeschichtliche Untersuchung zu den Ehetexten der frühen pariser Schule des 12. Jahrhunderts. Anhang: Edition des Ehetraktates der Sententie Magistri A.* Münster: Aschendorff, 1974

Teresa REGAN, *A study of the Liber de Spiritu et Anima: Its Doctrine, Sources and Historical Significance: A thesis...*, University of Toronto, 1948

Gérard RÉMY, Une lettre sur l'Eglise de Bossuet, in Anne-Élisabeth SPICA, *Bossuet à Metz (1652–1659): Les années de formation et leurs prolongements: Actes du Colloque international de Metz (21–22 mai 2004)*, Berne: Peter Lang, 2005, 97–113

René ROQUES, Introduction, in ANSELME DE CANTORBERY, *Pourquoi Dieu s'est fait homme*, Paris: Cerf, 1963 (SC 91), 9–190

Alessandro ROVETTA – Serena COLOMBO, Analisi iconografica del ciclo antelamico, in Giorgio SCHIANCHI (ed.), *Il battistero di Parma: iconografia, iconologia, fonti letterarie*, Milano: Vita e Pensiero, 1999, 137–168

E. Matthews SANFORD, Honorius, Presbyter and Scholasticus, *Speculum* 3 (1948), 397–425

William A. SCHACKLEFORD, *Replacing the Fallen Angels*, [s.l.]: Xulon Press 2007

Peter SCHAFER, *Rivalität zwischen Engeln und Menschen: Untersuchungen zur rabbinischen Engelvorstellung*, Berlin: De Gruyter, 1975

Felix SCHEIDWEILER, Studien zum Anegenge, *Zeitschrift für deutsches Altertum und deutsche Literatur* 1/2 (1944), 11–45

Giorgio SCHIANCHI, Iconologia del programma iconografico del cantiere antelamico, in Giorgio SCHIANCHI (ed.), *Il battistero di Parma: iconografia, iconologia, fonti letterarie*, Milano: Vita e Pensiero, 1999, 201–282

Martin A. SCHMIDT, Augustins "Bürgerschaft Gottes", *Theologische Zeitschrift* (Basel) 11 (1955), 45–67

Rolf SCHÖNBERGER et alii, *Repertorium edierter Texte des Mittelalters aus dem Bereich der Philosophie und angrenzender Gebiete*, Bd. 1–4, Berlin: Akademie Verlag GmbH, 2011

Fabian SCHWARZBAUER, *Geschichtszeit: über Zeitvorstellungen in den Universalchroniken Frutolfs von Michelsberg, Honorius' Augustodunensis und Ottos von Freising*, Berlin: Akademie Verlag, 2005

Manlio SIMONETTI, Alcune osservazioni sull'interpretazione origeniana di Genesi 2, 7 e 3, 21, *Aevum* 36 (1962), 370–381

Manlio SIMONETTI, Longus per divinas scripturas ordo dirigitur: Variazioni altomedievali su un tema catechetico agostiniano, *Romanobarbarica: contributi allo studio dei rapporti culturali tra mondo latino e mondo barbarico* 6 (1981–1982), 311–339

Beryl SMALLEY, Glossa ordinaria, in *Theologische Realenzyklopädie*, Bd. 13, Berlin-New York: Walter de Gruyter, 1984, 452–457

Lesley SMITH, *Glossa Ordinaria: The Making of a Medieval Bible Commentary*, Boston (MA): Brill Academic Publishers, 2009

R. W. SOUTHERN, *Saint Anselm and his Biographer: A Study of Monastic Life and Thought 1059–c. 1130*, Cambridge: Cambridge University Press, 1963

Ralf M. W. STAMMBERGER, Die Edition der Werke Hugos von Sankt Viktor († 1141) durch Abt Gilduin von Sankt Viktor († 1155) – Eine Rekonstruktion, in Rainer BERNDT (ed.). *Schrift, Schreiber, Schenker: Studien zur Abtei Sankt Viktor in Paris und den Viktorinern*, Berlin: Akademie Verlag, 2005, 119–231

Loris STURLESE, Zwischen Anselm und Johannes Scotus Eriugena: der seltsame Fall des Honorius, des Mönchs von Regensburg, in Burkhard MOJSISCH – Olaf PLUTA (eds.), *Historia philosophiae Medii Aevi: Studien zur Geschichte der Philosophie des Mittelalters*, Bd. 2, Amsterdam-Philadelphia: B. R. Grüner, 1991, 927–951

Carole STRAW, Gregory I, in Allan D. FITZGERALD (ed.), *Augustine through the Ages: An Encyclopedia*, Grand Rapids, MI: W. B. Eerdmans, 1999, 402–405

Dominik TERSTRIEP, *Weisheit und Denken: Stilformen sapientialer Theologie*, Roma: Editrice Pontificia Università Gregoriana, 2001

Roland J. TESKE, Origen and St. Augustine's First Commentaries on Genesis, in Robert J. DALY (ed.), *Origeniana quinta: historica, text and method, biblica, philosophica, theologica, Origenism and later developments*, Leuven: Peeters, 1992, 179–185

Jean-Pierre TORREL, *Initiation à saint Thomas d'Aquin: sa personne et son oeuvre*, 2. édition, Paris: Cerf, 2002

Novella VARISCO, Dal Cur homo al Cur Deus homo: un percorso sulla via della consapevolezza, in Paul GILBERT – Helmut KOHLENBERGER – Elmar SALMANN (ed.). *Cur deus homo: Atti del Congresso anselmiano internazionale Roma, 21–23 maggio 1998*, Roma: Centro studi S. Anselmo, 1999, 561–572

Antonio VIÑAYO GONZÁLEZ, San Martín de León, el primer español que cita a Pedro Lombardo, *Scriptorium victoriense* 1 (1954), 51–62

Adalbert de VOGÜÉ, Avertissement, in GRÉGOIRE LE GRAND, *Commentaire sur le premier livre des Rois*, tome 3, Paris: Cerf, 1998 (SC 432), 9–10

Adalbert de VOGÜÉ, Introduction, in GRÉGOIRE LE GRAND, *Commentaire sur le Premier livre des Rois*, tome 1, Paris: Cerf, 1989 (SC 351), 18–125

Adalbert de VOGÜÉ, Introduction, in GRÉGOIRE LE GRAND, *Commentaire sur le premier livre des Rois*, tome 4, Paris: Cerf, 2000 (SC 449), 9–42

Samuel VOLLENWEIDER, Luzifer – Herrlichkeit und Sturz des Lichtengels: Eine Gegengeschichte zu Demut und Erhöhung von Jesus Christus, in Jörg FREY – Gabrielle OBERHÄNSLI-WIDMER (eds.), *Das Böse*, Neukirchen--Vluyn: Neukirchener Theologie, 2012, 203–226

René WASSELYNCK, La part des "Moralia in Job" de S. Grégoire-le-Grand dans les "Miscellanea" victorins, *Mélanges de science religieuse* 10 (1953), 287–294

René WASSELYNCK, La présence des "Moralia" de S. Grégoire le Grand dans les ouvrages de morale du XIIe siècle, *Recherches de théologie ancienne et médié-vale* 35 (1968), 197–240; 36 (1969), 31–45

René WASSELYNCK, Les compilations des "Moralia in Job" du VIIe au XIIe siècle, *Recherches de théologie ancienne et médiévale* 29 (1962), 5–32

René WASSELYNCK, Les "Moralia in Iob" dans les ouvrages de morale du haut moyen âge latin, *Recherches de théologie ancienne et médiévale* 31 (1964), 5–31

René WASSELYNCK, L'influence de l'exégèse de S. Grégoire le Grand sur les commentaires bibliques médiévaux (VIIe-XIIe s.), *Recherches de théologie ancienne et médiévale* 32 (1965), 157–204

Heinrich WEISWEILER, La "Summa Sententiarum" source de Pierre Lombard, *Recherches de théologie ancienne et médiévale* 6 (1934), 143–183

Ronald G. WITT, *The Two Latin Cultures and the Foundation of Renaissance Humanism in Medieval Italy*, Cambridge: Cambridge University Press, 2012

Index of proper names

Vojtěch Novotný

Cur homo?
A history of the thesis
concerning man as a replacement
for fallen angels

English translation by Pavlína and Tim Morgan

Published by Charles University
in Prague, Karolinum Press
Ovocný trh 3–5, 116 36 Prague 1,
Czech Republic
http://cupress.cuni.cz
Prague 2014
Editor vice-rector Prof. PhDr. Ing. Jan Royt, Ph. D.
Cover and layout by Jan Šerých
Typeset and printed by Karolinum Press
First English edition

ISBN 978-80-246-2519-5
e-ISBN 978-80-246-2586-7 (pdf)